ENCYCLOPEDIA OF THE
Animal World

Vol 15   Otter — Platypus

Bay Books Sydney

OTTER, a carnivore belonging to the weasel family and living a semi-aquatic existence. It comprises five freshwater genera and one marine genus. The Lutrinae, as the otter subfamily is called, is one of the most widely distributed groups of mammals, absent only from large oceanic islands, Australasia, Madagascar and the polar regions.

Otters are well adapted to their semi-aquatic life. Covered with a close, water-proof underfur and long guard hairs, their body is muscular and lithe, built for vigorous swimming. The limbs are short and the trunk cylindrical. The paws, each with five digits and non-retractile claws, are generally webbed and the forefeet are shorter than the hind ones. The fully-haired tail, thick at the base but quite flexible, tapers to a point and is flattened on its under surface. Below its base are situated two scent glands (except for the Sea otter in which they are absent) which give the otter a characteristic mustelid odour, sweet and pungent. Adults may use these glands when suddenly frightened, but do not direct the scent towards the aggressor like a skunk *Mephitis*. Considerable colour variation exists, partly geographic (tropical species are usually lighter than their northern counterparts), partly seasonal (the fur is paler before the moulting season), ranging from black-brown to a pale grey hue. Stiff vibrissae, or whiskers, are numerous around the snout, reminding one of a seal, and smaller ones appear in tufts on the elbows. Used for tactile purposes in dark or muddy waters, they are very sensitive, detecting the slightest turbulence. When swimming under-water, the nostrils and small, round ears are kept shut and the otter must rely on its facility in swimming, on its sight, whiskers, and in some species manual dexterity, to detect and catch its prey. Contrary to popular opinion, the otter's diet is extremely varied. While in most cases, small, easily captured non-game fish form the bulk of the diet, eels, crayfish, frogs and small rodents are also readily eaten. Insects, worms and some vegetable matter may be ingested at times. The Sea otter's diet is more specialized.

River otters are among the most playful animals, and both Canadian and European otters slide down mud banks and tunnel through snow, while the 'clawless' species are very agile jugglers. When captured young, otters make engaging pets but require proper feeding as well as superhuman patience on the owner's part in the face of their boundless energy and inventiveness.

The European otter *Lutra lutra*, is not in fact confined to Europe but extends from the British Isles, across Russia to Japan and is also found in North Africa. In Asia, a number of subspecies are recognized, the most southerly occurring in Sumatra. Smaller than the Canadian otter *Lutra cana-*

Short-clawed otter showing the almost webless forepaws which are remarkably dextrous.

densis, the European otter measures 36–48 in (91–122 cm) and weighs 10–25 lb (4·3–11·4 kg). It is a territorial animal, the male's home range covering approximately 10 miles (16 km) of stream or lake. Generally solitary and nocturnal, they rarely vocalize and are the shyest members of the otter group. Pairs or small family groups can be found only at certain times of the year. One to five cubs, but more usually two or three, are born at any season after a nine week gestation.

A family of Asian Small-clawed otters. The female on the bank, is retrieving a cub with her forepaws, not with her mouth as does the European otter

An African subgenus of *Lutra* is currently recognized, the 'Spot-necked' otter *Lutra (Hydrictis) maculicollis,* which lives in the lakes and fast-running streams of East and West Africa. Mainly a fish eater, but more vegetarian than other otters, it does not compete with the large African 'clawless' otter *Aonyx capensis.*

The Canadian otter is restricted to North America south to Texas. The genus, however, spreads down through South America to Terra del Fuego, separating into seven other species along the way. The specific differences are based on the shape of the nose pad and skull variations but these otters are very similar in appearance and behaviour. For instance, the Canadian and South American otters share a common vocal repertoire which includes a low, chuckling greeting call unique to otters of the New World. An adult may measure 36–50 in (91–127 cm) and weigh 11–35 lb (5–15·8 kg). Females are smaller and lighter, especially in tropical forms. One South American Pacific species, *Lutra felina,* is distinct from the others in having become almost exclusively marine. Nothing is known of its habits, being extremely rare.

American otters are found in streams, lakes and estuaries. Seasonal variations occur in their diet when certain, preferred foods such as crayfish, softshell turtles, crabs or small fish become available. They may hunt alone or in pairs, usually by night but also by day in remote areas, and eat at least 2 lb (1 kg) of food a day. They appear to be even more sociable and playful than European otters but during the breeding season fighting may occur. The males, in search of females, wander far from their usual territory and mating takes place in the water. Delayed implantation occurs in the Canadian otter: the embryos lie dormant in the uterus for eight months after fertilization and are not implanted until two months before birth, lengthening the gestation to 10 or 12 months overall. Both European and American otter cubs must be coaxed into the river by their mother at two months old, as they do not take readily to water on their own. The cubs remain with their mother for at least a year and often until they reach sexual maturity when two years old.

The Indian 'Smooth-coated' otter *Lutrogale perspicillata,* is heavier-set and larger than the European otter. It can be found in marsh areas from Iraq to Borneo. Characterized by its short, dense fur, the Smooth-coated otter also has a flattened tail and thickly webbed paws with thick nails which enable the animal to be remarkably agile in manipulating and retrieving small objects. An adult male will total nearly 48 in (121 cm) in length and weigh 25 lb (11·4 kg). The shortened face and high cranium house massive molar teeth, which indicate a largely crustacean diet and, in certain areas, a semi-marine existence. The Smooth-coated otter also seems to adapt itself to a partly terrestrial life during seasonal droughts. Unlike the European otter, it is quite vocal, keeping up a constant 'conversation' of bird-like notes, coos, nasal whines and chirps with its companions. Its repertoire of sounds and calls is closer to that of the 'clawless' and Brazilian otters than to the European or American species.

Southeast Asia possesses the smallest of all otters, the Asian Small-clawed otter *Amblonyx cinerea.* Adult males may not exceed 30 in (75 cm) in total length or weigh more than 11 lb (5 kg). Usually dark brown with a contrasting whitish throat, a large grey subspecies exists on the hills of northern India. The forefeet have long agile fingers, only partially webbed, with tiny spike-like claws. Aptly called 'Finger otter' in German, these otters use their sensitive fingertips to search for prey under stones and pebbles in shallow water or mud, averting their glance to one side much the way raccoons do while 'washing' their food. Although European and Smooth-coated otters may occur in the same areas, no direct competition seems to take place between them, each being adapted to a niche or slightly different way of life. The Small-clawed, nearly clawless, otter can easily catch crabs, mussels and snails with its forepaws, while the European otter spends its time in fast moving streams rather than the shallows, and the Smooth-coated otter is

quite at home in marshy estuaries or swamps. No breeding season has been reported in the wild but in captivity cubs are born in winter or summer. Very vocal animals, they give high-pitched squeaks while moving in pairs or groups reminiscent of the 'coos' of the Smooth-coated otter. When suddenly alarmed they emit an explosive snort used to startle the enemy and, if cornered, attack with an ear-splitting scream.

The Clawless otter *Aonyx capensis,* is found from Ethiopia down to the Cape of South Africa. Usually it prefers the slow, shallow streams of the rain-forests but traces of its passage may also be found on the sand bars of the wide, deep rivers. These large otters measure 64 in (160 cm) and can weigh over 50 lb (23 kg). Coloration varies from a deep brown to a frosty grey with lighter cream white on the chin and neck. The forepaws are webless and the clawless fingers have an almost monkey-like dexterity. Even the thumb shows a surprising freedom of movement when manipulating or lifting small objects. The Clawless otters are the only mammals, apart from the Primates, which use their hands in such a skilful fashion. The hindfeet have a small web and the middle toes are nailed. The usefulness of these nails is immediately evident when the otter pauses to scratch itself with a hindfoot. Perhaps the same evolutionary process which acted to make the fingers more sensitive through nail loss, retained the hindclaws which likewise serve a purpose. Like the Oriental Small-clawed otter, the Clawless also catches its prey with its forepaws and carries it directly to the mouth, clutched in one paw, instead of picking it off the ground with its mouth as most other otters and carnivores do. They are mainly mollusc and crustacean eaters but dig for worms in soft

mud and eat small fish also. More terrestrial than other otter genera, they may wander far from water without discomfort when travelling from one stream to another, sleeping under boulders or thick vegetation along the way. Two to four cubs are born in the spring after a two month gestation, remaining with the mother for at least a year. The Clawless otters have the most complex vocal repertoire of all the otters with a wide variation of calls. A clear, flute-like whistle to call its companion, a long whine in greeting or a snarling scream are just a few of the sounds in their large 'vocabulary'.

The Giant Brazilian otter *Pteronura braziliensis,* can measure up to 8 ft (2·3 m) and weigh 75 lb (34 kg). It is found in the main rivers of South America, from the upper reaches of the Amazon south to Argentina. The massive head with the haired nose pad as well as the overall size of the animal, make it quite distinct from other South American otters. Yellowish-white patches on the chin, neck and chest contrast sharply with the dark brown body fur. Its wide tail is flattened and fer-de-lance shaped. The large feet are thickly webbed, impeding rapid locomotion on land. Brazilian otters prey on a variety of animals, but fish and waterfowl seem to be preferred. Quite active by day, they can be found in noisy groups of four or five, giving a short bark when alarmed and retreating to dens under the banks. Two or three cubs are usually born in March or April after a gestation of three months. Its diurnal habits have made it an easy target for pelt hunters and now this large otter is on the verge of extinction.

First announced to the world by Steller in 1751, the Sea otter *Enhydra lutris,* was subsequently so persecuted for its valuable fur that by the end of the 19th century it was close to extinction. Protected in 1911, it is

now making a satisfactory recovery, the entire population numbering between 30–40,000 individuals. While the Sea otter's range originally extended from the Kurile islands in Japan, across the Aleutian chain and down the west coast of America as far south as Lower California, colonies today are only local within this area. The most un-otterlike of all the genera, the Sea otter is exclusively marine, rarely coming ashore. The massive head with a short, blunt face and large nose is much paler than the body, which varies from shades of brown to almost black, sparsely covered with guard hairs. Unlike other otters, it has a short tail, seal-like flippers and small, compact forepaws. Adults will reach a little over 5 ft (1·5 m), including a 12 in (30 cm) tail and weigh up to 80 lb (36 kg). Their unique molars are broad and rounded, perfectly adapted to crushing Sea urchins, abalones and mussels. Diurnal, it floats peacefully in small colonies of 10–90 animals near kelp beds. Food is eaten while the animal is on its back, and stones brought from the ocean floor serve as an 'anvil' to break the urchin or mussel shell. The Sea otter is one of the few tool-using mammals. It lays the stone on its chest and holding a Sea urchin or a clam between its forepaws crashes it down onto the stone. It tucks its anvil under its arm while diving and uses it for several consecutive shell-breaking attempts. One young is born, rarely twins, at any time of the year after a nine month gestation. The cub is in a more advanced stage of development than any other mustelid at birth: eyes open, well furred, it also has a complete set of milk teeth and can immediately float in the water next to its mother or on her chest when nursing. The cub remains with her for at least a year, probably more as the females only give birth every two years. Sexual maturity is reached in the third year. No fighting occurs between the males during the breeding season. The Sea otter's natural enemies are the Killer whales, perhaps sealions and, unfortunately, man. SUBFAMILY: Lutrinae, FAMILY: Mustelidae, ORDER: Carnivora, CLASS: Mammalia.   N.D.

OTTER MONSTER. It has been suggested that some reports of monsters in lakes are based on the observation of a family of otters swimming in line. Such is the explanation of the ogo-pogo that is said to inhabit Canadian lakes. Lake Naivasha in Kenya, was said to harbour a monster so when Theodore Roosevelt, who was on the lake in a boat in 1911, saw three humps nearby, the supposed monster, he shot at the middle one. The other two disappeared, the third stayed on the surface. The skin of the otter is now at the American Museum of Natural History.

Small-clawed otter eating a fish. This is the smallest otter.

OTTER CIVET *Cynogale bennetti*, ranging from China to Borneo, which has adapted to an aquatic existence. See civets.

OTTER SHREWS, large otter-like insectivores, up to 2 ft (60 cm) long, living in West and Central Africa. There are only three species known and these are sometimes classified with the tenrecs which they closely resemble. Otter shrews are mainly nocturnal and semi-aquatic. See Insectivora. FAMILY: Potamogalidae, ORDER: Insectivora, CLASS: Mammalia.

OUNCE *Uncia uncia*, an alternative name for the *Snow leopard.

OUZEL, also spelt 'ousel', the Old English name for the blackbird *Turdus merula* but also applied to other Eurasian species of dark-plumaged birds, particularly the Ring ouzel *T. torquatus* and the Water ouzel or dipper *Cinclus cinclus*. The Ring ouzel is very similar to the blackbird but has a pale crescent on the breast, lives in rougher country and is less widely distributed. The Water ouzel lives around fast-flowing streams from which it finds its food by walking and swimming beneath the surface.

OVENBIRD, a family of about 220 species of small to medium-sized South American perching birds, usually with brown or chestnut-brown plumage.   The ovenbirds are a very diverse group of dull-coloured birds found from the high Andes to the sea coasts of South America. Most of them are drab birds with plumage of some shade of brown, some have rufous or chestnut upperparts and a few have white undersides or white wing markings. Only a very few species have any bright colours, though some of the genus *Asthenes* have a small patch of reddish-chestnut on the throat, and the White-cheeked spinetail *Schoeniophylax phryganophila* has a patch of bright chrome yellow colour on the chin. The true ovenbird or Pale-legged hornero *Furnarius leucopus* is also one of the more brightly coloured species, being a bright chestnut-brown above and white below.

Ovenbirds vary from about 4–9 in (10–23 cm) in length, but they show considerable diversity in the proportions of the various body parts. The bill is usually short, rather weak and straight, ending in a point. However, it is long and downcurved in the earth-creepers of the genus *Upucerthia*, short and slightly downcurved in the miners, such as the Common miner *Geositta cunicularia*, and short and triangular with the upper mandible somewhat curved upwards in the Rufous-tailed xenops *Xenops milleri*. In general species inhabiting the equatorial forests of South America have short, soft, rounded wings, while the species found in

southern Chile, Patagonia and elsewhere at temperate latitudes have longer, stiffer and more-pointed wings, probably because a higher proportion of them migrates. The legs and feet are usually rather strong, and are particularly so in the true ovenbirds (genus *Furnarius*) and the cachalotes (genus *Pseudoseisura*) which live mainly on the ground in open country. Only a very few species have crests on the head, these include the plainrunner or Lark-like bushrunner *Coryphistera alaudina*.

The vast majority of the ovenbirds are insect-eaters, although a few species and genera have adapted to feeding on a very wide variety of foods, especially representatives of some of the groups found in the southern part of the South American subcontinent. Species such as the Blackish cinclodes *Cinclodes subantarcticus* and the Dark-bellied cinclodes *C. patagonicus* are always found near to water, whether it is a small stream high in the mountains, or a broad lowland river. They live on small crustaceans and other aquatic animals which they catch by swimming in the water and paddling in the shallows, after the manner of the European dipper. Some species of this genus have even been seen feeding on floating masses of kelp and other large seaweeds, thus it seems that they are the only perching birds (Passeriformes) to have adapted, even partially, to a marine environment. Some of the miners and similar genera feed on seeds, leaves and other vegetable matter, though most of these birds probably take insects as well.

A very wide variety of habitats is exploited by ovenbirds, though the majority of species are found in the vegetation of wooded areas. Many species, such as the White-eyed foliage-gleaner *Automolus leucophthalmus* and the Montane foliage-gleaner *Anabacerthia striaticollis* hunt for insects and larvae among the twigs and leaves of forest trees, like warblers. The Sharp-billed treehunter *Heliobletus contaminatus* and the White-throated treerunner *Pygarrhichas albogularis* creep up the trunks of trees, probing into the bark for insects, and hacking at decaying wood in search of beetles and insect larvae. Some species hunt among the dead leaves of the forest floor, flicking leaves aside and tossing them in the air like thrushes as they search for concealed food.

This family also shows a great diversity in nesting habits. Some of the ground-living species nest in holes, either natural ones in banks, rocks or stony ground, tunnels dug by the birds themselves (as in the Common miner) or in burrows excavated by mammals. Some such as the Thorn-tailed rayadito *Aphrastura spinicauda* and the Tawny tit-spinetail *Leptasthenura yanacensis* nest in tree holes, and a number of species related to these nest in cracks behind the bark peeling

off dead trees or the disused, domed nests of other birds. In striking contrast to these the Wren-like spinetail *Spartonoica maluroides* and a few other species build neat cup-shaped nests in bushes and trees. Most remarkable, however, are the huge domed nests built by the true ovenbirds, the name ovenbird having originated in the resemblance that these nests bear to an old-fashioned stone oven.

The White-throated cachalote *Pseudoseisura gutturalis* builds a gigantic nest. The bird is only 8 in (20 cm) long, but the cavity inside the nest is big enough to contain a turkey, and it is said that a man can stand on the domed roof of the nest without causing any damage. The Firewood-gatherer *Anumbius annumbi* builds a large, domed nest of large twigs, the finished structure being several feet in diameter. It often builds its nest in a tall tree necessitating the carrying of large twigs some distance, a surprising feat for a bird that is only 9 in (23 cm) long. The Brown cachalote *Pseudoseisura lophotes* also makes a huge, barrel-sized nest, but many other ovenbirds build smaller nests of mud or mud and sticks. The Black-faced spinetail *Phleocryptes melanops* makes a neat domed nest on a tree branch. The main structure consists of twigs and leaves, which are daubed together with mud, animal dung and perhaps with the birds' own saliva. Nearly all of the 'oven-builders' make their large nests in trees, but one of the species of spinetail builds its nest on the ground concealed in thick vegetation.

The nests of most of the 'oven-builders' are comparatively well known because they are so conspicuous, but less is known of what goes on inside the nest than with the species using less well defended sites. So far as is known all of the ovenbirds lay unmarked white eggs, except the Black-faced spinetail *Synallaxis tithys* which lays bright blue eggs and one or two other species that lay very pale blue or cream eggs. As many as seven, eight or nine eggs have been reported in the nests of the White-throated spinetail or Pale-breasted spinetail *Synallaxis albescens* and a few other species, but most ovenbirds lay clutches of from three to five eggs in the southern temperate regions, and two or three eggs in tropical South America. Incubation periods of from 15–20 days have been recorded in the few species that have been studied and fledging periods of from 13 to 18 days.

Ovenbirds are often very active, but many species live in thick forests or scrub and are inconspicuous because of their skulking behaviour. The ground-living forms found in open country are often more readily seen, though many of these remain unnoticed because of their concealingly-marked plumage and habit of running or walking away from intruders instead of taking flight. In general

Seiurus aurocapillus, one of the many ovenbirds, a group that has a wide variety of nesting habits. The species shown above does not make an oven nest.

the ground-living forms have a smaller repertoire of calls than those inhabiting woodland and undergrowth, probably because there is less need for calls that give 'messages' when the birds are in sight of one another for most of the time. Many ovenbirds have harsh rattling, jangling and jarring calls, but the miners of the genera *Geositta* and *Geobates* give high-pitched ringing calls that are often monotonously repeated. The true ovenbird gives a succession of clear, vibrant notes which are often produced as a duet by two birds singing near to each other. Yet others, such as the Brown cachalote and the Rufous-crested cachalote *Pseudoseisura cristata* give harsh, jay-like screeches.

The ovenbirds have often been classified by ornithologists into five subfamilies. The first of these, the Furnariinae, includes the true ovenbirds (*Furnarius* spp) and a number of rather aberrant-looking genera such as the miners (*Geositta, Geobates*), the tococo or Crag chilia *Chilia melanura* and the earth-creepers of the genus *Upucerthia*. Another large subfamily is the Synallaxinae, the spinetails, which are a more uniform group marked by the huge barrel-like nests built by many species and by the stiffened quills of the tail feathers. Because of the huge nests this subfamily is often termed the 'castle-builders'. The other large subfamily, the Philydorinae, includes the treerunners *Pygarrhichas*, hookbill or Chestnut-winged hookbill *Ancistrops strigilatus*, the Point-tailed palmcreeper *Berlepschia rikeri,* the cachalotes *Pseudoseisura* and several other genera. The few remaining species are classified into two subfamilies, the Margarornithinae and the Sclerurinae. The Sclerurinae contains the Sharp-tailed streamcreeper

Lochmias nematura and the six species of leaf-scraper of the genus *Sclerurus*. The Margarornithinae includes the Spotted barb-tail *Premnoplex brunnescens,* the Rusty-winged barbtail *Premnornis guttuligera* and the four species of treerunner of the genus *Margarornis*. FAMILY: Furnariidae, ORDER: Passeriformes, CLASS: Aves.   D.H.

OVUM, the fully developed female gamete or egg, prior to fertilization, containing the haploid number of chromosomes. In many animals the actual penetration of the sperm into the cytoplasm of the female sex cell occurs before the final maturation division of its nucleus, i.e. at the secondary oocyte stage, but the fusion of the male and female nuclei does not take place until maturation of the female gamete has been completed.

OWLET-FROGMOUTHS, a family of eight species of *nightjars living in Australia, New Guinea and adjacent islands. They perch with an upright, owl-like stance, on slender legs. The large rounded head has stiff curved bristles projecting from the forehead and around the bill like the vibrissae (whiskers) of a cat. The cryptically-patterned feathers are soft and downy, and almost conceal the large broad bill. The birds are large-eyed and nocturnal; feeding by swooping from a perch to take insects on the ground or, more rarely, in flight. The three or four white eggs are laid in a hole in a tree or bank. FAMILY: Aegothelidae, ORDER: Caprimulgiformes, CLASS: Aves.

OWLS, soft-plumaged, short-tailed, big-headed birds of prey, the nocturnal equivalent of the Falconiformes. They have large eyes

directed forwards surrounded by facial discs. The bill is hooked and the claws sharp. Owls vary in size from the sparrow-sized Pigmy owl to the huge Eagle owls. There are about 132 species and four others have become extinct in historical times. All owls are rather similar and taxonomists have chosen to take the degree of ear development and asymmetry as a means of classification. Owls are divided into two families: the Tytonidae and Strigidae. The former includes the Barn and Grass owls *Tyto* and the curious Bay owls *Phodilus*. The nine species of Barn owls are characterized by big heart-shaped facial discs and long tarsi, and by having the middle claws on each foot expanded into serrated 'combs'. *Tyto alba* must be one of the most widespread of birds since it is found in the New World as well as in Africa, Europe, southern Asia and Australia. The majority of the *Tyto* species are found in the Australian-New Guinea-Celebes region with isolated species in Madagascar and southern Africa. Two Afro-Asian Bay owls are intermediate between the Barn owls and the remaining species.

The majority of the Strigidae belong to the subfamily Buboninae which generally have reduced or flattened facial discs, i.e. are 'frown faced', and less well developed external 'ear flaps' than those of the other subfamily, the Striginae.

Many of the 17 genera of bubonine owls have only one species. The rare Maned owl *Jubula lettii* of West Africa, and the Crested owl *Lophostrix cristata* are given generic status. So too is the tiny Elf owl *Micrathene whitneyi*, on the basis of having only ten as opposed to 12 tail feathers. The New Guinea Hawk owl *Uroglaux dimorpha* shows significant differences from the 16 chiefly Australasian *Ninox* Hawk owls to which it is closely related.

The Snowy owl *Nyctea scandiaca* and the Hawk owl *Surnia ulula* have circumpolar ranges, the latter living farther south. The most widespread of the bubonine genera is *Bubo*, the 12 kinds of Eagle owls occurring in the New World and across to the Philippines. The Hawk owls *Ninox* replace the Eagle owls in Australasia, as they do the Eared, Scops and Screech owls *Otus* which stretch in a long chain of species from the Americas through Eurasia and Africa to the southwest Pacific islands. Lacking ear tufts are the three similar Eurasian 'Little' owls *Athene*. Tropical genera include the curiously marked Spectacled owls *Pulsatrix*, Wood owls *Ciccaba*, and the Afro-Asian Fishing owls *Ketupa* and *Scotopelia*.

The second subfamily, the Striginae, includes six genera characterized by their well-developed facial discs and sophisticated hearing. Best known are the 'earless', chiefly black-eyed, Wood owls *Strix*, most of which have feathered feet and rounded wings. They are chiefly found in temperate woodlands in

many forest owls, the wings are short and adapted for weaving among the trees. There are three African species of *Scotopelia* which have no ear tufts. None, however, has developed the typical white heads or underparts characteristic of Fishing hawks.

When most other birds are roosting the owl must find food and defend its territory against competitors. Mates have to be courted, and the almost insatiable demand for food by the owlets must be satisfied. These activities are carried out at night when the land is illuminated, at best, by a full moon. The success of owls under these exacting conditions depends upon the efficiency of their sense organs which are adapted to work in the dark, making the birds as much at home in moonlight or twilight as we are when bathed in sunshine or neon light.

Once the sun has set, illumination is reduced to a very low level, but owls make the best use of the available light. They seem to be capable of resolving as much detail from the night scene as we can by day, having vision estimated to be 35–100 times more sensitive than our own. Even on the darkest night, deep inside woodland, most owls have little trouble in seeing clearly enough to weave in and out of the branches. At this level of illumination we would be completely helpless. Their eyes are relatively enormous (a Snowy owl's eye being the same size as a man's), with very wide corneas that allow the maximum of light

the New and Old Worlds, excepting Australia and New Zealand. The Tawny owl *Strix aluco* is found over most of Europe and parts of Asia and North Africa. Six *Asio* owls are all 'eared', and the Long- and Short-eared owls, *A. otus* and *A. flammeus* respectively, are both widely distributed circumpolar species. The second of these, being found even in temperate South America, must be one of the most southerly of all owls. Four members of the genus *Aegolius* are rather like miniature *Strix* owls and lack ear tufts. There are three mono-specific strigine genera, the eared *Pseudoscops grammicus* and *Rhinotynx clamator* of the Caribbean and South America respectively and the non-eared, but large, Fearful owl *Nesasio solomonensis* from the southwest Pacific.

The owl family has not undergone so much adaptive radiation as the diurnal hawks. The Least pigmy owl *Glaucidium minutissimum* of Mexico and the Amazon valley is the smallest at $4\frac{1}{2}$–5 in (12 cm), and by comparison the 27 in (68 cm) Eagle owl is a giant. Between these two extremes, there is a range of size with smaller species tending towards insectivorous diets and increasingly large prey being taken by the bigger owls. As hunters, owls tend to sit, watch and pounce, or else to drop onto prey when patrolling at a

Spectre of the bird world, the Barn owl, seen here with its fluffy chicks, can be seen hunting before sunset.

The Long-eared owl of Eurasia and North America often lays its eggs in the deserted nests of squirrels, crows, hawks and other birds.

low height. They are not basically interceptors, although some, like the Screech owl *Otus asio,* catch insects with their bills, flycatcher fashion. The Hawk owl *Surnia ulula* is the nearest equivalent to a small falcon or hawk. It is diurnal, has 'hard' plumage, comparatively small eyes, while the facial discs and sense of hearing are not as well developed as in the nocturnal species.

Several species of owls are adapted to a terrestrial mode of life, and the Burrowing owl *Speotyto cunicularia,* a day-living owl, even sunbathes, while the Cape and Australian Grass owls, *Tyto capensis* and *T. longemembris,* have relatively long legs and run well. The seven species of Fishing owls are big and powerful birds, diurnal in habit, that scoop fish from the surface of the water with their talons. All have feet covered with spicules to assist the grip on the prey and some have bare toes and tarsi. The four eared Asian species belong to the genus *Ketupa.* Here the facial discs are reduced and, like so

The Tawny owl hunts at night for small animals. It locates its prey by sensitive hearing then drops silently onto it.

through to the retina. In the jargon of photography the cornea/lens system is 'fast'. The lens is rounder than in diurnal birds and resolves the light into a small, but nevertheless bright, image on the retina. As a consequence of its size and shape the power of the lens cannot be greatly changed and so owls' eyes are inefficient at focussing on very close objects. The retina is also adapted for use in dim light, being composed almost entirely of rods which are very sensitive photo-receptors. By night the iris is drawn right back to expose as much of the lens as possible, while by day it closes so that light can only enter through a very small aperture.

The sense of hearing of most owls is also extremely well developed, particularly in the Tytonidae and the strigine owls. This is indicated by the enormous semi-lunar ear openings and their attendant flaps, which fringe the facial discs. The part of the medulla of the brain concerned with hearing is also well developed, containing 95,000 nerve cells in the Barn owl compared with only 27,000 in a crow twice the weight. Long-eared and Tawny owls also have large numbers of auditory nerve cells in the medulla, whereas both the Eagle owl and Little owl have relatively few and it seems that the former

species may depend less on vision for hunting. The upper limit to hearing in owls is similar to that of man (between 15 and 20 KHz: 1KHz= one thousand cycles a second). Owls are, however less sensitive to lower frequency sounds. Long-eared and Tawny owls do not react to sounds of less than 0.1 KHz, whereas the Eagle owl can hear sounds as low as 0·06 KHz. Owls' ears are more sensitive to certain frequencies than others, and this is a measure of the tuning of the ear mechanism. Tawny and Long-eared owls can hear sounds of 2 KHz and 6 KHz, about ten times fainter than any we can hear. The maximum sensitivity of these species is around 6 KHz but the Eagle owl's ear is tuned similarly to our own, responding best to sounds of about 1 KHz.

The sensitivity to high frequencies is exploited by the Tawny owl and Long-eared owl in hunting because their rodent prey produces noises of these frequencies, either vocally or by scampering across dry leaves and twigs.

Perhaps the most remarkable discovery about owls in recent years is the fact that Barn owls (and probably other big-eared species) can catch living rodents successfully in absolute darkness, providing the prey

vocalizes or gives some other sound clue to its whereabouts. Barn owls were investigated by Roger Payne of Cornell University who trained them to fly at a loudspeaker placed on the floor transmitting mouse or rustling noises. He found that in a completely darkened room the owls could intercept live prey by launching themselves on a trajectory that was accurate to within 1°. The accuracy of the bird's aim could be reduced to 5°–7° if frequencies above 8·5 KHz were filtered out. If frequencies of less than 5 KHz only were transmitted, the owls refused to strike. Clearly high pitched voices gave the Barn owls their best directional clues, and this is achieved in the following manner. Each ear is directionally sensitive to certain frequencies. Basically, sounds between 5 KHz and 15 KHz will always seem loudest when they come from the direction of the line of sight. So that if a Barn owl orientates its head to perceive high pitched sounds (approaching 15 KHz) equally loudly in each ear, it will be staring straight at its prey.

The ears of many owls are further refined by the asymmetrical layout of the openings and flaps. The right ear opening of the tropical Mottled owl *Ciccaba virgata* is half as long again as that of the left one. This probably means that if a sound source moves away from the line of sight, the reception in one ear will decrease with extreme rapidity while in the other it does so less quickly or may even increase. It is therefore easier to track the movements of the prey.

The ears and eyes thus form a highly sophisticated system for prey detection. It seems, however, that ears as adjuncts to hunting are more useful in northern temperate regions than in the noisy tropical forests, at least if ear size is any indication of sensitivity.

Many owls, including the 6 lb (2·7 kg) Eagle owl, fly with hardly a whisper. Silent flight doubtless has two purposes; firstly no warning is given to the prey of impending attack, and secondly the owl's sensitive hearing is not 'jammed' by noisy pinions. The main adaptation concerns the flight feathers which are effectively covered by a velvet pile. Turbulence, a major source of noise, is thus reduced.

Further adaptations to living by night may be found in owls' communication behaviour. Animals usually carry their own recognition marks, which have been compared with national flags, but brightly coloured patterns are of limited use at night. However, when seen against the night sky, owls have quite distinctive silhouettes and in 57 species these are enhanced by the presence of ear-

The Eagle owl ranges across Europe, Asia and North Africa. It is the largest owl and has a wingspan of 4–5 ft (1.5 m).

tufts—groups of long feathers that project from the scalp. These vary enormously in size from species to species: in *Otus, Bubo, Rhinoptynx, Ketupa, Jubula* and *Lophostrix* they are well developed and often project from the head like devil's horns. In the genus *Asio* three kinds of nocturnal and woodland long-eared owls have conspicuous ear tufts more to the centre of the head than other 'eared' species; in the two more diurnal 'short-eared' members of the same genus, the tufts are rudimentary. The latter inhabit open country and their need for special recognition signals may be less than in their woodland relatives.

Owls are also vociferous and their hoots and screams make up a well developed language. On the whole, there is a relationship between the size of the owl and the basic frequency of the voice. Large species, like the Eagle owl and Great grey owl, have deep bass hoots, with a frequency range not extending much further than 1 KHz, whereas the diminutive Pigmy owl has a high pitched call with a frequency range extending from 2 KHz to 8·5 KHz. Even so, the majority of owls have relatively low frequency voices, giving them a human-like quality. Owls need to proclaim their hunting territories and communicate with their mates over large areas. The carrying power of low pitched notes is much greater than of high pitched or squeaky ones, which in any case would tend to be dissipated easily by foliage and the tangle of branches in forests. Hoots then act rather like fog horns, as sound beacons in the darkness.

If the hoots or songs of a range of owls are analyzed one cannot help drawing a rough analogy with the morse code. Each species has its own characteristic style of hooting, with the 'dots' and 'dashes' being replaced by short and long hoots. There are owls with simple voices, like the Long-eared owl with its single monosyllabic hoot. Others like the Great grey owl run together a series of hoots, or abbreviated ones forming a phrase, as in Tengmalm's owl. The Tawny owl and its close relative the Ural owl have syncopated song phrases with both short and long hoots incorporated. To aid identification of the sexes, many owls have calls uttered only by the hens which, except in the Snowy owl, are similarly coloured to the cocks. Furthermore, antiphonal singing between mates has been recorded for Barred, Spectacled, Eagle, and Little owls. Antiphonal singing probably occurs widely and again is a characteristic of birds that live in woods and forests or are active at night when it is difficult to keep in touch by sight. Owls which inhabit thick woodland areas are also much more vocal than those of open habitats.

Female Snowy owl: the males are almost pure white. Breeding north of the tree line, these owls are found in Europe, Asia and America.

Owls are basically hole-nesters, laying their eggs in crevices, open cavities, or inside the vacated homes of woodpeckers. The Elf owl often nests in cavities bored by Gila woodpeckers or Mearns gilded flickers in the giant Saguaro cactus. A cryptic site like this must be advertized and shown to the mate, so that there can be no doubt about its location. Voice plays an important role in this: Tengmalm's owl calls repeatedly from the nest entrance and Little owls scream a great deal while flying round the nest. Eagle owls, too, have a nest-site display and it is during these ceremonies, when the sexes are close together, that visual displays may come into play. In particular, movement of the throat when hooting often reveal white patches, thus visual signals synchronize with the vocalization. Like many hole-nesting species most owls have pale-plumaged chins and throats.

A few owls have taken to nesting on the ground, like the Snowy owl and the Short-eared owl. In the case of the Laughing owl *Sceloglaux albifacies* of New Zealand this habit has made it particularly vulnerable to the depredations of introduced carnivores and rats and it only survives in small numbers on South Island.

Some owls are fairly catholic in their

choice of nest-sites. *Bubo* species sometimes take over old nests of eagles or ravens, and corvid nests are used by the Long-eared owl. Owls, however, do not usually build their own nests, although the Dusky owl and Milky eagle owl, of India and Africa respectively, will sometimes build platforms. Among the *Strix* owls, only the Lapland owl habitually builds its own nest. Tawny owls have even been known to nest in old rabbit burrows. In the New World, the Burrowing owl is the most specialized of the terrestrial species. These small owls are usually associated with Prairie dog communities, nesting in burrows perhaps 10 ft (3 m) long, up to four pairs per acre. Although these owls can dig their own, they may take over the deserted burrows of Ground squirrels, viscachas, wolves, foxes, skunks and armadillos. However, the Burrowing owl has been greatly reduced in numbers by the changing pattern of agriculture in the United States.

Like the eggs of other hole-nesting birds, those of owls are white. Presumably they show up better than coloured eggs in dimly lit surroundings and, because of the protected nature of the sites, there has been no selection for camouflage. Even those species that nest in exposed sites, such as the Snowy owl and

the Short-eared owl, have white eggs. In all cases the incubating birds are well camouflaged. Further protection is given to the eggs and chicks by persistent attacks being made on likely predators wandering too near the nests. Owls of several species have evolved defence displays that are often performed near the nest sites. The feathers are fluffed, wings spread and rotated forward, and the bill is often clappered. The effect is made all the more frightening by the big staring eyes which always face the enemy. Even downy owlets are able to frighten off would-be assailants in this way.

Bubo owls lay a single egg, whereas the smaller species, like the Burrowing owl, produce as many as 11 eggs. Incubation is carried out usually by the hens (which are larger than the cocks) from the time the first egg is laid. During this time the cocks supply them with food. The period of incubation usually lasts between four weeks for the Long-eared owl, and five weeks for the Eagle owl. On the whole tropical owls lay smaller clutches than those species of more northerly latitudes; the average clutch in equatorial Africa is 2·5 as opposed to 4·6 in mid-Europe.

Except in the Pigmy owl hatching is

asynchronous, an adaptation to a varying food supply. By the time the last egg has chipped, the oldest chick may be as much as two weeks old. Should food be plentiful then the parents will be able to bring enough to satisfy the demands of several owlets, but in the event of shortage, the oldest and strongest chick will dominate the supply and the others will die.

The period of dependence of the chicks upon their parents for food is unusually long in the Tawny owl. For several months after leaving the nest the adults must supply all the food for the young, while the owlets (or more usually owlet) themselves develop their own skill at hunting. However, by autumn they have to find their own territory or starve.

Many owls prey on animals the populations of which undergo wide and often rapid fluctuations. The few species which have been extensively studied show a number of ways in which they have come to terms with a constantly changing food supply. The Tawny owl is perhaps typical of temperate woodland areas. At Wytham Wood near Oxford, up to 30 pairs nest in the 1,000 acre study area. Wood mice and Bank voles formed 60% of the diet, and over the years, these rodents varied in number between five and 50 per

The White-faced scops owl *Otus leucotis*, about 9 in (23 cm) long, is common in the African bush and also penetrates far into the Sahara and other desert areas.

The Oriental hawk owl *Ninox scutulata*, of eastern and southern Asia, 9 in (23 cm) long, hunts insects in forest edges and jungle clearings.

acre, depending upon the crop of beechmast and other fruits upon which they feed. Despite this widely varying food supply, the numbers of Tawny owls did not fluctuate, but their breeding output was affected. Whereas in more normal times at least three out of four pairs could be expected to lay eggs, during very lean rodent years, the owls made no attempt to breed. In good mouse and vole years the clutches averaged three eggs or so, but in leaner years, fewer eggs were produced, and perhaps only a quarter hatched. If food is scarce, the hens forsake the nest in order to hunt for themselves, and the eggs cool and fail to hatch. Fledging success is also reduced from an average of about 1·0 per pair in good years to 0·3 per pair in bad years.

However, in the simpler environments of the taiga and tundra, presumably where there are fewer checks on population, prey species periodically build up to plague proportions, then crash with dramatic effect upon the predators. Lemmings, hares, mice and voles of different kinds are preyed upon by Snowy owls and Short-eared owls. Both owls are nomadic, capitalizing upon rich supplies of food wherever the prey species are swarming. The denser the prey, the more owls settle, and the more prolific they are in their breeding. From 1874 to 1876 there was a plague of Short-tailed field voles of unprecedented proportions on the upland pastures of Eskdale, Scotland. About 500 pairs of Short-eared owls settled in the area and bred without intermission from February to September, and clutches of 10–12 were reported to be not unusual. The vole plague died out in 1877 and those owls that did not starve to death, left for better feeding grounds.

Following peak years in the rodent population cycles, the owls suddenly find food scarce. At this time they may 'irrupt' in search of food from their usual home ranges. This happens to the Snowy owl, a tundra species dependent upon Collaed and Common lemmings. During the great irruption of 1926–7, a great flight of these arctic owls made their way via the Great Lakes into the USA where 2,368 were recorded. At these times individuals often settle on ships on the North Atlantic sea routes, and they even turn up in such unlikely places as the Azores.

Between the nomadic opportunists and the sedentary species such as the Tawny owl and Eagle owl is the Barn owl, studied by M. R. Honer in Holland where there are about 3,000 breeding pairs. The Barn owl population oscillates and heavy mortality tends to occur every three to five years, reminiscent of the rhythm of rodent population cycles. The Barn owl is basically sedentary, each pair hunting over 70 to 80 acres, and when rodents are numerous (every third year in Holland) each pair of owls can raise nine young over two successive broods. When the food supply declines with the owl population at a peak, the

young and some of the adult owls scatter and disperse far and wide throughout Europe. In cases of drastic failure of food supply even some of the adults remaining on their home ground may starve to death.

To the Tawny owl, on the other hand, life may be best guaranteed by not moving away from its complicated woodland and scrub territory; to hunt successfully at any time may mean literally knowing every inch of the ground, and this takes time to learn. So even when food is scarce Tawny owls may be able to make enough kills on their own familiar ground to keep themselves, if not their chicks, alive. The Barn owl's preferred habitat is midway between open grassland and woodland, and it sometimes behaves like a typical sedentary species while at other times like a nomad.

Apart from those owls that periodically 'irrupt', several species are truly migratory, for example Scops owl *Otus scops,* and the Oriental hawk owl *Ninox scutulata.* It is thus no accident that islands have become colonized by these owls, where they may develop distinctive subspecies as, for example, on the Seychelles and Comoros, in the Indian Ocean. In fact most of the major land habitats

of the world have been colonized by one or more species of owl.

The story of owls starts 60 million years ago, in the Eocene period, when *Protostrix mimica* hunted over what is now Wyoming. Modern owls, however, probably evolved in Eurasia. French soil has yielded the earliest fossils of Eagle (*Bubo*) and Eared (*Asio*) owls in the Oligocene. By comparison, the Barn owls are modern, because their remains date from the late Miocene of 12 million years ago. Since then, they have established themselves all over the world (*Tyto alba* is world-wide in distribution with 36 forms), and vigorous speciation has taken place in the Australo-papuan region. One extinct species, *Tyto ostologa,* of the Caribbean was a giant, the size of a Snowy owl.

The rapid expansion of the rodent family was gathering momentum during the Oligocene and Miocene (40–12 million years ago) and this was precisely the time when modern birds of prey, both diurnal and nocturnal, were actively developing. The food supply represented by the large number of rodents and other small mammals was divided between the two orders of birds of prey. During the day they were taken by hawks and falcons

Little owl with earthworm. From its original range in continental Europe, Asia and North Africa, it has been introduced to England and New Zealand.

(Falconiformes) and by the owls at night. Owls are, however, not closely related to the hawks although they have similar structures, both having decurved bills, sharp talons and eyes well positioned for stereoscopic vision, so necessary for hunting by sight. This is the result of convergent evolution due to similar feeding habits. Owls differ from hawks in having no crop, a long alimentary caecum and two toes tending to face backwards. Owls also tend to bolt their food without much preparation. Only the falcons, among the hawks, resemble owls in their habit of not building their own nests. The Short-eared owl is the nocturnal equivalent of the Hen harrier both in hunting methods and in the prey taken and Cooper's hawk and the Red-tailed hawk are equivalent to the Horned owl. The Red-shouldered hawk is similar in its requirements to the Barred owl and so on. ORDER: Strigiformes, CLASS: Aves.   J.S.

OWL LORE, Owls feature in many legends and most often as a bird of doom, death and sorcery, no doubt because of their nocturnal habits, penetrating gaze and eerie shrieks. In the British Isles an owl perching near a house was widely believed to be an omen of death to one of the household, while in other parts of the world owls were thought to suck the blood of babies. Another deep-seated attribute of the owl is its wisdom, perhaps based on its human appearance—upright stance and a marked 'face' with eyes set together. The owl was the companion of Athene, the goddess of wisdom, who was at loggerheads with Dionysius, the god of drink and licentiousness. Following the mediaeval custom of using mythological opposites as antidotes to disease, we find that owl flesh was used as a cure for gout, known to be brought on by overdrinking and that owls' eggs were a cure for dipsomania and epilepsy.

OX, in common usage the name is applied to a castrated bull used for draught purposes or for its meat. Zoologically, the plural, for example, wild oxen, is used not only for the domesticated cattle but for some other members of the family Bovidae. Alternative names sometimes used for domesticated cattle are bullock and steer. A bullock meant originally a young bull or a bull calf. It is now always used for a castrated bull, or ox. The name 'steer' is also used for a young ox, especially one that has been castrated.

OXPECKERS, two aberrant starlings adapted for feeding on hides of large grazing animals. They are found only in Africa, where they have probably evolved in the environment provided by the extensive herds of large grazing animals on the African grasslands. The Yellow-billed oxpecker

Buphagus africanus is widespread over western and central Africa except in the Sahara and the Congo Basin, while the Red-billed oxpecker *B. erythrorhynchus* is confined to the eastern third of Africa from the Red Sea to Natal. In the central regions their distributions overlap and the two species may be found together without apparent interaction.

In their manner of scrambling over the bodies of large animals the oxpeckers have evolved a rather woodpecker-like manner, and they superficially resemble them in other features. They are about 7–8 in (18–20 cm) long, with a rather slender body. The longish, pointed tail is well-developed, with stiff-shafted tapering feathers which can help to prop the bird as it clings upright to a vertical surface. The legs are fairly short and stout with strong feet equipped with large sharp claws to give a firm grip. The wings are long and pointed. The bill is rather heavy, and broad at the base with an arched culmen to the upper mandible, while the lower mandible is deep, with flattened sides sloping outwards towards the cutting edge and with a sharp angle at the front. Oxpeckers are relatively dull in colour. Both species are a dull coffee-brown above, with a duller, paler brown on the head. The belly is light buff, grading into a dull olive-brown on the breast. The Yellow-billed oxpecker is a little larger than the other species and has pale buff on the rump and upper tail coverts. It has a bright chrome-yellow bill, the lower mandible being bright red towards the tip. The Red-billed oxpecker has a wholly red bill and also has a conspicuous ring of bare yellow skin around the eye. The bill of the first species is proportionally larger than that of the second, and the lower mandible is very deep and broad towards the base.

Oxpeckers tend to live and feed entirely on the skin of animals such as buffalo, rhinoceros, giraffes, zebras and various antelopes. Where human occupation has introduced domestic cattle, or replaced other grazing animals with these, the birds transfer their attention to the domestic stock. The oxpeckers usually occur in small groups. They shuffle over the bodies of the animals with considerable agility, but prefer to perch woodpecker-fashion, with head uppermost, and in this posture will move sideways or drop back or downwards in short jerky hops. The host animals appear to show little or no reaction while the birds move around the body and neck, up and down the limbs, and even over the face. They even tolerate the birds' attention to open sores. However, where the birds have been introduced to animals without previous experience of them, these show alarm on the first occasion that the oxpeckers settle on them. The principal activity of the birds is feeding on the blood-gorged ticks which they remove from

Red-billed oxpecker of eastern Africa. Much of its life is spent on the backs of large animals where it feeds on blood-sucking ticks.

the animals' bodies. They also take blood-sucking flies and remove any blood that shows. Experiments with captive birds have shown that the bills are well-adapted to rapidly removing every trace of blood from a surface using a sideways scissoring movement. They also remove scar tissues and, while their attention is mainly beneficial in removing the ticks, they may also do some harm in enlarging the wounds during this cleaning-up process. The extent to which these birds are dependent on ticks for food is shown by the way in which, when dependent on domestic cattle, oxpeckers disappear from areas where cattle are treated for external parasites.

Oxpeckers spend most of their time on the animals and have been seen sunbathing while they cling to the hide. Although in some instances the birds leave the animals and retire to roost communally in holes in trees or in reed beds they may also, on some occasions at least, roost on the bodies of their hosts. This association is not without other advantage to the animal host. The birds are alert to danger and will react to the approach of a potential predator by ascending to the back of the host and uttering loud hissing and rattling calls which warns the host. In addition to these alarm notes the birds have a high-pitched twittering flight note.

Courtship and copulation also occurs on the hosts. The display of the male is a bowing of the head and fluttering of the wings, accompanied by a chattering call. The birds must, however, leave the animals in order to nest. The nest is built in a hole in a tree or a cleft in a rock. It is a rough untidy mass of grass lined with animal hair. The three to five eggs are pale blue or white, spotted with brown or violet. The young may be fed by other adults besides the parents, up to four birds having been seen at one nest, and during this period the adults may have to search for suitable hosts. The young appear to be fed on ticks and blood. When fledged the young are similar to the parents but even duller in colour with some fine dark barring on the feathers and with dull brown bills. FAMILY: Sturnidae, ORDER: Passeriformes, CLASS: Aves.

OYSTERCATCHERS, sea-shore wading birds, about the size of a pigeon. There are usually considered to be four species and 21 subspecies of which seven are completely black while the remainder have pied plumage. The pied forms are very distinctive, having a black head and upperparts, white belly and rump, white tips to the primary wing feathers and patches on the secondary wing feathers forming a broad wing bar. The feet and legs of all species are stout with three toes and the colour varies from bright orange-pink to a pale pink depending on age and subspecies. The bill is long, laterally compressed and about $3\frac{1}{2}$ in (9 cm) long. It is bright orange in the breeding season, but becomes duller during the rest of the year. The iris is bright scarlet. The sexes are very similar but females are slightly larger and the bill size can be used to sex individuals in the hand.

Immature oystercatchers have brownish tinges to the plumage and also differ from the adult in having darker legs, a black tip to the bill and a brown eye iris. They have a white half-collar on the front of the neck which is also common to the adult bird outside the breeding season.

Oystercatchers are found on the shores of every continent except Antarctica. Most of them are separated geographically from their neighbours, but in certain areas two species exist together. In areas, such as South America, the Falkland Islands, New Zealand and Australia, one of the pair of species is pied, the other black. The pairs also differ in their feeding and breeding habits which helps to maintain the species separation and permits peaceful coexistence.

They are adapted to feeding on marine shellfish and worms and are hence restricted to coastal areas in winter. Most of them remain on coasts to breed on sand-dunes, among rocks and shingle or on small islands, but some move inland to breed,

The cosmopolitan oystercatcher at its nest where it lays three well-camouflaged eggs. The strong red bill is used for smashing open shellfish.

notably in parts of Europe, USSR and New Zealand.

Most forms are migratory and in early spring the oystercatchers arrive on their breeding grounds where they set up territories. Each territory, comprising part of a mudflat, mussel-bed or sand beach, enables access to a good supply of food and also includes an area which will, subsequently, be used for nesting purposes. Nests are simply scrapes in the ground, crudely lined with small flat stones or pebbles, pieces of seaweed, fragments of shell—any suitable material near at hand. Scraping appears to be of great importance and a large number of scrapes may be prepared before the final choice is made. The first eggs appear in May, about eight weeks after the birds arrive. A clutch of three is usual but two or four are not uncommon. The eggs are incubated by both parents for 25–28 days and the chicks are fed on shellfish and marine worms, again by both adults, until they fly at about five weeks of age.

The basic features of inland breeding are similar to those described above for coastal breeding. Inland breeding is not common and is only known to occur, to any extent, in northern Britain, the Netherlands (Friesland), New Zealand (South Island) and around the Aral Sea (USSR). In Britain the habit has increased very greatly in the past 35 years and continues to do so. Territories

are taken in arable fields, although some birds will be found nesting at altitudes of up to 2,000 ft (610 m) in the Scottish Cairngorms. In low-lying parts of Scotland eggs are laid in mid-April, over 90% being placed in newly-sown fields. The food of the adults and young consists of earthworms and leatherjackets.

On average each pair in Britain manages to raise between 0·7 and 1·0 chick to the flying stage, but coastal breeders, studied in Scotland, appear to be less successful, perhaps due to a greater number of predators or to human disturbance in some districts.

Many oystercatchers are specialist feeders on bivalve shellfish, a source of food tapped by very few other birds. They have evolved a complex pattern of behaviour to exploit this rich food supply. For example, when they are attacking mussels *Mytilus edulis* the oystercatchers pull the mussels off the bed, turn them over, hammer a hole in the flat surface and cut the strong adductor muscle which holds the two halves of the shell together. Once this muscle is severed the bird can use its bill as a lever prising the shells apart; the meat is then chiselled out with fine scissor-like movements of the bill. It has been shown experimentally that the ventral surface is the weakest area of the mussel shell and this fact ties in with the oystercatchers' behaviour which has become adapted to opening the mussel in the easiest possible manner. When the mussel is under-water the shell halves gape so that the bird can sever the adductor muscle with one quick stabbing action, without breaking the shell.

Oystercatchers are noisy birds, particularly in the breeding season, and much of this noise results from their 'piping'. The birds strut around, shoulders hunched forward with their bills pointing almost vertically downwards and a continuous, loud, rapid trilling accompanies these movements. Previously thought to be part of sexual behaviour (pairing, mating etc), it has recently been shown to result from aggressive tendencies (driving intruders from a breeding territory or from the vicinity of a feeding bird, for example). FAMILY: Haematopididae, ORDER: Charadriiformes, CLASS: Aves.   P.B.H.

OYSTERS AND OYSTER FISHERIES.
The Edible oysters, as distinct from the Pearl oysters and other so-called 'oysters', are bivalve molluscs belonging to the family Ostreidae. Although of great antiquity with many extinct genera and species, all living oysters belong to the three genera *Ostrea, Crassostrea* and *Pycnodonta*. The last of these, although containing the largest species, occurs usually in relatively deep water and never in numbers together. Its species are therefore of no commercial importance and may be disregarded. Despite their age, the Ostreidae continue to be highly successful in shallow coastal waters in all but the polar seas. However, in the more densely populated areas, notably along the Atlantic coast of Europe and in many areas around the shores of North America, the formerly extensive oyster reefs have been totally destroyed by

overfishing and the effects of other human activities.

In the primitive bivalve mollusc the two valves, which with the dorsal ligament constitute the shell, were connected by anterior and posterior adductor muscles and the animal moved slowly through soft substrates by means of a muscular foot with the body vertically disposed. But in the Ostreidae, which probably originated in the Upper Triassic, the anterior adductor is lost and the body has become reorganized around the remaining, centrally disposed, adductor, the foot was lost and, at a very early stage in these changes, the animal became cemented by the left valve to a hard substrate. The shell is either rounded or somewhat elongated from hinge to free margins, the lower (left) valve being cup-shaped and the upper one flat. Within a species the form of the shell is very

Outside the breeding season oystercatchers gather in large flocks, those from high latitudes migrating to warmer places. Despite their eye-catching plumage oystercatchers are normally remarkably inconspicuous, especially when perched on surf-splashed rocks.

variable depending on the nature of the surface to which it is attached and also, in a dense bed or reef, on the pressure of surrounding animals. The 'spat' settle most freely on adult shells.

Structure and life history can best be described with reference to the European flat oyster, including the British 'native', *Ostrea edulis*. The body, exposed after removal of the flat upper valve and the mantle flap which forms this, is organized around the central adductor muscle. This consists of two parts, a 'catch' muscle of smooth fibres which closes the shell for, if necessary, prolonged periods if exposed to the air or to unfavourable conditions in the sea, and a 'quick' muscle of striated fibres responsible for repeated sudden contractions needed for the ejection of sediment and other waste which collects within. These muscles act in opposition to the elastic ligament, that part of the shell which is uncalcified and unites the two valves at the hinge. The heart, displayed after opening the cavity in which it lies above the adductor, consists of two auricles which receive blood from the gills and pass this into the muscular ventricle. Above this again lies the visceral mass containing the alimentary system including the stomach and intestine with the style-sac in which a gelatinous rod, the crystalline style, rotates and serves both to stir the contents of the stomach and also

assist in their digestion by dissolving at the tip to release enzymes.

The pair of extremely voluminous gills, the 'beard' of the oyster, lies in a half circle around the adductor muscle. Each consists of two flaps, or lamellae, made up of great numbers of parallel filaments, attached from place to place and so forming a highly complex lattice-work covered with different series of highly active ciliary hairs. Those that line the sides of the filaments create a powerful inhalant current of water which passes through the lattice-work to emerge above and behind the gills and then leave the shell as a posteriorly directed out-flowing current. It carries with it waste products from the anus and from the kidneys.

Particles contained in the inflowing water are retained on the surface of the gills where, under the action of frontal cilia on these surfaces, mixed with mucus, they collect into streams along the base and free margins of each half gill (demibranch) where a further series of ciliary currents convey them to the mouth. The entrance to this is guarded on each side by a pair of fleshy lips or labial palps. The inner, opposed, faces of these are ridged and even more elaborately ciliated than are the gills, their function being to control the quantity of mucus-laden material which passes into the mouth. There is also, although it is a little difficult to determine

precisely how this is accomplished, some selection for quality. The food of oysters, like that of other bivalves, consists essentially of the largely microscopic plant life of the surrounding sea water and this is what almost exclusively passes into the alimentary system which is highly adapted for dealing with such finely divided material of plant origin. What is rejected by the palps, and to some extent by the gills as well, is dropped on to the surface of the mantle lobes, carried by cilia to their margins where it collects forming 'pseudo-faeces' which are expelled from time to time by sudden contractions of the quick muscle. It is the extreme efficiency of the feeding and digestive systems which is largely responsible for the great success of oysters. Where the water is extremely turbid, with high concentrations of suspended silt, this system may break down.

The reproductive organs ripen and spread over the two sides of the body during the summer months. Although at any one time an individual is either male or female, there is an alternation of sex, the speed of succession depending on temperature. Thus, at the northern end of its range, *Ostrea edulis* may function as male and then female in alternate years. In British waters it may often spawn in both capacities in the one year while in southern France oysters may spawn as females with intervening activity as males

Left: the 'native' oyster *Ostrea edulis* lying in the lower (i.e. the left) valve. Arrows indicate directions of inflowing and outflowing currents of water and the direction of circulation across the gills. Right: stages in the settlement of the American oyster *Crassostrea virginica*. 1–3, larvae swimming with the velum in the plankton (foot shown in 3 and 4 where the animal is 'searching' for a place to settle). 5–7, crawling with foot. 8, fixation on left valve. 9 and 10, settled 'spat' one or two days old.

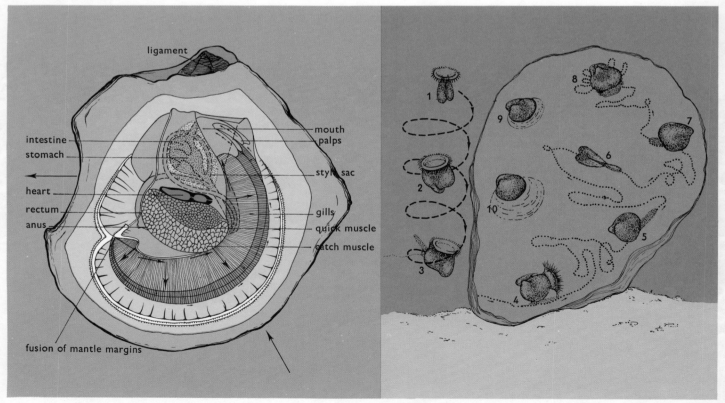

Edible oyster *Ostrea edulis* exposed by a low spring tide. Famed as food, many of the original beds have been destroyed by overfishing and pollution.

several times in the same season. Spawning begins when the sea temperature reaches about 59°F (15°C). Only in the male phase are the sexual products, the spermatozoa, released. In countless numbers they are carried out in the exhalant current and almost immediately drawn in by the inflowing current of individuals in the female phase, the eggs of which are fertilized as they issue from the oviducts. Surprisingly, the fertilized eggs then pass through the meshwork of the gills, that is against the flow created by the cilia lining the sides of the filaments, to be incubated in the mantle cavity, forming first a creamy mass, when the oyster is said to be 'white sick' and then, as pigment accumulates in the digestive organs, becoming grey or 'black sick'. After the initial discharge of sperm by perhaps only a single individual in the male phase, the presence of sperm in the water leads to a chain reaction, other males as well as females spawning so that the whole oyster bed is speedily in a state of intense reproductive activity.

Up to one million larvae may be incubated for a period of up to two weeks depending on temperature. When liberated, during the 'swarming' process, they are shelled and have a velum or ciliated sail used for swimming and for the collection of the most minute members of the plant plankton for food. For anything from one to two-and-a-half weeks these active larvae are members of the animal plankton at the mercy of water movements. Settlement involves change in both habits and

structure with the loss of the velum and the temporary appearance of a foot and sense organs, including an eye spot. These enable the larva to find a suitable substrate, when it turns over on the left side and attaches itself by a spot of cement. In general such settlement occurs in shady places and usually where other oysters have settled, so that oysters tend to aggregate in large numbers. Following this 'spatfall', the young assume the appearance of the adult with development of gills and palps. Shell growth proceeds by a series of sudden marginal extensions known as 'shoots'.

The genus *Crassostrea* which includes the more vigorous and, in these days, more successful Portuguese, American and Japanese oysters, *C. angulata, C. virginica* and *C. gigas,* differs both in structure and in life-history. The lower shell is always more deeply cupped, they have an additional passage, the promyal chamber, from gills to the exterior on the hinge side of the adductor, and in the female phase they liberate the smaller eggs, which may exceed 100 million. These are then fertilized and develop in the sea. The structural differences together with a greater functional adaptability enable these oysters to live in less saline, or more variably saline, and more turbid, water than do species of *Ostrea. Crassostrea* has proved the better able to withstand coastal changes produced by man and now includes much the most numerous and most abundantly exploited species.

Oyster cultivation is of great antiquity and developed independently in the Mediterranean and in Japan. Without precisely cultivating them, the Romans maintained *O. edulis* largely on ropes in Lago Lucrino and Lago Fusaro to the northwest of Naples. The animals seem to have been largely collected around Brindisi and were then 'fattened' in the warm saline waters of these small lakes in which grew a particularly rich plankton of microscopic plants. Such methods seem to have persisted until relatively recent times. The natural beds, particularly off the Atlantic coasts of Europe, were exploited without damage until the middle of the last century when increase in human populations and improved methods of transport led to overfishing and permanent destruction of the natural reefs. Study of the persisting culture methods in Italy led to the establishment of an elaborate system of oyster cultivation along the Atlantic and Mediterranean coasts of France. This has never happened in Great Britain where modern production is no more than 1% of what it was a century ago. Destruction caused by overfishing has been enhanced by pollution and by the introduction of foreign pests and competitors for settling space, notably the Slipper limpet *Crepidula fornicata* and the Oyster drill *Urosalpinx* (see whelk), both from North America, and the Australasian barnacle *Elminius modestus*. Cultivation has amounted to little more than the spreading of dead shells, or cultch, to provide settling surface and the 'relaying' of imported Seed oysters, usually *Ostrea edulis* but also the Portuguese *Crassostrea angulata* which grows well in British waters but, because reproduction involves a temperature of about 68°F (20°C), only spawns during occasional very warm summers.

Cultivation in France is on parcs which are exposed at low water. Originally this was exclusively of *Ostrea edulis* but, after accidental introduction, the much hardier *Crassostrea angulata* is now almost exclusively cultivated south of Brittany. The Japanese *C. gigas* is also being reared. Cultivation involves the continual care of the growing oysters which are laid on the flat sandy or muddy surface and kept above the continually falling silt which would otherwise smother them. Starfish, crabs and other native pests are removed (the American pests have not spread there). Palisades and stakes which separate adjacent parcs also keep out invading fish.

When the temperature rises appropriately in the early summer 'collectors' are positioned in regions where the larvae will leave the surface and the spat subsequently settle. This is not necessarily above the parcs which are situated where the plankton is rich and so growth most rapid. The larvae may then be carried away by the prevailing water movements. Although any convenient hard surface will provide settling surface, the standard 'collector' consists of half cylinder roofing tiles arranged, concave side undermost, in alternating rows, first in one direction and then the other, within a wooden crate-like framework. The collecting tiles are thinly coated with lime so that the young oysters can be flaked off when they reach an adequate size without damage to the tiles

which can be used indefinitely. However, if a suitably pliable collecting surface is used it is possible to detach the young oysters within a day after settlement and then to rear them under laboratory conditions until they reach a size when they can be laid out on the oyster beds. It is along such lines that experiments are now being carried out in Britain.

The production of oysters along the Atlantic coast of North America is based on collection, with some cultivation, of the Cupped oyster *Crassostrea virginica,* which occurs from the Gulf of St Lawrence to the Gulf of Mexico and probably comprises three subspecies spawning within different ranges of temperature. Although production is still very great, particularly in the Gulf of Mexico, many one-time flourishing beds along the Atlantic coast are now denuded. This is in part due to overfishing but still more to the effects of a variety of parasites and diseases; the oysters have also to contend with the attacks of enemies of which starfish and oyster drills are the most potent. The European *Ostrea edulis* has been introduced with some success along the New England coast.

The native oyster of the Pacific coast of North America is the small *O. lurida,* of minor importance and now displaced as far north as British Columbia by the large and enormously prolific *Crassostrea gigas*. This was, and continues to be, imported as 'seed' from Japan but is now completely established particularly in protected areas where the temperature rises locally to above 68°F (20°C) at which it spawns. It is a large and extremely vigorous species; if left it may attain lengths of up to one foot (30 cm), far too large for commercial use. But if adequately tended no species of oyster is so

prolific or so easy to cultivate. This is done on a large scale in Japan where a most impressive industry having no initial connexion with European cultivation now exists. Although a number of species of Edible oysters occur, *Crassostrea gigas* is much the most vigorous and is alone cultivated.

Cultivation would appear to have originated in Japan in the 18th century on palisades of bamboos and is now widespread along the east coast. Spat are collected on strings of spaced scallop shells which are usually suspended from rafts in sheltered inlets. Later the large scallop shells with their covering of small spat oysters are spaced further apart and transferred either within frameworks fixed to the bottom in very shallow water or else, and more commonly, suspended in strings from rafts which are buoyed up by large concrete floats. This suspended culture has the major advantage of exposing the oysters to layers of water rich in planktonic food and also keeping the animals well clear of the bottom and so away from the attacks of their most serious pests, starfish and Oyster drills. Vast numbers of these large rafts are maintained in suitably protected waters along the east coast of Japan, with greatest concentrations in the Inland Sea around Hiroshima.

The Japanese industry not only supplies internal demands but provides the Seed oysters which are exported to the United States and elsewhere including Australia where there is also a considerable industry based on the cultivation of the local *Crassostrea commercialis* mainly along the coast of New South Wales. Other species of oysters are exploited in New Zealand. FAMILY: Ostreidae, ORDER: Eulamellibranchia, CLASS: Bivalvia, PHYLUM: Mollusca. C.M.Y.

Early method of oyster culture practised in Japan, the spat settling on bamboo fences and being raked off when full grown. Modern methods (right) of collecting and growing oysters include strings of old oyster shells hung from rafts and also piles of curved tiles stacked on the beach.

P

PACA *Cuniculus paca,* a rodent found in tropical America, from Mexico to southern Brazil. It belongs to the same family as the agoutis and acushis, but is rather larger, up to 2 ft (60 cm) in length. Like its relatives it has almost no tail, but it is distinguished by a pattern of bold white spots and lines on the back and sides. The skull of the paca is unique amongst mammals in having the cheek-bones grossly enlarged and inflated, with a peculiar honeycombed texture, perhaps acting as resonating chambers. Pacas are vegetarians and sometimes damage crops. FAMILY: Dasyproctidae, ORDER: Rodentia, CLASS: Mammalia.

PACARANA *Dinomys branicki,* a South American rodent superficially resembling the *paca, although it is placed in a different family, of which it is the sole member. Like the paca it is a heavily built animal about 22 in (56 cm) long and it has a similar pattern of rows of white spots on a background of dark brown. It differs from the paca, however, in having a conspicuous tail, about 8 in (20 cm) long. The pacarana is confined to the lower slopes of the Andes from Colombia to Bolivia. It is a poorly known animal and appears to be becoming very rare. Its survival is not helped by its temperament, being unusually docile and slow-moving for a rodent. FAMILY: Dinomyidae, ORDER: Rodentia, CLASS: Mammalia.

PADDLEFISHES, primitive fishes related to the sturgeons and sharing with them a skeleton of cartilage and a spiral valve in the intestine. There are only two species of paddlefishes, one from the Yangtse in China (*Polyodon gladius*) and one from the Mississippi basin (*P. spathula*). The body, although naked, resembles that of the sturgeons except for the prolonged snout which is extended into a flat sword. This 'paddle' is sensitive and easily damaged and is not used, as might be expected, as a probe or digger in feeding, since these fishes tend to swim with their mouths open and gather their food in that way (small planktonic organisms). The barbels that are characteristic of the mouth of sturgeons are reduced to small protuberances

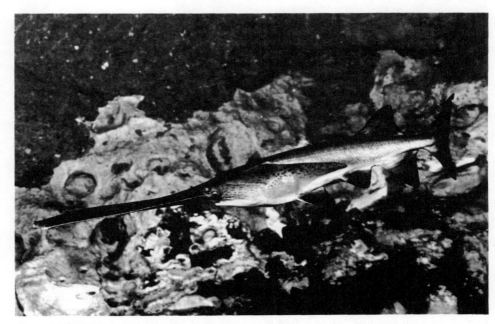

The use to which the grotesque 'spoonbill' of the paddlefish is put is still speculative.

under the paddle. The Mississippi paddlefish rarely grows to more than 150 lb (68 kg). The Chinese paddlefish is reported to reach 20 ft (6 m) in length. Paddlefishes spawn in turbulent waters and it is only in recent years that their larvae have been identified and studied. Like the sturgeons, the paddlefishes have become rarer owing to pollution of rivers. FAMILY: Polyodontidae, ORDER: Acipenseriformes, CLASS: Pisces.

PAIN, a sensation which can be experienced only by an individual, who may describe it as pricking, burning, stabbing, shooting and so on. As it is subjective, pain in others can only be inferred by the description given and, in certain circumstances, the reactions and symptoms of the sufferer. Animals cannot communicate a description of their pains so their particular suffering must, to a considerable extent, be interpreted and understood with reference to experiences of our own.

Nevertheless there is scientific evidence that the nervous pathways in other mammals at least closely correspond to those in humans and that the stimulation or irritation of a sensory nerve-ending will be quickly conducted along specific nerve fibres to a particular region of the brain and consciousness. At a Symposium on pain Lord Brain concluded his presidential address with these words:

'Since the diencephalon (part of the forebrain) is well-developed in animals and birds, I at least cannot doubt that the interests and activities of animals are correlated with awareness and feelings in the same way as my own, and which may be, for aught I know, just as vivid.'

Many people with personal experience of pain will probably agree that crushed limbs and violent stomachache or colic, are both exceedingly painful and distressing conditions. Yet the pain endured in either case is a condition which is basically in the interests of the individual (human or animal) concerned, since the affected limbs will be rested and not used, so permitting healing to commence, while the violence of the colic will take away the animal's desire for food and hasten the passage of the noxious material

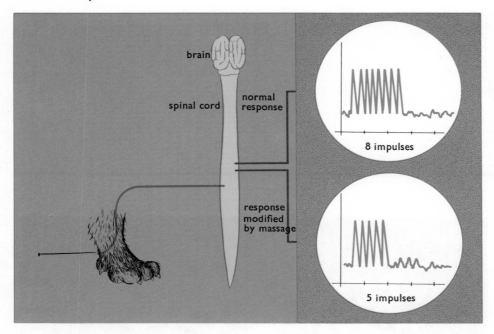

The normal response to a pin-prick on a cat's paw is shown here as 8 impulses recorded on an oscilloscope connected to an electrode in the spinal cord. By simultaneously massaging the area that is pricked, the response can be reduced to only 5 impulses. This seems to confirm the value of rubbing away pain.

through the intestines and its evacuation. Pain is, therefore, beneficial as a warning sign that something is wrong. This is of great importance to the recovery of individual animals which might otherwise continue to use the particular organs affected.

The pain in an injured limb can be reduced by injecting a local anaesthetic around the nerve involved but if this is done then the animal has no sensation in that part of the limb and may injure it further without any warning signs being given. It is not possible to give instructions to animals to lie down and rest, but it is possible to sedate them so that their activity is reduced and movements less frequent.

The classical example of stomach pain is provided by a description of the symptoms of colic in the horse: the animal looks anxious or worried, refuses to move or does so only with difficulty, frequently lies down or rolls, grunts, groans and thrashes about the floor. Somewhat similar signs of intestinal pain may be seen in rats, mice or other small animals which have eaten certain cruel poisons such as phosphorus and arsenic.

Animals in pain can be extremely dangerous. Only people who are absolutely confident of their ability to do so should attempt to handle them, and the attentions of a veterinary surgeon should always be obtained as soon as possible. W.N.S.

PAINTED SNIPE, a family of marsh-frequenting snipe-like birds one species of which is found from Japan to Australia and west to Africa and the other in South America. The first is the Painted snipe *Ros-* *tratula benghalensis,* with the Australian population subspecifically differentiated from that in Africa, southern Turkey, India, China and Japan, and the second is the American painted snipe *Nycticryphes semicollaris,* found from southeastern Brazil to northern Argentina. The two species are rather similar in plumage but differ in a few minor characters such as the amount of webbing between the toes, and the conformation of bill and tail. Resemblances with the true snipe are superficial and due to the convergent evolution of the two families because of a similar way of life in like environments. Painted snipe are more closely related to *jacanas and have some features in common with the cranes.

In size and shape Painted snipe are comparable with true snipe, but have rather shorter legs and a shorter bill, only slightly longer than the head, and a little decurved towards the tip. Like snipe, the tip of the bill is pitted and sensitive to the movement of the worms, insects, crustaceans and molluscs for which the bird probes in mud. The eyes are set at the sides of the head so that Painted snipe have monocular vision through the entire 360° field, and probably have binocular vision in front of and behind the head. Like snipe too, the plumage is cryptically patterned, olive above with creamy lines over the forehead and crown, through the eyes and over the shoulders, and buff spots and bars on the wings and tail. But here the similarity ends, for Painted snipe are more

The marsh-dwelling Painted snipe *Rostratula benghalensis* on its nest, in Kashmir.

richly coloured, especially the female, which is a little longer than the male and takes the initiative in courtship although playing a minor role in nesting.

In the Old World Painted snipe it is the female who displays towards the male, and she may be polyandrous. In a spectacle which few have recorded, the wings are spread and brought forward to display to best advantage to the male their rich pattern of buff circles on an olive ground, and to offset the cinnamon breast and face with its white spectacles. The male builds a simple nest on marshy ground, concealed by tall sedges or a tangle of thorny shrubs, and incubates the clutch of four or more glossy whitish eggs with handsome black or purple blotches. He rears the downy young, while the more aggressive female defends the territory. In the American painted snipe the reversal of the roles of the sexes has not proceeded so far, and the female incubates.

Lacking the aerial courtship flights of some of the true snipe, the lives of Painted snipe are conducted close to the marshy ground they love. They tend to be crepuscular and solitary, although they may be concentrated by drought on to a few pools, when several together can be flushed by day. When flushed, they fly weakly on rounded wings, with legs trailing like a rail, to drop down into cover again as soon as possible, where they stand guardedly bobbing the body up and down like a sandpiper. They certainly wander a good deal, but regular migration has not been established, although

several have been caught in the early morning at a particular season in suburban localities in Africa, circumstances suggesting regular nocturnal migration. FAMILY: Rostratulidae, ORDER: Charadriiformes, CLASS: Aves. C.H.F.

PAIR BOND. When two adult individuals of a species associate closely with one another, show co-operative behaviour and are not overtly aggressive towards one another, they can be said to have formed a pair bond. The pair normally consists of a male and a female but it is not unusual in aviary or domesticated birds for two males to form a pair.

The pair bond forms after an initial period of courtship but mating often occurs a considerable time later so that a period of 'engagement' follows the establishment of the bond. The length of time for which the pair bond lasts varies from a short period during the breeding season in mallards *Anas platyrhynchos* to the life-long union of the Grey lag goose *Anser anser* and jackdaw *Corvus monedula*. A pair bond occurs not only in birds but also in some species of fish, for example the Jewel fish *Hemichromis bimaculatus* and in some mammals such as the wolf *Canis lupus* and the badger *Meles meles*. The majority of the higher Primates are promiscuous or polygamous but the Lar gibbon *Hylobates lar* which lives in small family groups containing two adults shows a long-lasting pair bond.

Human beings are the only species of social primate which shows a pair bond and, unlike most other mammals, a prolonged period of courtship occurs in our own species.

Lorenz has described how the members of a pair of geese greet one another with a display of aggression directed away from the mate and this he has termed the 'triumph ceremony'. A number of other types of behaviour are associated with the pair bond which suggest an affectionate relationship. Mutual grooming is common amongst both birds and mammals; adult members of a pair often adopt juvenile behaviour towards one another and, in many birds for example, the female may solicit food from her mate by adopting juvenile begging behaviour.

The death of one of the partners breaks the life-long pair bond and the behaviour of a bereaved Grey lag goose has been described by Konrad Lorenz. The bird searches for its mate travelling further and further afield, it loses status and its condition deteriorates so that it becomes easy prey to a fox.

It seems probable that the establishment of a pair bond may have different functions in different species. Most commonly it serves to keep the parents together at a time when they are rearing their young so that they can co-operate in the feeding and defence of their offspring. This is the situation in the Jewel fish and in seasonally pairing birds such as the European robin *Erithacus rubecula*.

In the mallard, however, the pair bond breaks after coitus and the cryptically coloured female alone rears the young. In this case it is possible that the function of the pair bond is to ensure that the pair are physiologically attuned so that they breed successfully. The work of Daniel Lehrman on the Ring dove *Streptopelia risoria* has shown that the proximity of a courting male influences the female's physiological state and reproductive behaviour. The presence of the male facilitates the development of sexual maturity in the female for if a male is absent or only a castrated male is present, the female does not select or build a nest and will not mate. T.B.P.

PAIR FORMATION, the establishment of a special bond between members of the opposite sex for breeding purposes. The term is used especially for birds. The pair bond may be temporary, seasonal, or permanent and in the strict sense should indicate a monogamous state. It usually involves complex movements or vocalizations and elaborate displays.

PAIRING, a term used with at least three shades of meaning. It is used for the pairing of chromosomes in *meiosis (reduction division) in which homologous chromosomes come to lie side by side. It is also used for the association of animals in pairs for a shorter or longer period for purposes of reproduction. This is of great importance in animals in which there is prolonged care of the young in which both parents take part. And it is an euphemism for copulation.

PALAEONISCIDS, an order of fossil fishes which, together with the bichirs and sturgeons, comprises the Chondrostei of the subclass Actinopterygii or ray-finned fishes. See also fishes, fossil; and the classification table of fishes. ORDER: Palaeonisciformes, INFRACLASS: Chondrostei, SUBCLASS: Actinopterygii, CLASS: Pisces.

PALEARCTIC REGION, one of the six major zoogeographical regions, it includes all of the Eurasian continent north of the tropics, with Iceland, the British Isles and Japan, and also a small corner of Northwest Africa which, isolated from the rest of Africa by the Sahara, has been colonized mainly by animals from Europe.

Most of the southern edge of the region, from the Middle East through the southern USSR, western China and Mongolia, is covered by arid or desert country. This, together with the Mediterranean to the west and the high Tibetan plateau to the east, almost completely isolates the Palearctic region from the tropical faunas of the Ethiopian and Oriental regions. Only in the extreme east is there a gradual transition between tropical Southeast Asia and the mainly deciduous forests of southern China. North of the desert zone there is a transition through grasslands to deciduous and mixed forest up to about 60°N. North of this there is a broad zone of coniferous forest. The regions above the Arctic Circle and most of Siberia, are covered by tundra.

As might be expected from this climatic pattern, the richest fauna of the Palearctic region is to be found in the forests of southeast China. Here the fauna also includes some tropical animals extending north from the Oriental region, such as the alligator and the Monitor lizard *Varanus*.

The isolation of the rest of the Palearctic region is comparatively recent. In the Tertiary the climate of Eurasia was much warmer and moister, so that tropical and subtropical animals were widely spread through the region. Only in the late Pliocene and the Pleistocene did the climate become progressively colder and drier, culminating in the Ice Ages. As a result, the more warmth-loving animals migrated southwards, and the

Map of the Palearctic region, which includes Europe, most of Asia as well as a strip of north Africa.

fauna remaining in most of the Palearctic region contains only the more tolerant and climatically resistant animals. Since these qualities permit most of them to range widely through the world, hardly any Palearctic animals are confined to that region— the only exceptions are the hedge-sparrows, the Mole rats, the Bactrian camel and the pandas.

There are, then, virtually no exclusively Palearctic animals, and the Palearctic region itself is not uniform but is strongly zoned climatically. As a result, it is best considered as a series of fringing zones, of successively more severe climate, bordering the more hospitable tropics. The faunas of these zones differ from one another in the successive disappearance, as one travels northwards, of the less resistant animals. For example, it is in the Mediterranean and Balkan regions that the amphibian and reptile fauna is most diverse, including such forms as the salamanders, the frogs, the tortoises *Testudo*, pond-turtles, colubrid snakes, poisonous Pit vipers and several types of lizard (geckos, agamids and skinks). Individual genera or species of these cold-blooded vertebrates, such as the newt *Triturus*, the frog *Rana*, the toad *Bufo* and the viper or adder *Vipera*, extend somewhat farther north. Nevertheless, the more northern terrestrial vertebrate faunas are predominantly composed of the warm-blooded birds and mammals, and even these are greatly reduced. Thus there are only 37 families of bird that are widely distributed in the Palearctic region (and some of these are mainly summer migrants), compared with 56–7 in the tropical Ethiopian and Oriental regions. A few mammals, such as the beavers, bears and deer, appear to be specially suited to colder regions and occur in such parts of both the Old World and the New World (the Nearctic region). Nevertheless, most of the mammals are, again, members of groups that are more numerous and diverse in the tropical regions—for example, pigs horses, bovids and murids (rats and mice).　　　C.B.C.

PALEO-ECOLOGY, the study of the inter-relationships between organisms and the environments of the past. It brings together the disciplines of paleontology—the study of extinct animals and plants—and sedimentology, in which the process of deposition of sedimentary rocks is investigated. Broadly speaking, the paleoecologist attempts to answer two kinds of question: first, how did variation of the physical environment affect animal and plant communities and their distribution; and secondly, how has change of the environment during geological time affected the evolution of both organisms and their community structures?

These questions can never be fully answered because the paleo-ecologist is limited by the nature of the evidence available for study. For example, not all environments encourage the preservation of animal and plant material in the form of fossils. In upland areas the rate of deposition of sediment is often very slow, or even does not occur at all, and the chances of any organic remains surviving long enough to be included in these sediments are correspondingly very slight. Conditions for preservation are optimal in areas where there is rapid deposition of fine sediment, but even under these conditions as little as 0·1% of the original population may be eventually preserved. The only organisms which are readily preserved are those which have a hard skeleton, or which secrete a shell and consequently the fossil record of animals such as flatworms and jellyfish, and plants such as fungi and algae is virtually non-existant. Another limitation of paleo-ecological studies arises from the fact that the only physical conditions that can be known are those which have influenced sedimentary deposition.

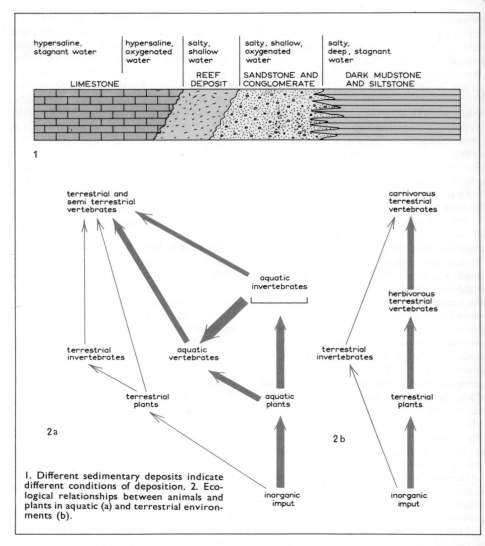

1. Different sedimentary deposits indicate different conditions of deposition. 2. Ecological relationships between animals and plants in aquatic (a) and terrestrial environments (b).

In spite of these limitations, the paleoecologist is able to reconstruct a picture of some past environments with a fair degree of certainty. For example, a variety of physical conditions have caused both faunal variation and sediment (facies) variation in the Permian deposits of Texas and New Mexico, which were studied by N. D. Newell in 1957. Here a single sedimentary horizon was found to change from dark mudstones and siltstones, to sandstones and conglomerates, thence to reef deposits, and finally to limestone. This facies variation indicates that the sediments were deposited on either side of a reef, on one side of which was a deep sea in which dark muds and silts were deposited, and on the edge of which collected sands and gravels. The reef separated the sea from a lagoon in which the limestone was deposited. By an analysis of these sediments, and by comparison with present day conditions, it could be inferred that the lagoonal water was well aerated and had a high concentration of salt, while the sea was of normal salinity, well aerated near the edge of the reef, but increasingly stagnant in deeper water. The

fossil content of these rocks confirmed this interpretation. Except at the edge of the reef where some crinoids or Sea lilies were found, few specimens were obtained from the lagoonal limestones, presumably because conditions had been too saline. In the reef deposits themselves, there was a varied fauna of sponges, algae, lampshells and bryozoans. Along the edge of the reef there were sponges, echinoids and molluscs but, further out, where dark silts indicated a lack of oxygen, fossils were few and consisted only of fragments derived from the inshore faunas. Under present-day conditions a similar faunal sequence can be seen in lagoonal and reef environments, thus the hypothesis was confirmed that the Permian environment of Texas and New Mexico was similar to that seen in other parts of the world today.

In this way variation of fauna and environment can be traced along a single facies representing deposition during a discrete period of geological time. An alternative approach attempts to follow changes of fauna and environment through a vertical succession of geological horizons, in other words over a period of time rather than over an area.

A good example of such a study comes from the Triassic of South Africa where a series of continental deposits indicate a gradual change from wet, swampy conditions (Lystrosaurus zone of the Lower Triassic) to a dry desert climate (Cave Sandstone and Red Beds of the Upper Triassic). During this climatic change, which took place over a period of about 45 million years, the fossil flora and fauna changed also. Thus, there was a gradual change from a flora typically containing plants such as horse tails, to one dominated by the seed fern *Dicroidium*. During Lystrosaurus zone times there were small carnivorous mammal like reptiles but the main elements of the fauna were semi-aquatic reptiles such as *Lystrosaurus* and *Chasmatosaurus,* and amphibians. With drier conditions this fauna gave way to one in which small, active mammal like reptiles predominated. By Upper Triassic times the climate was hot and dry, and these conditions seem to have stimulated the great adaptive radiation of reptiles, of which the dinosaurs were now an important element.

Apart from correlation of past organisms and environments, it is also possible for the paleo-ecologist to speculate upon the ecological relationships between the organisms themselves. When beds occur in which fossils are abundant, tentative models can be made representing past communities. These are based upon the feeding habits of the animals present, and upon an identification of their supposed habitats. This type of paleo-ecology, which was largely pioneered by E. C. Olson, can show for example, that, in the Early Permian, the community was primarily based upon aquatic plants. This can be deduced from the fact that the dominant vertebrates of that period, the pelycosaurs, were themselves aquatic or semi-aquatic. However, by Late Permian times the community was one in which the dominant vertebrates—carnivorous and herbivorous mammal-like reptiles—were terrestrial.
P.H

PALLAS, Peter Simon, 1741–1811, famous traveller and naturalist, was born in Berlin, son of a surgeon, and himself was trained in medicine. He settled in Holland and in 1766 published his Elenchus Zoophytorum, one of the earliest works on the lower invertebrates. Because of this and his Miscellanea Zoologica, published the same year, he was invited by the Empress Catherine to accept the chair of natural history in the Imperial Academy of Sciences in St. Petersburg and from then on he spent many years travelling across Russia, into Central Asia and Siberia investigating the natural history.

PALMCHAT *Dulus dominicus,* a thrush-sized bird confined to Hispaniola and Gonave in the West Indies, regarded by some as a relative of the waxwings and silky-flycatchers, but treated by others as the sole representative of its own family. It is brown above with a greyish-olive wash, and yellowish on the flight feathers. Below it is white with profuse, short brown streaks. The wings are rounded, the head heavy with a short, laterally-compressed bill with a strongly curved culmen. The palmchat feeds on berries and flowers and is very sociable. The nest is bulky and built of twigs, usually around the frond-bases of a palm. The nest is sometimes built on its own but is more frequently found grouped with others to form a continuous large structure, up to 3 ft (1 m) across. Each pair occupies a cavity lined with finer material and opening to the outside. The same nest is refurbished and used each year. Clutches of four heavily-blotched white eggs are laid. FAMILY: Dulidae, ORDER: Passeriformes, CLASS: Aves.

PALOLO, the South Sea Islanders' name for a marine bristleworm *Eunice viridis* which swarms at the surface of the sea at certain times of the year. The adult worm lives on the sea bottom in muddy sand, amongst rocks or in crevices in coral. It is superficially like a ragworm but the head end bears five short tentacles or antennae and two additional tentacles just behind the head. The body is long with many segments and with gills arched over the back. As the worm becomes sexually mature the rear half of the body becomes loaded with ova or sperm, and it looks then quite different from the front half. At the spawning season the worms leave their shelters on the sea-bed, the rear half of their body breaks away and swims to the surface where it splits shedding its ova or sperm into the water. This mass of eggs is netted by the people of Fiji and Samoa, taken ashore and cooked. The season of spawning is precisely determined, the worms maturing under hormonal influences governed by a combination of factors related to the lunar cycle and to light. This ensures that all the worms which normally live independent lives on the sea bottom release their genital products at the surface at the same time, giving maximum opportunity for the ova to be fertilized.

The average date of the appearance of the great swarms was November 27th in data gathered up to 1921. In fact swarming occurs seven, eight or nine days after the full moon. Very careful analysis of the timing of the breeding behaviour during the day shows that this also is remarkably regular.

Swarmings of other kinds of worms, in the warmer parts of the Atlantic as well as other parts of the Pacific, are sometimes called palolo, although wrongly, as for example Japanese palolo. FAMILY: Eunicidae, CLASS: Polychaeta, PHYLUM: Annelida.   R.P.D.

PAMPAS DEER *Ozotoceros bezoarticus,* the most elegant of the South American *deer, inhabiting the open plains.

PANCAKE TORTOISE *Malacochersus tornieri,* of Tanzania, also known as Loveridge's tortoise, has a flattened, flexible shell, and can squeeze into narrow crevices and between rocks. By slightly inflating its body it can resist being pulled out.

PANCHAX, small egg-laying freshwater fishes belonging to the family of toothcarps and found in Africa and Southeast Asia. Many of the panchaxes are now included in the genus *Aplocheilus,* but their former placement in *Panchax* earned them their common name. In Africa, members of the

Pachypanchax playfairi, one of the panchaxes, living in the freshwaters from East Africa to Madagascar and the Seychelles.

genus *Micropanchax* are also referred to as panchaxes. The Asian species grow to about 3 in (8 cm) and the African species to about 2 in (5 cm). The Dwarf panchax *A. blocki* from Ceylon has a shining blue-green underside which has given it the alternative name of Green panchax. The Blue panchax *A. panchax,* found from India across to Malaysia, is rarely imported into Europe although it is extensively kept and reared in the Far East. The African panchaxes, and especially *M. macrophthalmus,* are often on sale in Europe and are attractive additions to an aquarium. FAMILY: Cyprinodontidae, ORDER: Atheriniformes, CLASS: Pisces.

PANCREAS, a gland present in vertebrates lying between the stomach and the first loop of the intestine. In many mammals it is rather diffuse, but in other vertebrates it is usually a fairly compact structure. The pancreas has two quite separate functions. It secretes a mixture of digestive enzymes, including trypsin, lipase and amylase, which passes via the pancreatic duct into the intestine. Groups of cells, not involved in enzyme production, known as the Islets of Langerhans act as an endocrine gland secreting the hormone insulin which passes directly into the bloodstream and helps control the blood sugar level. Failure of the pancreas to produce enough insulin results in the disease diabetes mellitus.

PANDA, GIANT *Ailuropoda melanoleuca,* one of the rarest, most puzzling and yet very popular mammals known today. Since the first live black and white panda reached a zoo in the western hemisphere in 1936, only 14 others have been kept in captivity outside China. The Giant panda's inaccessible and restricted range is no doubt one of the factors responsible. It lives in a most inhospitable environment: densely vegetated mountains which are either covered in snow or shrouded in mist while deep gorges and ravines form such efficient barriers that it takes weeks for a man to contour them. The beishung, as the Giant panda is known locally, lives in the bamboo and rhododendron forests of Yunnan and Szechuan in an area approximately 500 m (800 km) wide. Because of these formidable odds, the panda was only discovered in 1869 by Père David, a French zoologist explorer. Ever since then, taxonomists have been at a loss to decide its correct classification, whether it belongs to the bear family Ursidae or the raccoon family Procyonidae which includes kinkajous, coatis, olingos and cacomistles. The Giant panda weighs 160–400 lb (75–180 kg) and measures 44·5 to 63 in (1–1·6 m) including the diminutive tail. The fur is white or yellowish, contrasting with black limbs, shoulders, ears and eye patches. Once considered a monophage, subsisting on bamboo to the exclusion of all else, the panda

can actually survive for long periods without it, feeding on a variety of juicy plants instead. Captive pandas sometimes even eat cooked meat. However, bamboo forms the major part of its diet in the wild. Young shoots in particular are eaten while the hardened stems are broken off and discarded. While foraging, the Giant panda sits on its haunches, legs spread, and holds the delicate branch with one forepaw, using a remarkably strong 'pseudo-thumb' to grip it. This unusual 'sixth digit' is in reality a modified wrist-bone under the pad of the foot which has evolved to a thumb-like size and flexibility, permitting precise plucking movements. The only other mammal to have a 'sixth-finger' is the Lesser panda, in which it is vestigial, but no bear shares this astonishing adaptation. The head has also evolved an impressive musculature to reduce this hard food to a pulp. The molars are wide and flat, and the skull is much broader than a bear's narrow, small-toothed head. Once the bamboo is thoroughly crushed, it then passes through the oesophagus and stomach, equally impervious to splinters or fibrous bulk, which are as tough and muscular as a chicken's gizzard. Contrary to other vegetarian mammals, the intestine is very short (more so than any bear's) which would indicate that the panda's ancestors were carnivorous and the adaptations of the upper digestive system were sufficient to cope with the bamboo. Because the food is so quickly digested and contains little protein, the panda must spend over twelve hours a day chewing to obtain

sufficient nourishment. No wonder that pandas do not stray far from the dense bamboo thickets. They have never been observed galloping like bears but instead use a slow, pigeon-toed, rolling shuffle, swinging the heavy head from side to side. The fastest gait is a jog-trot which surprised early hunters who concluded that it was a stupid animal because it did not flee at top speed. One could argue that such a hampered mammal must have some other means of defence. Elusive habits, remote habitat and bone crushing jaws useful in close combat are the only life-saving attributes of the panda. There is also the puzzle of its conspicuous markings. Perhaps these are an effective camouflage against snow-covered slopes.

Superficially pandas are bear-like because the skeleton must be sturdy enough to carry such a large head. Another argument towards placing Giant pandas in the Procyonidae is the structure of the reproductive system. Both Giant and Lesser pandas have inconspicuously small genitalia while in the bears, they are more apparent and dog-like. But there is a counterpoint: Giant panda cubs are born after a short 120–140 day gestation, weighing 5 oz (142 gm), approximately $\frac{1}{800}$th of the adult weight. Bear cubs are also completely helpless and tiny at birth. Other comparisons show that a panda's blood serum is identical with a bear's, but on the other hand the chromosome count is the same as a raccoon's. Until more is known about the panda's habits in the wild, the animal's relationships will not be clarified.

Giant panda, adopted by the World Wildlife Fund as a symbol of endangered animal species.

Lesser panda, or Red panda, was the first of two species to be given the Nepalese name, panda. The latter name was later also applied to the Giant panda of China.

The Giant panda's behaviour in captivity is quite different from a bear's. It does not bellow or whine but bleats and also hisses and spits like the Lesser panda, the kinkajou and the coati (all procyonids). Furthermore, solitary most of the year, Giant pandas possess scent-glands used by the male to mark territorial boundaries and by the female to indicate sexual receptivity. Bears do not do this. They use their urine and droppings. The bear and the Giant panda shared a common ancestor 40 million years ago which looked like a civet. The descendants of this mammal, over the next few million years, evolved simultaneously towards a dog-like form, and elsewhere towards arboreal cacomistle-like raccoons. These arboreal forms were found in the New World but a few, the present day pandas, spread across Asia and continued evolving into super-raccoons. FAMILY: Procyonidae (or Ursidae?), ORDER: Carnivora, CLASS: Mammalia. N.D.

PANDA, LESSER *Ailurus fulgens,* also known as the Red panda, discovered by Hardwicke in 1821, was only described by Frédéric Cuvier four years later, in 1825. It remained the only panda known to science for nearly 50 years. Like the Giant panda it favours remote bamboo forests between 7,000 and 12,000 ft (2,300–4,000 m) but it is more widespread and may be found from Yunnan and Szechuan, southward to Sikkim and westward to Nepal. The 'fire-fox' as it is aptly called in China, has an elongated body covered in soft, dense fur of a brilliant chestnut red. The tail, 2 ft (60 cm) long, is bushy, faintly ringed with creamy orange and russet. In contrast with the body, the triangular face and large pointed ears are usually a light fawn colour. A dark stripe circles each eye and runs down to the chin.

The Lesser panda's broad paws with hairy soles and semi-retractile claws are well adapted to the rigours of its environment, being both useful in climbing trees and gripping icy boulders. Although heavy-limbed in appearance, this medium-sized mammal weighs only 7–12 lb (3–5 kg) and measures 32–44 in (80–112 cm) including the tail. The 'fire-fox' is crepuscular and arboreal, resting during the daylight hours either curled up in the fork of a tree or sprawled along a branch. Descending to browse in the bamboo groves, it eats young shoots, fruit and, should it stumble across them, an occasional egg or nestling. This small panda feeds in the same manner as its larger relative, plucking bamboo leaves with either forepaw which has a special callosity on the pad allowing certain prehensile movements. Such a vegetarian diet is surprising for a carnivore but as most procyonids (raccoons, coatis, kinkajous, etc.) are omnivorous to a great extent, the Lesser panda has just specialized its diet further. Even though it is much more agile than the Giant panda, both share the same swaying, pigeon-toed, plantigrade walk (the sole of the foot resting on the ground with each step). But in the trees, Lesser pandas venture out on the thinnest branches and climb down the steepest trunks head first without the slightest clumsiness. They travel usually in pairs, at least until the young are born, in a tree trunk or rocky crevice, when the mother remains constantly with them as they are blind and helpless for a month. The family group is often not broken up until the next litter. Should one of the four cubs stray (twins are not rare), it will give a long 'wah!' bleating call until the female has located and retrieved it, carrying it in her mouth. Not surprisingly for animals living at such elevations, delayed implantation may take place which lengthens

the overall gestation period from three to five months. This applies almost always to the northern race, Styan's red panda *Ailurus fulgens styani,* a slightly larger subspecies. Other vocalizations include a hiss ending with a spit or snort, depending on whether this usually docile animal is defensively or more aggressively inclined. When hard pressed, it will rear up and cuff the intruder with both forepaws or clasp and bite. FAMILY: Procyonidae, ORDER: Carnivora, CLASS: Mammalia. N.D.

PANDAS IN ZOOS. The status of Giant pandas in the wild is unknown as their range lies within the borders of the Chinese People's Republic and there have been very few seen in zoos outside China. In 1967 the only Giant pandas in captivity were 16 in China, two in Korea, and one each in London and Moscow. The first to be taken outside China was Su-lin which reached Chicago Zoo in 1936. Another, Mei-Mei, arrived there in 1938. In the same year a female, Ming, and two males, Tang and Sung, were brought to London Zoo. The males died before Ming and she only survived to 1944. Lien-ho then lived in the London Zoo from 1946 to 1950. Now, the only Giant pandas in the west are Chi-Chi, a female at London and An-An, a male, in Moscow. Attempts have been made to mate them, Chi-Chi being taken to Moscow in 1966 and An-An making the reciprocal visit in 1968. Nothing resulted, but the Chinese are reported to have had more success, three pandas having been born in Peking Zoo, apparently the result of artificial insemination.

PANGAEA, the single land mass which existed before it was split into separate continents by *continental drift.

PANGOLINS, also known as Scaly anteaters, are mammals with the body covered with scales that overlap in an imbricated manner, like slates on a roof. Only the abdomen, the inner sides of the extremities, the throat and part of the head are free from scales. These are covered with hair. The scales are outgrowths of the true skin and are coated with epidermis. The head is conical the eyes are small and the outer ear is also small. Since pangolins have no teeth, they feed by means of the very long, wormlike extensile tongue. They have short, sturdy legs and the front paws have claws. The terrestrial types have a strong, muscular tail, approximately the same length as the body, which is completely scaly. In arboreal types the slender tail is longer than the body with a bare patch at the tip of the tail (about the size of a finger) and is used as a prehensile limb when climbing.

The seven living species are as follows. The Indian pangolin *Manis crassicaudata,* found in India and Ceylon, with a head and body length of 2 ft (60 cm) and a tail 18–20 in (45–50 cm) long. The scales are pale yellowish-brown and the skin is brownish. The Chinese pangolin *M. pentadactyla,* found on Formosa and in southern China, has a head and body length of 20–24 in (50–60 cm) and a tail 12–16 in (30–40 cm) long. The scales are blackish brown and the skin greyish-white. The Malayan pangolin *M. javanica* inhabits the Malay Peninsula, Burma, Indo-China, Laos and the islands of Sumatra, Borneo, Java and others. Its head and body length is 20–24 in (50–60 cm) with a tail 20–32 in (50–80 cm) long. The scales are amber to blackish brown and the skin is whitish. These three Asiatic types differ, among other things, from the African species by the presence of hair between the scales. On the African continent four types are distinguished. The Small-scaled tree pangolin *M. tricuspis,* of the tropical rain-forests from Sierra Leone to the Central African trough fault, has a head and body length of 14–18 in (35–45 cm) and a tail 16–20 in (40–50 cm) long. The scales are brownish-grey to dark brown and the skin white. The Long-tailed pangolin *M. tetradactyla* also inhabits the rain-forest areas of Africa, but is rarer than the Small-scaled tree pangolin. Its head and body length is 12–14 in (30–35 cm) and its tail 24–28 in (60–70 cm) long. The scales are dark brown with yellowish edges and the skin dark brown to blackish. The Giant pangolin *M. gigantea* is also an inhabitant of the tropical rain-forests. Its head and body length is 30–32 in (75–80 cm) and its tail 22–26 in (55–65 cm) long. The scales are greyish-brown and the skin whitish. The Temminck's pangolin *M. temmincki* lives in the East African savannahs, from Ethiopia to the Cape. Its head and body length is 20 in (50 cm) and the tail 14 in (35 cm) long. The scales are dark brown and the skin light with dark hairs.

The pangolins, according to type, have 12–16 dorsal vertebrae, 5–6 lumbar vertebrae, 2–4 sacral vertebrae and 21–47 caudal vertebrae. The Long-tailed pangolin has the largest number of caudal vertebrae (46–47) of all mammals. The ensiform process of the sternum, which in *M. javanica* and *M. pentadactyla* terminates in a 'blade-shaped' structure is also worthy of mention. In the case of *M. tricuspis* and *M. tetradactyla* the xiphisternum (ensiform process) is drawn out in two long cartilaginous members, which are united at their ends and then have a cartilaginous process on either side, drawing forwards. These modifications are related to the powerful elongation of the tongue. Pangolins have no clavicle.

The Small-scaled tree pangolin and the Long-tailed pangolin are purely arboreal.

The scales of pangolins, resembling fur cones, overlap like roof-tiles. They live in caves, which they leave at dusk to search for insects and worms and plants. They have no teeth and catch insects with a long round tongue; the insects are pulverized between the protuberances of the wall of the stomach and little stones which they also swallow. The long strong tail is used for climbing.

Vertical tree trunks are mastered by 'climbing', the body carrying out caterpillar-like movements. First, the two frontlegs are extended, then the body is drawn along and the hindlegs then get a grip in the bark of the tree just behind the forelegs. The toothed-edge scales of the tail ensure an additional support. When changing over from one branch to another the animals, by means of hindlegs and the prehensile tail, obtain such a sure grip that they can release the forelegs and lift the trunk off the branch at right angles.

These two arboreal types can also hang from a branch by the tail. If they cannot find a hold with the forelegs, they climb up 'themselves'. The two other African types, the Giant pangolin and Temminck's pangolin, are terrestrial. The column-like hindlegs, with their large soles, play the major part in the forward movement. The animals often go in a slightly raised position, the forefeet barely touching the ground. The extended tail, slightly raised from the ground, acts as counterpoise. If the animals are exposed to the weather, they erect the front part of the body and sit on the rear limbs and the tail. The Asiatic types move along the ground with great security, but are also good climbers. All pangolins have the ability to roll themselves up more or less into a ball. The arboreal types make the most complete balls, the tail close to the body and surrounding it. They sleep in this position in the fork of a branch or in epiphytes on the trees. The ball shape, however, is also a defensive position and it requires considerable force to unroll one of these animals. If this is done, the pangolin defends itself by squirting urine. Apart from human beings, the only enemies are the large felines. The terrestrial pangolins dig holes in the ground which, in the case of

the Giant pangolin may be up to 15 ft (5 m) long. They sleep rolled up in the burrow, without making a special sleeping place. All the pangolins are nocturnal and sleep during the day. At night they hunt for food, ants and termites. The arboreal types prefer ants, which live in soft cardboard-type nests, and the various tree-termites whose nests are also made of soft material. The terrestrial pangolins, owing to their extraordinary strength, are able to tear open even the hardest termite hills. The insects are picked up by the sticky tongue, which is kept moist all the time with the fluid from the enormously developed salivary gland. The stomach acts as a kind of 'masticating apparatus'. Since pangolins are toothless, the ants and termites pass into the stomach without being cut up and have to be ground up there. For this reason the stomach, instead of the mucous membrane, is lined with a horny stratified 'pavement epithelium' with 'horny teeth'. Opposite this, at the end of the small bend in the stomach there also rises a member provided with horny teeth and set in motion by powerful muscles. It is claimed that some pangolins swallow small stones with their food, which help in grinding up the insects. A Small-scaled tree pangolin will eat up to 7 oz (200 gm) of insects in one night. The stomach of the Giant pangolin will take even more. The range of distribution of the Chinese pangolin coincides with that of the two types of termites most frequently to be found there. The larger pangolins, however, would not be satisfied by the amount of insects obtained by digging out the termite hills and they also eat the types of ants and termites which move about at night in columns. During the digging out of a termite hill, the terrestrial pangolins anchor themselves to the ground by the hindfeet and tail.

The powerful claws of the forefeet dig close to the snout, which penetrates into the ever-deepening cavity, the tongue searching for termites, in the small tunnels. Since pangolins are very rarely seen, their presence in the open 'hunting grounds' is usually only betrayed by the excavated termite mounds. The soldier ants and termites, of course, attack the pangolins, by biting into and clinging to all the bare parts of the body and between the scales. In order to free themselves from the insects on chest and belly, the pangolins slither along the ground with all four legs extended. In order to get free from the insects which are firmly gripping the base of the scales, the pangolin forces its way between branches and other objects so that the scales, pressing heavily on each other, squash the insects.

The special food needed makes it difficult to keep pangolins in captivity outside their normal range. The Asiatic and the two large African pangolins have already been kept successfully in several zoological gardens. *Manis crassicaudata* and *M. pentadactyla* have lived in the Prague Zoo for up to 20 months. The Antwerp Zoo has had *Manis gigantea* for years and the Basle Zoo had *Manis temmincki*. The Long-tailed pangolin has never yet been kept successfully: the Small-scaled tree pangolin may thrive in captivity under favourable conditions if fed with ants' eggs. The composition of the substitute food varies with each zoo. Those in the Prague Zoo were offered the following mixture: boiled and raw minced meat, grated eggs, carrots, curds, ants' eggs and a little salt. The Giant pangolins at the Antwerp Zoo are given cornflakes, unsweetened condensed milk, water, scraped fish, ants eggs, wheat germ oil and a few drops of formic acid. For a year we have been giving our Giant pangolins a viscous pulp consisting of three grated hard-boiled eggs, one fresh egg, 3 grammes Nesmida (formic acid), one drop protovit, some fodder additive, boiled rice and milk. The animal thrives in this way without ants' eggs or insects. Water is taken by rapid projection and withdrawal of the tongue, foam forming at the tip of the snout with more or less large bubbles. The excrement is cylindrical, usually surrounded by a mucous membrane and according to the food, ants or termites, is blackish or brown.

The only sounds made by a pangolin are hissing, puffing and humming, all are probably due to heavy breathing and not to actual vocal expressions. We still know very little about reproduction in pangolins. The gestation period is unknown. African pangolins produce only one young at a birth, but there are records of three young in Asiatic pangolins. In all species the newly-born young

are approximately the same length, $11\frac{1}{2}$–13 in (28–32 cm). They are pink and the scales light and not yet imbricated. In the two African arboreal pangolins and in *M. javanica,* soon after birth the young begin to climb on the mother's tail base, hold on to the edge scales of the tail by the claws of their forefeet and ride on the mother. In the burrowing pangolins the young are born in the sleeping chamber and probably spend their early days there. The tail base of a Giant pangolin is also too broad for the new-born to be able to cling, although the baby will try to climb on. In both the African arboreal species the young animal cuddles up close to the mother's belly to sleep. If the mother rolls up, they both form a ball, thus completely protecting the young from anything outside. Female pangolins have a few nipples on the chest. The Small-scaled and Long-tailed pangolins are individualists and lead a solitary life, male and female meeting only in the mating season. It is reported of Asiatic pangolins that they live in pairs in underground burrows (or caves) and the pygmies say the same thing about the Giant pangolin.

At one time, pangolins were classified with the Edentata, together with sloths, anteaters and armadillos. Nowadays they are placed in an order of their own, the Pholidota. Remains of fossilized pangolins were found in the Oligocene and Miocene ages of fifteen million years ago. The range of distribution at that time also comprised parts of Africa and Asia. FAMILY: Manidae, ORDER: Pholidota, CLASS: Mammalia.   U.R.

PANIC, the term used for the habit of a flock of gulls and terns taking suddenly to the air en masse, often silently, and for no reason apparent to the observer. This is also known as a 'dread'.

PANTHER, a black or melanistic variety of the *leopard. The name was in use in mediaeval England for the leopard itself but was later used by sportsmen in India for the black variety. It has also been applied to the puma or cougar, in North America, and to the jaguar of South America.

PAPER-MAKING WASPS, gregarious insects common in the tropics, sub-tropics and the warmer parts of the temperate regions. The term 'paper-making wasp' can be applied to a number of different groups all of which construct their nests from a paper-like material manufactured by chewing woody plant tissue and mixing it with saliva to make a pulpy mass. Hornets are well-known paper-makers, but the term is sometimes used in a narrower sense to denote members of the genus *Polistes*. These are slender wasps, sometimes referred to as 'yellow-jackets' in the United States, on account of their bright yellow bodies striped with black. They are common near human habitations where they make small horizontal comb-like nests, consisting of a cluster of hexagonal cells suspended by a paper stalk from the underside of the eaves. An egg is placed in each cell and the larva which hatches from this is fed on insects captured by the worker wasps. The various paper-makers show differing degrees of social complexity which is often reflected in the structure of the nest. In some instances, several horizontal combs are constructed, one below the other, suspended by a central paper filament. The majority of such nests, unlike those of the hornet, are not enclosed in a protective envelope, although in some species a partial awning may be provided, occasionally a complete covering. In temperate latitudes the paper nests are abandoned before the onset of winter during which many members of the population die. A hibernating queen survives the winter and builds up a new colony the following year. FAMILY: Vespidae, ORDER: Hymenoptera, CLASS: Insecta, PHYLUM: Arthropoda.   J.A.W.

PAPER NAUTILUS *Argonauta argo,* a cephalopod mollusc related to the common octopus which it closely resembles in its general structure. It has a rosette of eight sucker-bearing arms around a beaked mouth, a rather large brain which is typical of all modern cephalopods, prominent eyes and a bag-like body containing the digestive and reproductive organs. Below the main

Male paper nautilus *Argonauta argo* which is shell-less and one tenth the size of the female.

part of the body there is a pouch—the mantle cavity—containing the gills and the openings of the reproductive and digestive systems and the kidney ducts. The animal lives in the surface waters of the Mediterranean and other warm seas. Exceptionally large specimens may have a shell of 10 in (25 cm) or more in diameter.

It is a very remarkable mollusc in a number of ways. Thus, it has a shell that is not a shell in the normal molluscan sense. Instead of being a rigid calcareous structure attached to the rest of the animal by connective tissue and muscles, it is thin, almost papery as its name implies, and the octopod inside can crawl out and leave at will. This papery false shell is secreted by glands on the edge of the webs bordering the first pair of arms, and appears to act both as protection (the animal can withdraw inside) and as a float (since nearly all specimens captured seem to have air trapped in the upper part of the shell). The unchambered shell also serves as a cavity in which to hang the eggs: *Argonauta*, like other octopuses, broods its eggs until they hatch.

This last use of the shell introduces a second oddity of the Paper nautilus because the shelled animals are all females. The males of the species are minute—1–2 in (3–5 cm) long—and at first sight a quite different kind of animal. They are clearly octopods and characteristically bear an enormously enlarged third right arm which acts as a receptacle for the sperm packets produced by the animal. This arm is inserted into the mantle cavity of a female, where it breaks off. The male then swims away to regenerate another arm. Early taxonomists were puzzled by the apparent absence of males, which they failed to collect or recognize, and by the presence of the curious suckered objects found in the mantle cavity of female Paper nautiluses. Cuvier described the 'hectocotylus' left in the mantle cavity as a parasitic worm and other authors, following his lead, went as far as to identify the ganglionated nerve chain of the arm with the central nervous system·of more orthodox annelids. This zoological nonsense was dismissed when Muller caught and described male Paper nautilus in 1853. The animal is now recognized as showing an extreme example of sexual dimorphism and is a very interesting descendant of the bottom living octopods that has secondarily returned to the pelagic life of its remote ancestors, the squids.

Even today its habits are still something of a mystery, for nobody knows what it eats or how it catches its prey. In aquaria the Paper nautilus ignores small fish although small movements of its eyes indicate that it can see objects swimming close to it. It will grasp pieces of fish touched against its arms and transfer them to its mouth. If anything touches against the expanded webs of the first pair of arms the web is swept by the fourth arm on the side touched and quite possibly this is an adequate means of catching prey for an animal living in the populous regions of the sea-surface. ORDER: Dibranchia, CLASS: Cephalopoda, PHYLUM: Mollusca. M.J.W.

PARADISE FISH *Macropodus opercularis,* one of the labyrinth fishes found in China and Southeast Asia. It grows to about 4 in (10 cm) long and has a browny-blue body with a dozen vertical, thin orange-red stripes. The tail fin is also red and there is a red edged black spot on the gill cover. Samuel Pepys wrote in his famous Diary, towards the end of the 17th century, of 'a prettily marked fish living in a glass of water' which was then a recent import. This has often been cited as the first mention of a goldfish in England, but it has been suggested that it was a Paradise fish because of the marks. The Chinese had been breeding these fishes for a long time and as they are fairly hardy this interpretation is feasible. FAMILY: Anabantidae, ORDER: Perciformes, CLASS: Pisces.

PARADOXICAL FROG *Pseudis paradoxa,* a remarkable frog, of Trinidad and the Amazon basin, in which the tadpole is more than three times the length of the adult. See Pseudidae.

PARAKEETS, a loose name given to small or medium-sized parrots, usually those with long tails. There is no natural group of parakeets, the name having been given to many species which are not closely related to one another. Examples from different genera are: the now extinct Carolina parakeet *Conuropsis carolinensis* of North America, the green parakeet *Myiopsitta monachus* of Argentina, the Rose-ringed parakeet *Psittacula krameri* of the Old World Tropics, the Ground parakeets *Pezoporus* of Australia and the Crested parakeets *Cyanoramphus* of New Zealand. To add to the confusion, the familiar budgerigar is sometimes called a Grass parakeet, and the diminutive lorikeets, which have quite short tails, are alternatively called Hanging parakeets.

Here only the members of the genus *Psittacula* are described. All have long, finely-pointed tails and have vernacular names ending in 'parakeet'. Most *Psittacula* parakeets have a distinctive and colourful pattern on the head which relieves the overall green of the body and wings. One of the most beautiful is the Alexandrine parakeet *Psittacula eupatria*. The head of the male is banded with red, purple, black and turquoise. The body and wings are bright green with a red flash on each shoulder and the long tail is azure-blue.

Indo-Malaya is the home of most of the

A golden-headed South American parakeet, *Aratinga*, of the kind sometimes referred to as conures.

Psittacula species, but one of them, the Rose-ringed parakeet *Psittacula krameri* has an extremely wide distribution: from Senegal in the far west of Africa to Indo-China. Like most of its relatives, the Rose-ringed parakeet lives in semi-arid country where, however, it keeps largely to the trees. Only a few species inhabit heavily forested regions and these seem to prefer the more open parts. The Long-tailed parakeet *Psittacula longicauda* of the Malayan Peninsula and the Indonesian Archipelago is a common bird of the lowlands which were once completely clothed in jungle. It shuns the remaining rain-forest areas, however, and is most often seen in cultivated regions. Its original home was possibly the narrow strip of open woodland which occurs naturally on poor sandy soils along the coast.

For much of the year parakeets are gregarious, flying around in noisy flocks, but when the breeding season begins they pair off and nest singly or in small colonies. Mating is preceded by elaborate and comical courtship displays in which the male struts along a branch towards the female and the pair engage in rhythmic swaying and 'necking' exercises. Like most other parrots, parakeets are hole-nesters. The natural site is a hole in a dead tree or branch, but where parakeets live in towns and villages, as in India, temples, bridges and other man-made constructions provide many good nest sites. Two or three dull white eggs form the usual clutch and are laid at the bottom of the cavity with scant or no nesting material.

The natural food of parakeets is largely fruits, nuts, buds and flowers. A tree bearing ripe fruit may attract hundreds of birds, yet the observer may have great difficulty in seeing a handful of them, so well are they camouflaged among the foliage. When they are disturbed, however, the tree seems to explode as parakeets fly out noisily in all directions. Because of their liking for ripening cereals and soft fruit, several parakeets have become a great nuisance to farmers. In India, Ceylon and Burma, huge flocks of Rose-ringed parakeets, sometimes accompanied by other species, inflict very heavy losses in wheat fields, rice paddies, and orchards. In southern Malaya, the Long-tailed parakeet *Psittacula longicauda* has recently taken to stripping the valuable pulp from oil-palm nuts. Thousands of these beautiful birds are being shot every year on certain palm estates, in an attempt to reduce the damage. FAMILY: Psittacidae, ORDER: Psittaciformes, CLASS: Aves.   P.W.

PARAMECIUM, the best known *ciliate, formerly called the Slipper animalcule, and one which has been studied intensively not only at school and university level but also in the wider fields of cell and molecular biology. Eight species of *Paramecium* are known, but

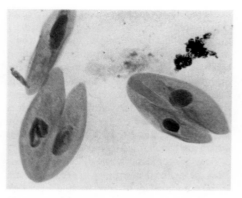

Two pairs of *Paramaecium* in conjugation. The large central body in each individual is the meganucleus. In the left-hand pair the micronucleus is dividing into four and the products of division appear as darker bodies against the meganucleus.

some authorities recognize more. All are free living in fresh or stagnant water and one occurs in brackish water. The ciliates are elongate and round in cross section. To one side is the conspicuous mouth lying in a deep groove called an oral groove. The ciliate is covered with a uniform layer of cilia and those in the region of the mouth are essentially no different from those covering the rest of the body, although they beat more strongly. The ciliate swims by revolving about its axis and does not feed while swimming. When stationary the ciliate creates a vortex by beating the cilia in the oral region and this actively draws fine particles into the oral groove and thence into the mouth.

Paramecium feeds on bacteria and particles of plant material and is selective in its choice of food, for it can reject unsuitable particles before they enter the mouth. The food taken in enters a food vacuole which forms in continuity with the mouth and which eventually breaks off to circulate around the body while the food contained in it is being digested. By feeding the ciliate yeast stained with the dye congo red the changes in alkalinity and acidity can be traced, the acid vacuoles being blue and the alkaline ones red. Eventually waste products are egested at a permanent excretory pore called a cytoproct. As it lives in freshwater, water is continually entering the ciliate and has to be removed. The water passes into two contractile vacuoles which grow as the water in them accumulates and eventually discharge their contents to the outside via a permanent pore. *Paramecium* is very sensitive to changes in its habitat and actively avoids unfavourable conditions. It can do this by reversing its ciliary beat so that it moves backwards and then moves forward again along a different path. This pattern of behaviour is called an avoidance reaction.

Paramecium possesses one macronucleus and one or more micronuclei depending on the species. Among the better known species,

P. aurelia possesses two micronuclei and *P. caudatum* one. *Paramecium* divides by asexual fission at right angles to the length of the animal and the new mouth grows in continuity with the old. Division is frequent and occurs three to five times a day. Three different forms of sexual reproduction occur in *Paramecium* and the best studied of these is the process known as conjugation in which two individuals come together, the macronuclei disappear, the micronucleus divides and one daughter micronucleus migrates to the partner and fuses with the stationary micronucleus. The macronucleus is regenerated from the micronucleus and the two individuals separate to begin a series of asexual divisions. This is the basic form of sexual reproduction in ciliates, and is complicated only by the fact that in species like *P. aurelia* there are two micronuclei and one of these has to disappear first and later be reconstituted. The second kind of sexual reproduction, which is called autogamy, resembles conjugation except that no mating occurs and two daughter micronuclei fuse with one another in the same individual. The third sexual process is called cytogamy and although two individuals come together the micronuclei are not exchanged and the result is very like autogamy. Species of *Paramecium* exist in a number of varieties and mating types. It is convenient to regard the varieties as equivalent to species of higher organisms and the mating types as equivalent to sexes. Mating occurs only between different mating types of the same variety. The mating types differ from sexes in that there is no morphological difference between mating types and also there can be more than two in any variety; for example, *P. bursaria* has eight.

Populations of *Paramecium* have interesting histories. At first the population is immature and multiplies solely by asexual division. During the next period, that of maturity, conjugation occurs and during the final period, of senescence, autogamy or cytogamy occurs. *Paramecium* is also interesting at the cellular level for the cytoplasm of several species contains a number of particles which are capable of multiplying by themselves. The best known of these particles are those called Kappa, and paramecia with Kappa can kill those without, the former being called killers and the latter sensitives. Mu particles cause the death of the mate during conjugation. The interesting thing about these particles is that their activity is under the control of the genes of the *Paramecium*.

Paramecium is a member of the order Hymenostomatida which is regarded by experts on ciliates as the group about which the evolution of the Ciliata revolves. *Tetrahymena* is another member of this order. Of the two, *Paramecium* is the more specialized

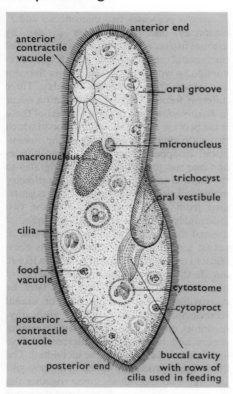

anterior end

anterior
contractile
vacuole

oral groove

micronucleus

macronucleus

trichocyst

oral vestibule

cilia

food
vacuole

cytostome

cytoproct

posterior
contractile
vacuole

buccal cavity
with rows of
cilia used in feeding

posterior end

The single-celled Paramecium or Slipper animal-cule, free living mostly in fresh or stagnant water, the best known of the ciliates.

and it is unlikely that it has given rise to any other major group. It is probable that *Paramecium* has evolved from a more primitive hymenostome with a simple mouth and has become specialized by elaborating its oral region to such an extent that the structure occupies the whole of one side of the animal and completely dominates its way of life. ORDER: Hymenostomatida, CLASS: Ciliata, PHYLUM: Protozoa.   F.E.G.C.

PARAPINEAL ORGAN, alternative name for the *parietal organ. See also pineal organ.

PARASITES AND PARASITISM, the latter being an association between two organisms of different species in which one, the parasite, is for some part of its life-history physiologically dependent on the other, the host, from which it obtains nutrition and which may form its total environment. Nearly all the major groups of organisms from viruses to vertebrates have some parasitic members. The most important parasites, besides the viruses which are a wholly parasitic group, occur in the bacteria, Protozoa, Platyhelminthes (flatworms) and Nematoda (roundworms). Study of the parasitic worms, the platyhelminths, nematodes and acanthocephalans, is termed helminthology. Blood-sucking arthropods, such as mosquitoes, Tsetse flies and ticks, are also important because they transmit parasitic diseases and serve as vectors or transport-

hosts for other parasites. Examples of vector transmitted diseases are malaria, caused by the protozoan *Plasmodium* spp and transmitted by anopheline mosquitoes, sleeping sickness caused by trypanosome protozoans and transmitted by Tsetse flies *Glossina* spp, bubonic plague produced by a bacillus transmitted by Rat fleas, yellow fever, a virus disease transmitted by *Aedes* mosquitoes and elephantiasis caused by filarial nematodes which are transmitted by mosquitoes.

The phenomenon whereby one parasite is itself parasitized is termed hyperparasitism. It is common in insects such as sawflies *Ichneumon* spp, which lay their eggs on insect larvae already parasitized by sawfly larvae of another species. These parasitic larval insects are termed parasitoids because they destroy the host; most true parasites cannot afford to harm the host because it would jeopardize their own livelihood.

There are many kinds of parasitic relationship ranging from the brood parasitism shown by, for instance, cuckoos and honeyguides which depend on other birds to rear their young, to the extremely intimate relationship existing between a tapeworm and the vertebrate host on which it is completely dependent. Parasites such as mosquitoes, leeches and the Fish louse *Argulus* are periodical parasites and visit the host only for a blood meal. Others, like lice, tapeworms and some nematodes, are permanently associated with their hosts so that the host comes to form the environment for the parasite. These forms are usually obligate parasites which have become so committed to a particular kind of existence in association with a particular host that they are unable to survive without that host. In contrast, other organisms are usually free-living but can become parasites if the opportunity arises (facultative parasites). Certain tropical blowflies may lay eggs in skin wounds of man and the maggots that hatch, which usually feed on decaying meat, feed on the living flesh and cause horrible deformities. Some organisms are accidental parasites. Certain free-living protozoans, worms and maggots, when accidentally ingested by another animal, can survive for fairly long periods of time in this new environment and may even avail themselves of host tissues and fluids. Some animals are parasitic only as juveniles and are free-living as adults. It is difficult to realize that the large freshwater Swan mussel *Anodonta* has a parasitic larval stage called a glochidium which attaches to the gills of passing fishes, embeds itself in host tissue and feeds there for a while, breaking out later to assume the free-living sedentary existence of the adult.

There are parasites specialized for life in almost every organ and tissue of the host body. In general a distinction is made between ectoparasites which live on the out-

sides of their hosts (e.g. Vampire bats, mosquitoes and lice), endoparasites which occupy the gut, organs and body cavities (e.g. most flukes, tapeworms and roundworms) and the haemoparasites or blood-living forms (e.g. Malaria parasites, typanosomes, the Blood flukes *Schistosoma* and microfilarial stages of the nematodes *Wucheria* and *Brugia*).

Because the parasitic way of life demands certain kinds of adaptive specialization, it is not surprising that parasites from widely different groups of animals may come to resemble one another by convergent evolution. Parasites tend to lose their locomotory organs and develop attachment organs which ensure constant contact with the host. These may consist of suckers, spines, hooks, a proboscis which penetrates deep into host tissue or an adhesive glandular surface. Many endoparasites finding themselves bathed in host tissues rich in nutrients tend to lose the gut and absorb the food across the body wall. The tapeworms and acanthocephalans lack a gut and so do many parasitic copepods. Some parasites, such as

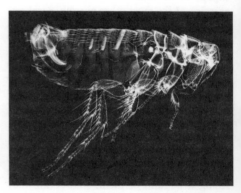

One of the 16 different kinds of flea that may be found as ectoparasites on the European mole.

the copepod *Sacculina,* which causes parasitic castration in crabs, have solved the problems of both attachment and food absorption by adopting a branching root-like body-form which has a large surface area for nutrient uptake. This parasite can only be recognized as a copepod because it retains a free-swimming nauplius larva, characteristic of Crustacea in its life-history. The physiology of parasites is also highly specialized—for instance, many gut parasites seem to be facultatively anaerobic, forms like tapeworms produce few digestive enzymes and rely on the presence of pre-digested host nutrients, while blood-feeders produce anticoagulents to prevent the blood they eat from clotting. Parasites often have very complicated life-cycles which may involve several intermediate hosts before the adult stage is reached in the definitive host. For instance, the Liver fluke *Fasciola hepatica* has sporocyst, redial and cercarial stages in

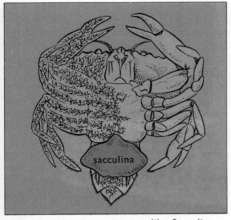

A crab carrying a mature, sac-like *Sacculina* on the underside of its abdomen.

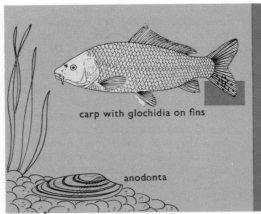

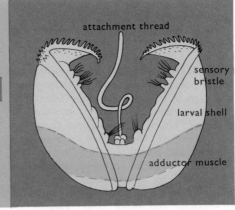

The glochidia larvae, shown enlarged on the right, of the freshwater mussel *Anodonta*, shown at the bottom, spend a parasitic period on the fins of fishes such as carp.

A victim of elephantiasis with the various stages in the life-cycle of *Wuchereria bancrofti* or *Brugia malayi*, similar worms which cause this condition. 1. Female and 2. male adults, life size. 3. Head of female and 4. tail of male of *W. bancrofti*, showing, respectively, circumoral papillae and spicules with perianal papillae. 5. Mosquito, with microfilariae entering the oesophagus as it feeds on the blood of a patient, reaching the stomach, and penetrating into the hemocoele, where short 'sausage' forms (first- and second-stage larvae) can be seen. An infective (third-stage) larva is seen in the region of the mosquito's mouthparts. 6. The microfilaria and three larval stages, shown at the same magnification, illustrate metamorphosis and growth within the insect vector. 7. Microfilaria (sheathed larva) with human erythrocytes.

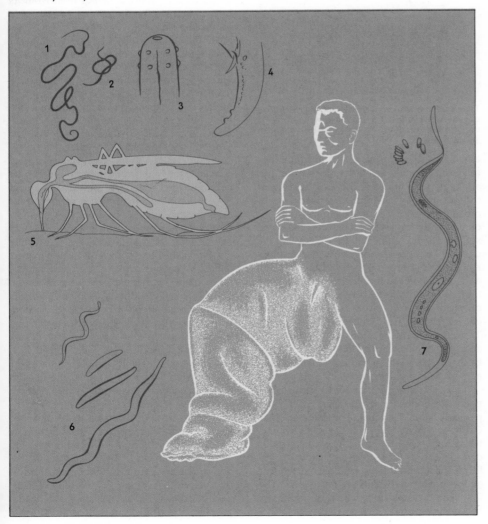

snails before becoming adult in the bile ducts of sheep. In many instances a resistant stage is incorporated into the life-cycle; the Liver fluke has a resistant metacercarial stage which encysts on grass, and nematodes have extremely resistant eggs and sheathed larval stages. This increases the chances of survival between the different phases of the life-cycle. Transition from one stage to another is often in response to specific chemical stimuli or trigger mechanisms. Some tapeworm larvae are stimulated to excyst (i.e. break out of the cyst) in the definitive mammalian host by certain kinds of bile and sheathed nematode larvae are activated by a high carbon dioxide concentration. Many parasites tend to become host specific, that is, so closely adapted to conditions in one particular host that they are unable to live in any other. Another way in which a parasite becomes attuned to its host is to become adapted to the host's immune reactions. As host antibodies are present in blood and lymph, haemoparasites are obviously in a vulnerable position. The Blood fluke *Schistosoma*, which causes the disease bilharzia, has resolved this problem by coating itself with host antibodies so masquerading as host tissue and avoiding the immune response. Parasites also have had to increase their reproductive capacity or biotic potential relative to free-living forms to compensate for the hazards of locating the various hosts involved in the life-cycle. Not only are a great number of eggs produced but many parasites also reproduce asexually. A single miracidium larva of a fluke, after infecting a snail intermediate host, divides asexually to produce many thousands of rediae and cercariae larvae. Tapeworms bud off proglottids (new segments of the tapeworm) from a neck region behind the adhesive scolex.

As there are many different kinds of parasitic association, there are many ways in which different parasitic relationships could have arisen. The tendency of symbiotic and commensal organisms to exploit the relationship and the phenomenon of accidental parasitism provide clues showing some of the factors favouring the development of parasitism. K.L.

PARASITIC ISOPODS, small crustaceans whose parasitism ranges from those which are slightly modified in shape from their free-living relatives to forms in which all traces of *isopod and crustacean characters have been lost. They are all fundamentally ectoparasitic; even those which lie within the body cavity of the host are separated from the body fluids by a membrane. The normal biting mouthparts give way to suctorial mouthparts and other body features are modified. In general the sexes are separate but in some families protandrous hermaphroditism (first male, them female) occurs and additional larval stages are incorporated in the life-history.

The least modified forms are found in the suborder Flabellifera in which the adults, for example, *Aega* and *Anilocra*, of some families are ectoparasites of fishes. They show broad flattened bodies in which the first three pairs of legs are modified to hold onto the surface skin of fishes; these legs are short with the end joint curved into a hook. The mouthparts tear the skin and rasp the flesh of the host. The larval stages are free-swimming and, as in *Anilocra*, for example, over their third to fifth moult become fully developed functional males. From the sixth to the ninth moult spermatogenesis ceases and the ovary which has been developing gradually, even during the male stages, becomes functional. The body also changes its form from male to female.

This is an example of protandrous hermaphroditism. If under experimental conditions a male is kept isolated from any contact with a female its development into a female is rapid but if paired with a female its development is slowed down and may not be completed until the female is removed. Further experimentation shows that a male in process of changing into a female develops more rapidly if a young male is introduced. It is not known what stimuli cause these reactions or how they act.

In the suborder Gnathiidea the species in their young stages are ectoparasitic on fishes and free-living as adults. The life-history of *Gnathia maxillaris* is a good example. The young larva is free-swimming. Then, it becomes attached to the fins of a fish to take up its ectoparasitic habit. Its normal biting mouthparts become modified for penetration and suction, closely packed together and forming a cone. The mandibles become styliform with a serrated edge for cutting through the skin and into a blood vessel. The maxillules and maxillae also become stylet-like and together with the stylet-tipped maxillipeds form a suctorial channel for the

blood. The second thoracic segment becomes fused to the head and its appendages closely applied to the oral cone; the last joint becomes hooked and assists in the feeding process. The larva moults three times and takes two successive meals of blood which swell the thoracic segments five, six and seven to produce a characteristic late larval stage known as the praniza. This stage moults to give adult males and females $\frac{1}{4}$ in (6 mm) long. They seek shelter under stones and in crevices and also burrow into mud. There is a well marked sexual dimorphism in that the male has a large dilated anterior region involving the head and thoracic segments three and four. It possesses a pair of powerful mandibles which are stated to be used for

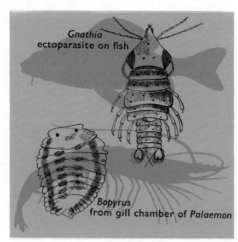

Two parasitic isopods *Gnathia* and *Bopyrus*. The degeneration due to a parasitic way of life is usually less marked in ectoparasites than in endoparasites.

burrowing to make the niches in which they are found, a male and a female together. As adults they do not feed; the mouthparts and the gut atrophy and they lose all traces of modifications for a parasitic habit. They exist on the food they have stored during the larval stages, which is sufficient also to develop the gonads. The eggs are not released for development inside a brood-pouch but are retained and the whole embryological development takes place within the parent's body and the offspring are born as first stage larvae. Only one generation is produced by each female. Thus the Gnathiidea are characterized by showing a metamorphosis in their life-history, parasitism in the larval stages only and marked sexual dimorphism in the adults.

The suborder Epicaridea show pronounced modifications associated with the parasitic habit. They are all parasitic on other Crustacea at all stages in their life-history, which involves two hosts. The adults differ considerably from each other but the larval forms living in the same kind of environment and with the same habits are much alike. The first larval stage that emerges from the brood-pouch of the female is the epicardial

stage. This is like a young isopod with modifications for a parasitic life on free-swimming copepods in the plankton of the seas. The antennules are small but the antennae are well developed and may assist in swimming and possibly in the identification of the copepod host. The mouthparts are adapted to penetrate the cuticle of the copepod and to suck out food. In all stages of all epicarids the mouthparts are unusual in that the upper and lower tips together form an oral cone in which the stylet-like mandibles function. Maxillules and maxillae are not developed. Feeding is assisted by the lamelliform maxillipeds lying on the posterior margin of the cone. The thorax has six pairs of short legs which are prehensile showing well-developed hooked claws. The abdomen carries five pairs of natatory pleopods enabling the larva to swim as a member of the plankton to find its copepod host. More than one species of copepod may serve as host to each species of parasite although in general each species of isopod is more attracted to one species of copepod host than another. The larva undergoes six moults while attached to the copepod, slowly changing in shape until it finally detaches itself from its host to become free-swimming and searches for the final host.

In the family Bopyridae, as in *Bopyrus fougerouxi* parasitic on the prawn *Palaemon serratus* and *Iona thoracica* parasitic on the burrowing prawn *Callianassa*, the late stage larva enters the gill-chamber of its host and moults to a further larval stage, known as the bopyridium, which retains the legs for attachment to the wall of the chamber and the suctorial mouthparts for feeding; the pleopods are reduced. It has been shown in *Iona thoracica* that if only one bopyrid is present it develops into a female and a subsequent bopyridium into a male. When several larvae enter the gill-chamber together they all show signs of development into females but only one matures. If experimentally a very young female is taken and placed on a more mature female it becomes a male. If a young male is taken from a female and placed in an uninfected gill-chamber it becomes a female. Thus bopyrid larvae are capable of development into either males or females depending on their position and sex is not irrevocably determined at fertilization. The females suck blood and grow rapidly, moulting once as the hosts moult. When fully grown the females have flattened segmented bodies, asymmetrical, with reduced legs particularly on the asymmetrical side. The five pairs of brood lamellae completely arch over the ventral side of the thorax and the pleopods are flat respiratory lamellae. The males retain the bopyridial larval form and become mature, at this stage, an example of *neoteny, that is, persistence of the larval form, and *pedogenesis, or reproduction in the larval form.

The males remain small and lie on the ventral side of the abdomen permanently attached.

In the family Entoniscidae which parasitize true crabs, examples being *Portunion maenadis* on the Shore crab *Carcinus maenas* and *Pinnotherion vermiforme* on the Oyster crab *Pinnotheres,* the adult females are found within the body cavity of the host surrounded by a sheath and feeding through a small hole in the sheath. In *Portunion* this sheath is formed by the lymphocytes of the host. The females of all the entoniscids enter the body cavity from the gill-chamber at a moult when the cuticle is soft. For a time the original connection with the gill-chamber is lost but it is eventually regained to allow the release of the young larvae. These forms are often referred to as endoparasites. The adult female loses all her legs, the pleopods are raised into crumpled folds and contain extensive blood spaces, into which oxygen is drawn from the blood of the host. The brood-pouch is extensively developed to completely cover the thorax and to extend forward to overhang the head. The male remains amongst the pleopods, in the bopyrid stage.

In the family Cryptoniscidae, an example being *Hemioniscus balani* parasitic on the intertidal barnacles of rocky shores, the late larva enters the mantle cavity of the barnacle. The life-history illustrates, as in *Anilocra,* a case of protandrous hermaphroditism. After functioning as a male it gradually changes and becomes a female. The head of the female becomes embedded in the tissues of the host, feeds and stores food in its gut. As eggs are produced the shape of the body becomes much distorted. The head may retain its isopodan characters for some time but eventually the whole body becomes a sac, filled with eggs, in which the alimentary canal and nervous system degenerate and external segmentation is lost, and with it all traces of crustacean characteristics. This sac eventually splits and actively swimming larvae, looking like typical isopods and known as epicaridean larvae, emerge.

In the parasitic isopods generally the parasite does not effect such profound changes on the host as in the case of the parasitic cirripedes although some male crabs may be feminized. Also the occurrence of protandrous hermaphroditism and of sex reversal in the young stages is indicative of an instability of sex in the Crustacea.   E.E.W.

PARASITIC MITES, these are mainly of three types: those that use other animals as a means of dispersal and distribution between discontinuous food sources; those that live in the nests of other animals, feeding on the detritus which accumulates in nests; and those that live on the nest owner's body, feeding on debris derived from the skin, such as exudates, skin scales or both.

A typical example of the first is the association between mites and Dung beetles. The adult female mites are often found clinging to the 'hairs' on such beetles and, thus, get carried to new deposits of dung, where they prey on other small arthropods or on the eggs of insects. Many species of mites have a special instar after the first nymphal stage adapted to clinging to the surfaces of arthropods or, in some cases, the fur of mammals. Not all the individuals of a species necessarily pass through this stage.

The nests of birds and mammals and of the social insects all carry considerable mite populations, acting as general scavengers or preying on such scavengers. In small mammals' nests, for example, species of *Labidophorus* and *Xenoryctes* are such scavengers

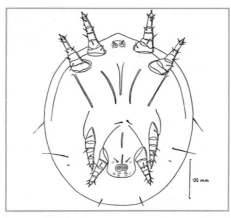

Specialized nymph (hypopus) of the non-parasitic grain mite *Acarus siro* which attaches to insects for dispersal.

and with them are found their predators, such as *Haemogamasus, Laelaps* and *Cheyletes.* Animals like *Haemogamasus pontiger* can be found on small mammals, such as rats, and may contain blood, they can also occur on grain with other mites and do not, then, contain blood and are, presumably, preying on the other mites. This species can be reared in culture on wheat germ and, in fact, it illustrates the ease with which transitions can occur between one food habit and another.

Acarid mites are found not only in the nests but on the nest owners, feeding on desquamated skin scales and skin debris generally. Rodents, particularly, carry listrophorid mites, whose appendages may be very remarkably adapted for clinging onto hair. Moving along the hair, such mites rasp off scales from its surface. Similar mites are found in a great variety of forms on birds, feeding on the secretion of the preen gland and scales off the feathers. Such mites attract their predators onto the hosts. Mites such as these which cannot really be regarded as true parasites may well have given rise to species which, as it were, grew impatient and rasped scales off the surface of the body and obtained partially keratinized cells which are, presumably, more nutritious and, perhaps,

even obtained a seepage of tissue fluid. Forms, such as *Myocoptes musculinus* on the mouse show such an intermediate stage between the listrophorid type and those mites, such as *Psoroptes* which cause irritation, exudation of fluid, loss of coat and the typical symptoms of mange. This change of feeding habit, which after all is the essential of parasitism, does not involve any drastic modification of the animal.

From the abrasion of the skin surface to actually burrowing into it is a relatively short step. The Itch mite *Sarcoptes scabei* of man is a typical example. It burrows down through the keratinized cells into the region of partial keratinization, the stratum spinosum. Thus, it enters a region of living cells and

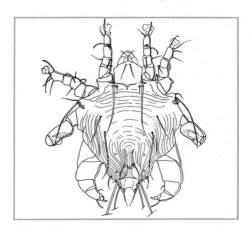

Male of *Myocoptes musculinus*, an ectoparasitic mite occurring on mice, causing them to develop mange.

tissue fluid, a richer source of food than the surface rasper can get at. The walls of the tunnels it makes cornify behind it, its presence irritates the skin and the malpighian layer becomes more active, producing cells faster in an effort to slough off the invader with the cornified layer. The tunnels and cornified cells are, of course, raised toward the surface by this activity and, ultimately lost. The mite is always found at the end of the burrow, feeding just above the malpighian layer on cells and tissue fluid. There is, thus, a constant struggle between the mite and the processes of growth and cornification of the skin. It is noteworthy, in this respect, that healthy well-fed hosts are better able to resist the effects of infection than those in poor condition.

Parasites, such as we have been considering, show little modification of the feeding apparatus. They do, however, exhibit a general reduction in hard sclerotization of the skeleton and present a finely wrinkled appearance. Their legs and claws may be highly modified for adhering to the surface of the host. Their other main modification must be in their sensory physiology to produce the correct behaviour patterns.

Living as predators on the scavengers or

ectoparasites of the nest owner, there occur predacious mites which by manipulation of their rather long chelicerae and probably by indulging, to a certain extent, in external digestion, eat the soft inside of their prey and leave an empty skin. Their gut does not contain fragments of their prey, but a sort of soup of partially digested and very finely divided material. This is still more emphasized in those mites with mouthparts very highly modified for piercing and sucking and there is a very well-developed complex of salivary glands. The prey is held by the pedipalps, pierced by the chelicerae, saliva digests the inside of the prey and this is sucked back and the empty skeleton discarded. Predators of both these groups, therefore, have the required type of feeding apparatus to take the further step of piercing the surface of the nest owner and feeding on its blood or tissue fluid. Moreover, they are attracted onto the body of the host by their prey. It is not surprising to find mites, such as *Dermanyssus* and *Ornithonyssus* (see gamasids), sucking the blood of birds and small mammals. The mouthparts of the trombids are rather short for this type of work and cannot get down to the really nutritive part of the skin. Modification of the salivary complex enables these mites to attain their objective another way. Part of the salivary secretion dissolves a canal down through the skin, the walls of this canal harden and it forms a tube up which the mite can suck nutriment. Whether the hardening of the wall of the tube is a host reaction or due to a salivary secretion is not known; it can pull out of the host when the mite is forcibly detached.

Man is also to be numbered amongst those animals which build nests either individual or social. These inevitably attract mites similar to and in some case identical with those to be found in other less elaborate structures; such as squirrels' drays or starlings' nests. These mites feed on stored food, organic detritus, such as skin, scales and mould, which occur in human habitations. A similar sort of transition can be found here as in other nests. Of recent years, it has been shown that allergic asthma is often caused by a mite, *Dermataphagoides pteronyssinus,* which feeds in house dust on desquamated skin scales and is a relatively common inhabitant of houses and can be found in the dust on mattresses, for example. There are, however, recorded cases of this mite being found in numbers on the skin of people, feeding on surface scales and dandruff, thus showing the first tentative step towards an ectoparasitic habit; or perhaps it is a species which has evolved in the opposite direction, a member of the family Epidermoptidae most of whose relatives live on birds or mammals, feeding on skin.

Amongst the mites which burrow into the skin or feed on its surface, it is usual to find that the life-cycle includes a free egg. Parasitic mites are often viviparous, producing larvae or nymphs. It is the general rule that parasites of these two groups are parasitic throughout their life-cycle. There are many mites parasitic on lizards in all instars, but there are also a great many species which are only parasitic as larvae. These parasitic larvae are known collectively as *chiggers. In various parts of the world, they are a source of danger to man since they act as vectors of pathogenic organisms, such as rickettsias.

Amongst these parasitic larvae are forms which parasitize arthropods. Water beetles and a good many insects with aquatic immature stages come into contact with the larvae of aquatic mites. By parasitizing the insect, the mite secures not only food but a means of transport to other water masses. If the host is an immature insect, the mite must stay with it at its moults in order to get carried by the adult to a fresh habitat. This calls for a complex behaviour pattern, linked with the changes occurring in the host. It is possible that there is some connexion between the changes in circulating hormone and the response of the mite to moulting in the host. This type of gearing of mite to host is well shown by a group of acarid mites parasitic on birds, commonly pigeons. These mites in the active stages live and feed on the skin and feathers of the host, this part of their life-cycle being very brief. Intercalated into the cycle is a hypopial nymph which is produced during the nesting period when the nestlings are young. These hypopi (non-feeding stage usually produced for distribution purposes, see above) penetrate the skin of the young birds between the feather tracts; how this is achieved mechanically is not known. Arrived in the subcutaneous tissues, they remain quiescent but grow in size. Since they lack mouthparts it is to be presumed that they absorb nutriment through the body surface. In this condition they remain until the host itself is nesting, when at the appropriate time they emerge as active nymphs, become adult and reproduce themselves. It is, too, highly probable that the mites' cycle of activity in the pigeon is controlled by hormonal changes occurring in the bird.

A move from the surface of the host into the interior can for these small creatures be easily carried out by invasion of the respiratory tract. Blood-sucking mites have invaded the nasal cavities of seals and some species of birds, whilst in primates, other than man, one species *Pneumonyssus* invades the lungs. Relatives of the Feather mites are found in the lungs and air sacs of pheasants. The tracheal system of insects has been colonized, too. The most investigated case being that of the honeybee parasitized by the mite *Acarapis woodi,* relatives of which are found as external parasites of insects or living free in the nests of social insects.

It is as ectoparasites that mites have, in the main, adopted the parasitic habit and before leaving the subject it is worthy of note that man's habitations include the nests of other creatures, such as birds and small mammals. When, for various reasons, these nests are vacated by their owners, blood-sucking mites left behind may often turn to man as a source of food. Man has domesticated a number of animals and their parasites may effect a transfer of host. *Notoedres cati,* for example, which causes mange in cats, can live, at any rate for a time, on man.

Mites with piercing mouthparts are often plant parasites, which feed by piercing plant tissue and digesting cell contents by injected saliva and sucking up the food thus obtained. In temperate regions, the life-cycle is regulated to the foliar cycle of the plant, by the photoperiod. The mites may overwinter as eggs or adults. Winter eggs which diapause are produced in response to shortening day length. Some of these parasites evoke the formation of galls on the host plant; the blister galls and nail galls are caused by them. Others, it is said, induce the formation of witches' brooms on silver birch and willow, but whether they are directly responsible or introduce a fungal causative agent is unsure. Like the chiggers, however, they can act as vectors of virus diseases, but of plants. ORDERS: Astigmata, Mesostigmata and Prostignata, CLASS: Arachnida, PHYLUM: Arthropoda.   T.E.H.

PARENTAL BEHAVIOUR, behaviour concerned with the care of the young including the preparations made before they are hatched or born, so that nest-building, for example, is a part. Most invertebrates have no contact with their young, laying their eggs and then leaving them. However, incipient parental care is seen in earwigs: the female remains beside the group of eggs which she has laid, cleaning them and keeping them free of moulds until the young hatch. Many solitary wasps leave provisions for their larvae by capturing and paralyzing insects or spiders and storing them in a hole in the ground. Before closing the hole, an egg is deposited on top of the pile of food. Other species of wasp show progressive provisioning, for they leave less food with the egg but return at intervals to re-stock as the larva consumes the stores. Elaborate though the care of the young larvae is in a colony of social insects, this care is usually given by the workers, the offspring of the queen, and not by the queen herself, once the colony has been established.

Some decapod crustaceans carry their eggs fixed to swimmerets on their abdomen

When two Prairie dogs *Cynomys ludovicianus* meet they exchange a 'recognition kiss'. When one is juvenile, this is the prelude to the adult grooming it, nibbling its fur all over.

Some others keep them aerated by moving the abdomen slightly. Many scorpions carry their young on their backs, but apart from transporting them and protecting them, give them no other aid.

It is among vertebrates that parental care is most intense culminating in the long period of infancy in Primates and especially in man. The eggs of some fishes and of birds are kept in nests. A male stickleback makes a nest in which the female lays its eggs and, after fertilizing them, the male guards the nest and even chases off the female. By vigorous movements of its fins and tail the male drives freshwater through the tunnel of the nest and over the eggs, ensuring that they have a good supply of oxygen. Some species of the cichlid genus *Tilapia* are *mouth-brooders. The female takes the eggs and sperm into her mouth and she subsequently holds the fertilized eggs in her mouth until they hatch. On hatching the young are allowed to leave, but return to the parent's mouth rapidly at the approach of danger.

Fishes, unlike birds and mammals, do not feed their young. The strain upon parent birds of bringing food to a nest of voracious young is considerable as several hundred visits to the nest in one day by a parent bird is not unusual. Young birds have evolved many special behaviour patterns in connection with this habit, the most important being the inducement to the parent bird to regurgitate food on seeing the coloured inside of the throat and mouth of the young. Later when the young leave the nest, but are still being fed by the parents, they develop a begging call which has a similar effect.

Physiological changes take place in the breeding bird which not only affect its reproductive organs. For example a patch on the breast, the brood patch, becomes abundantly supplied with blood vessels and the feathers in that area may moult. The result is that a bird can settle itself down on to its eggs bringing the warm patch into contact with them. The need to incubate involves remarkable feats of endurance. An Emperor penguin parent will hold its single egg on its feet, covered by a fold of skin, for seven or eight weeks while its partner is away at sea feeding. The parents exchange places, taking their turn in feeding and incubating. Nest sanitation is of the greatest importance, not only for reasons of hygiene but also because the white droppings may make the nest conspicuous. So parent birds remove the droppings of the very young which, when they are older, move to the edge of the nest to defaecate. Pieces of egg-shell are also removed from the nest.

Some mammals also make nests for their young. Rabbits, for example, build nests lined with hair which the female plucks from her body. Toward the time of birth the hair on the parts of the mother's body that she can most easily reach becomes loose and can easily be plucked out.

Young mammals must suck the mother's nipples to obtain the milk they need and yet the ability to locate the milk source seems to be a matter of experience. The parent often helps the young animal in its search by pushing it into the right position. A mother cat will leave her kittens to feed herself for an hour or so. On her return she wakes the kittens by nudging them, circles around them and then settles down, enclosing them in an oval formed by her body and legs. This restricts their search to the underside of her body and so aids their learned feeding behaviour.

Care of the newborn extends also to their bodily functions. Kittens, after birth, are unable to urinate or defaecate without their mother's help. It is entirely due to her licking and stimulation that they are able to rid their bodies of waste products in the first few days of their life. Without her attention they would die. This behaviour probably arises from the fact that in the wild state it is certainly safer for the mother to collect the excrement and keep the lair clean much in the same way as the parent bird keeps the nest clean. There is, of course, much evidence that mammals teach their young some of the activities which are essential for life, for obtaining food, for example. Often the young are encouraged to imitate a parent or are punished if they go to a place which is unsafe.　　　　　　　　　　　　J.D.C.

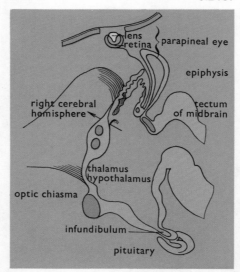

Right half of the diencephalon (part of the forebrain), midbrain and associated structures in the tuatara to show the parapineal or parietal eye.

PARIETAL ORGAN, the anterior partner of two tiny processes which develop middorsally from the posterior part of the forebrain in some reptiles, amphibians and primitive fishes, and project upward towards the roof of the skull. An alternative name is parapineal organ, and the posterior member of the two processes is the *pineal organ. In amphibians the two processes appear to fuse, and in higher vertebrates the parietal organ disappears. Both these organs may be the vestiges of a second pair of eyes that in some ancestral forms appeared on the top of the head. The tip of the parietal organ may be modified in some animals to form a light-sensitive structure, usually known as the 'parietal eye'. It is sometimes referred to as the 'pineal eye', but this term is more correctly used for the posterior member of the pair of outgrowths.

The parietal organ is best developed in the *tuatara *Sphenodon*, and is well developed in some lizards, but is small or absent in most adult reptiles. In *Sphenodon* the parietal organ is often called the 'third eye', though it is only visible externally in very young animals, being completely covered over by skin and scales in the adult. It has a relatively elaborate structure, with a lens and retina (light-sensitive layer), but no iris. It is extremely small, with a diameter of only about $\frac{1}{50}$ in (0.5 mm). A translucent tissue covers the lens and also fills the tiny hole in the skull immediately above the organ. The parietal organ of *Sphenodon* appears to have no optical function, not only because it is covered by opaque skin and scales, and the nerve leading from it to the brain has degenerated, but because extensive experiments have failed to show any ability of the organ even to detect light. Other experiments designed to test whether the function of the organ is to 'inform' the animal of changes in the temperature of the environment have so far given rather inconclusive results.　　J.R.

PAROTID GLANDS, on the back of the neck of frogs and toads, their secretions constituting an important protective device against predators. The treefrog *Hyla vasta* produces a secretion which causes inflammation of the skin of anyone handling it. In general parotid secretions are harmless to members of the same species. They have an action similar to digitalis when injected into higher vertebrates and some progress has been made with their chemistry. In South America hunters have used such secretions to tip arrow heads. Any bird or smaller mammal hit by such an arrow succumbs to paralysis.

PARROTBILLS, a small subfamily of 20 species of songbirds, Paradoxornithinae, with stout, parrot-like bills. The name is also used at times for those members of the honeycreeper family of Hawaii which have parrot-like bills. The typical parrotbills are most closely related to the babblers. They are almost all confined to southeastern Asia, north to the Himalayas and northern China, but with a single species, the Bearded reedling *Panurus biarmicus* present in reedbeds from Manchuria westwards and northwards into

Europe as far as eastern England and the Baltic. In general parrotbills are dull-coloured birds, the plumage being mainly brown and ranging from greyish brown to light chestnut, with some vinous pink on some of the smaller birds. The heads of most show some variegation in the form of areas of black, grey, and more rarely white, producing contrasting patterns. White and black streaks on the edges of flight feathers also occur on some species. The body plumage is soft, dense and silky. The wings tend to be short and rounded; the tail well-developed, rather long, and graduated at the tip. The legs and feet are not conspicuously large but are strong, and enable the birds to be very agile and acrobatic in their movements, clinging in a variety of postures. The feet can be used for clamping down food items.

The striking bills of most species are short and stout, laterally flattened and very deep, the culmen strongly arched and the cutting edge of the upper mandible dipping slightly towards the base, then curving upwards and over, arching downwards again to form a strong hook at the tip, the lower mandible being shaped to fit. Exceptions to these are the bills of the largest species, the Great parrotbill *Conostoma aemodium* and of the Bearded reedling, both of which are of a more slender and conventional shape. The latter species also differs from others in that the sexes differ in plumage, the female lacking the grey head and black moustache stripes of the male.

The species vary considerably in size, the Great parrotbill being about 11 in (28 cm) long and the smaller species only 3–4 in (8–10 cm) long, including the tail. Save for the tiny stout bills the smallest species resemble the Long-tailed tits in their general appearance, thick plumage and behaviour.

Parrotbills are birds of low cover, such as thickets of forest floors, but are in particular associated with bamboo thickets and, in more open habitats, with bamboos or reedbeds. The heavy bills are used for tearing open the stems of reeds or bamboos or removing bark from trees, in search of insects. Green shoots and seeds may also be included in the diet. The nests are compact cups of grasses and leaves, often bound together with spiders' webs, and placed in a low site such as a bamboo clump. The eggs are plain blue or paler and heavily patterned. There are usually two to four in a clutch but the Bearded reedling may have five to seven. FAMILY: Muscicapidae, ORDER: Passeriformes, CLASS: Aves.

PARROTFISHES, a family of colourful tropical marine fishes related to the wrasses. The name parrotfish has sometimes been applied to superficially similar but unrelated fishes but is best restricted to the Scaridae. Parrotfishes are moderately deep-bodied and have a fairly long dorsal fin but shorter anal fin. The fin spines are rather weak. The teeth in the jaws are fused to form a 'beak' and this, together with their very bright colours, earns them their common name. Parrotfishes feed on coral, biting off pieces and grinding them very thoroughly with the pharyngeal teeth in the throat. This is then swallowed, the food extracted and the calcareous matter excreted, often in regular places where small piles of coral debris accumulate. Parrotfishes are, in fact, responsible for most of the erosion that occurs on reefs. Many species show strong homing instincts, returning to the same spot after foraging for food, and schools of parrotfishes have been seen regularly following the same route through the coral landscape. At night, some species, such as the Rainbow parrotfish *Pseudoscarus guacamaia,* secrete a tent of mucus around themselves. This may take up to half an hour to produce and as long to break out of in the morning. This mucous envelope would seem to be a protective device which perhaps prevents the odour of the fish from reaching predators.

Parrotfishes usually reach 2–3 ft (60–90 cm) in length, but a Tahitian species has been reported to attain 12 ft (3·6 m). In some species, such as *Scarus coeruleus* of the Atlantic, the larger individuals develop a curious bump on the forehead. The extraordinarily bright colours of the parrotfishes (often vivid patches of varying green and red) have made identification of species difficult. The young fishes are often quite different from the adults and the latter may show striking sexual differences, sometimes greatly complicated by sex reversal with or without the appropriate change in colour. In the Surf parrotfish *Scarus fasciatus* of the Atlantic this sexual dichromatism is so pronounced that the male and female can hardly be recognized as the same species. The species known as *S. taeniopterus* and *S. croicensis* were long thought to be distinct species until it was realized that only males of the first had ever been found and only females of the second.

The parrotfishes make excellent eating and in some areas are of commercial importance. FAMILY: Scaridae, ORDER: Perciformes, CLASS: Pisces.

PARROTS, a family of about 320 species, widely distributed in the tropics and southern temperate regions. Parrots are 4–50 in (10–130 cm) in total length and are mostly brightly coloured, although there are some drab grey, brown, green or black species. The family is sharply set apart from other groups of birds, although they are probably more closely related to the pigeons than to any other group. The hooked bill, bulging cere at the base of the bill, more or less rounded wings, short legs, zygodactyl feet and other characters, as well as general appearances

Hyacinth macaw, or Blue ara *Anodorhynchus hyacinthus*, a Brazilian parrot.

enable all parrots to be easily recognized as such.

The family is divided into four subfamilies (more in older classifications) of very unequal size. The first subfamily the Strigopinae, includes only the peculiar *kakapo or Owl parrot *Strigops habroptilus* of New Zealand. This is a large flightless bird which lives in burrows among tree roots during the day, emerging at night to feed on the leaves, flowers and berries of low growing plants.

The 17 or so species of *cockatoo in the subfamily Cacatuinae are distributed from Australia to the Philippines. They are mainly medium-sized to large with rather short tails.

Green-cheeked Amazon parrot *Amazona viridigenalis* ot northeastern Mexico.

Over 200 species of parrot are classified in the subfamily Psittacinae. The members of this large group are 4½–40 in (11–100 cm) or more long, and are found in the Americas, Africa, Asia and Australasia, as well as on many islands in the Pacific and Indian Oceans and the Caribbean. All American parrots belong to this subfamily, and the total of approximately 130 species is greater than the total number of parrot species inhabiting any other continent. American parrots vary in size from the huge, long-tailed *macaws to the sparrow-sized Andean *parakeets of the genera *Bolborhynchus, Amoropsittaca* and *Forpus*. Many of the larger American parrots, for example the genera *Ara, Anodorhynchus* and *Amazona,* including the macaws and Amazons, feed mainly on fruit and seeds from forest trees. Some of the smaller species eat fruit pulp, small seeds and nectar and pollen collected from flowering trees, as for example trees of the genera *Touit* and *Brotogeris*; and some species inhabit open country in temperate South America or on the Andean plateau, feeding mainly on the seeds of low-growing plants, for example the genera *Amoropsittaca* and *Bolborhynchus*.

So far as is known all American parrots nest in holes in trees but sometimes in holes in cacti, ants' nests, rocks or buildings. The Hooded parakeet *Myiopsitta monachus* is unique among parrots in building huge communal nests of sticks in the branches of trees, each pair having a separate nest chamber within the main structure.

The extinct Carolina parakeet *Conuropsis carolinensis* was the only parrot with a range extending into the northern temperate regions of North America. It was formerly very abundant in the Gulf and middle United States but was wiped out by human persecution. Several macaws and Amazon parrots on the islands in the Caribbean have also

become extinct in the past few hundred years. Some of these are known only from skins and other identifiable remains, while others are known only from contemporary descriptions and paintings, so that it is not clear how many different species there were. A trade in young parrots for the pet industries of Europe and North America has flourished for many years in the West Indies, so that other island species of parrot may well be threatened with extinction if the trade continues unchecked.

Africa has surprisingly few species of parrot, perhaps because of the aridity of large areas and the relative scarcity of fruiting forest trees in the wetter areas. The African grey parrot *Psittacus erithacus,* a medium-sized, short-tailed species, is found throughout tropical Africa, and the Ring-necked parakeet *Psittacula krameri* has an extensive range which includes much of southern Asia and most of tropical Africa. The seven species of the genus *Poicephalus* are small to medium-sized parrots found over much of the southern two-thirds of Africa, feeding on fruit, seeds, and sometimes the nectar and pollen of flowering trees. The *lovebirds *Agapornis* are also peculiar to Africa.

One species of lovebird and two species of Vasa parrot, *Coracopsis vasa* and *C. nigra,* are peculiar to Madagascar. All three inhabit forests, the lovebird feeding mainly on seeds and the Vasa parrots mainly on fruit from forest trees. Several extinct parrots are known from islands in the Indian Ocean, the most distinctive among them being *Lophopsittacus mauritianus* of Mauritius, the size of a large cockatoo, with a huge bill about 1¼ in (3 cm) wide.

Many species of the subfamily Psittacinae are found in southern Asia, in Australia and on the islands of the Indo-Malayan, Moluccan and Papuan regions. The heavy billed, fruit-eating members of the genus

Tanygnathus, the racquet-tailed species of the genus *Prioniturus,* and the long-tailed Ring-necked parrots of the genus *Psittacula* are among the large species found in the Indo-Malayan and southern Asian regions. The Eclectus parrot *Eclectus roratus* and the New Guinea Hawk-headed parrot *Psittrichas fulgidus* are large, forest inhabiting species found in the Papuan region, both of which eat mainly fruit from forest trees.

The Hanging parrots, Bat parrots or *lorikeets of the genus *Loriculus* in the subfamily Loriinae are found from India to New Guinea and New Britain, and other small parrots, *Psittinus, Geoffroyus, Psittacella,* are also found in this region.

Several genera of the subfamily Psittacinae are found in Australia, including *Aprosmictus,* of which the Red-winged parrot *A. erythropterus* is a familiar Australian bird.

The fourth subfamily Loriinae includes the *lories and lorikeets, the Pygmy parrots, the Fig parrots, the Kaka *Nestor meridionalis* and *Kea *N. notabilis* of New Zealand and the Australian Broadtailed or platycercine parrots. Various of these groups have been considered as separate subfamilies in earlier classifications.

The six species of Pygmy parrot *Micropsitta* are 4–4½ in (10–11 cm) long, so that they are the smallest of all parrots. They are found from New Guinea to the Bismarck Archipelago and the Solomon Islands. All six are forest birds. The Red-breasted pygmy parrot *M. bruijnii* and the Geelvink Bay pygmy parrot *M. geelvinkiana* are green with buff, yellow and blue markings, and red breasts in the males. The other four species do not have red breasts, although several species have tufts of red feathers on the flanks and the breast of *M. meeki* is bright yellow.

The Pygmy parrots are probably unique among birds in feeding on fungi. They scrape slime-like fungi from decaying wood with their stumpy, weak bills and suck it into their throats through a tube-like tongue. Termites, lichen and seeds are also eaten at times, although little is known of the diet of several species. The Blue-breasted pygmy parrot *M. pusio* and the Red-breasted pygmy parrot often nest in holes which they excavate in the nests of tree-dwelling termites. Several adult birds have been seen at individual termite nests, implying that more than two birds are involved in rearing the young, something that is unknown in other parrots.

The five species of Fig parrot *Opopsitta* and *Psittaculirostris* are small, stout parrots with brilliantly coloured plumage, brilliant shades of red, orange, yellow, green, blue, black and white being arranged in sharply contrasting patterns in the different species.

These heavy-billed parrots are forest dwellers which live mainly on the fruit and seeds of forest trees.

The Australian Broad-tailed or platycercine parrots are a group of about 31 species, most of them confined to the Australian mainland, but some occurring in New Zealand, New Caledonia and even the Society Islands. The *budgerigar *Melopsittacus undulatus,* a familiar cage-bird, is the smallest of the platycercine parrots and it is found only in arid areas of Australia. Two other distinctive and rather peculiar platycercine parrots are the Australian Ground parrot *Geopsittacus occidentalis* and Night parrot *Pezoporus wallicus.* The latter is very rare, if not extinct, and restricted to bushy and grassy areas in the arid interior. The Ground parrot is found on swampy grasslands on or near the coast. Both species feed on the ground and nest in grass tussocks or in hollows under vegetation, and both have concealingly marked plumage with elaborate yellow, brown and green patterns.

The other platycercine parrots are all long-tailed, and most of them have bright plumage with contrasting shades of red, yellow and blue predominating. They nearly all inhabit open areas with scattered trees or patches of scrub, and feed on the seeds of low-growing plants, sometimes fruit or flowers. The New Caledonia parakeet *Purpureicephalus cornutus* is the only member of the group to have a crest, consisting of elongated feathers from the back of the crown.

Because of their bright plumage and diet of seeds the Australian platycercine parakeets have been favourites with aviculturists for many years. FAMILY: Psittacidae, ORDER: Psittaciformes, CLASS: Aves.   D.T.H.

PARTHENOGENESIS, sometimes popularly termed virgin birth, is the development into a new individual of an ovum that has not been fertilized by a sperm. It is usually regarded as an aberrant form of sexual reproduction. The offspring, which may resemble the parent exactly or differ from her in material features, inherits all genetical information from the one parent, and to this extent parthenogenesis resembles asexual reproduction.

Parthenogenesis is the sole method of reproduction in a few arthropods, while in many arthropods, mainly insects and crustaceans, both parthenogenetic and normal sexual reproduction may occur. In bees, fertilized eggs give rise to diploid females and workers, unfertilized eggs to haploid males. In *aphids, all individuals, whether they arise parthenogenetically or after fertilization, are diploid (a modified diploidy in the males). Parthenogenesis that leads to the formation of a new adult is known to occur in other groups than the arthropods,

in rotifers, nematodes and some molluscs, for example, and can be encouraged experimentally in many types of animal. The ova of Silk moths, starfishes, Sea urchins, Marine worms and amphibians have been made to develop into embryos or larvae by pricking them with a needle, shaking them, changing the temperature, washing them in acids, alkalis, salt solutions and other fluids. In mammals there is no convincing evidence that complete development can occur by parthenogenesis although abortive parthenogenetic development is a normal feature of some species.

Most naturally occurring parthenogenesis is associated with a modified *meiosis that leaves the egg diploid or restores diploidy to the egg (see genetics). There is little evidence concerning the nature of stimuli that cause haploid eggs to develop, in nature, into haploid individuals. Experimental work, mainly on vertebrates, has shown that many stimuli (chemical, mechanical, temperature shock) may initiate abortive parthenogenesis. This may be of two kinds: gynogenesis, the development of an egg after entry of a sperm but without the participation of the sperm nucleus, and androgenesis, the failure of the female nucleus after entry of the sperm, its role being taken over by the male nucleus. Both phenomena are akin to parthenogenesis.
                                                       A.F.

PARTNERSHIPS, a term sometimes used in popular natural history writings for a variety of associations between two or more, often dissimilar, animals. They include commensalism, symbiosis, inquilism, mutualism and phoresy. There is another association which because of its detriment to one of the associates is seldom spoken of as a partnership. This is parasitism. All these are dealt with under their separate headings but in fact they tend to intergrade and it is not always possible to make a sharp distinction between these six kinds of associations, which is why 'partnerships' is often the preferable term. An early term used for the first time in 1876 spoke of animals living together for mutual benefit as 'messmates'. This was later replaced by 'commensalism' for a one-sided association between two organisms in which one obtained shelter or food, or both, from the other, the second partner reaping little or no benefit. Then the term 'symbiosis' came into use in 1879. This means literally 'a living together' and was used for any association from commensalism to parasitism.

PARTRIDGES, game birds distributed throughout Europe, Asia and Africa. They include the little Stone partridge *Ptilopachus petrosus* which is found in the rocky parts of West and East Africa and the even smaller 'Bush quails' *Perdicula* of India which are

The hen of the Grey or Common Partridge, well-known gamebird, settling on her eggs.

really dwarf partridges. The See-see partridges *Ammoperdix* are sandy-coloured desert birds to be found in the Middle East and western India.

Most well-known of all is the Grey or Common partridge *Perdix perdix*, 12 in (30 cm) long, with a chestnut horseshoe on its breast. This famous game bird is monogamous and coveys usually consist of one pair with their offspring from the previous summer. The coveys break up early in the new year when the birds pair off and take up their breeding territories. Unlike many game birds the cock partridge is a devoted parent and helps the hen in the care of the chicks.

The Grey partridge is also found in Europe, east to the Caspian area but is replaced in Turkestan, Mongolia and northern China by the closely related *Perdix barbata* and in Central Asia and the Himalayas at high altitudes by *Perdix hodgsoniae*. The partridge population of the British Isles and other areas has declined in recent years because of changing agricultural methods including the use of pesticides and the grubbing up and removal of hedgerows which provided shelter and nesting cover.

The Red-legged partridge *Alectoris rufa* is a more colourful bird than the Grey partridge. It originated on the continent of Europe but has been introduced as a game bird to the British Isles. It is more at home in wooded and rocky country as well as in mountains. The chukar *Alectoris graca* is very similar to the typical Red-legged partridge in appearance. It is found from the Alps eastwards to Manchuria, while its near ally *A. barbara* inhabits North Africa and the giant *A. melanocephala* lives in Arabia.

Snowcocks *Tetraogallus* are generally included under the general heading of partridges. They live at high altitudes in Central Asia, the Caucasus, Asia Minor, the Himalayas, northwestern China and Mongolia. They are large birds almost as big as pheasants. The Snow partridge *Lerwa lerwa* is found high up from Afghanistan to Sikkim and western China. The 16 species of Tree partridges *Arborophila* spp are more colourful and are found in forests from eastern India to southern China and Malaysia.

The Black wood partridge *Melanoperdix nigra* is found in Malaya, Sumatra and Borneo, while the very rare Crimson-headed partridge *Haematortyx* is confined to northern Borneo. The Ferruginous wood partridge *Caloperdix oculea* and the large Long-billed partridge *Rhizothera longirostris* both come from Malaysia and have short spurs. They are closely related to the francolins.

Most beautiful of all the partridges is the roulroul *Rollulus roulroul* from Malaysia. The plumage of the male is predominantly green with blue and red markings and a vivid crimson crest.

The Bamboo partridges *Bambusicola* spp

Passenger pigeon, famous North American pigeon which once existed in countless millions but was shot out of existence, the last survivor dying in a zoo almost at the moment World War I began in Europe.

are found only in India and resemble small pheasants in shape. The cocks sometimes have as many as four spurs on each leg, while the hens usually have only one or two. There are two species in India and one in Ceylon. FAMILY: Phasianidae, ORDER: Galliformes, CLASS: Aves. P.W.

PASSENGER PIGEON *Ectopistes migratorius,* extinct bird of the pigeon family, Columbidae, which bred in very large numbers over much of the eastern part of North America well into the 19th century. It had disappeared by 1914, its end being hastened by human activities.

The Passenger pigeon was closely related to the Mourning dove *Zenaida macroura*. It was smaller than a feral pigeon and slimmer and had a long pointed tail. The plumage was blue-grey above with a pink breast shading to white under the tail. The flight feathers of the wing were almost black and the central tail feathers not much lighter. There were also black streaks on the scapulars and black spots on the wing coverts. The outer tail feathers were almost white. On each side of the neck there was a purple-pink iridescent patch. The legs, feet and irides were red. The female was basically similar to the male, but much duller.

A century ago the Passenger pigeon was famous because of its prodigious numbers. The American ornithologist, Alexander Wilson, estimated one flock at over 2,230 million birds. In 1871, in one area of central Wisconsin, an estimated 136 million birds bred within an area of 850 sq miles (2,200 sq km). Such numbers were by no means un-

usual. Audubon described the multitudes in what were then the backwoods of Kentucky, Indiana and Ohio, and in 1687 the enormous numbers of Passenger pigeons around Montreal had so damaged the crops of the colonists that they had to be exorcised like devils.

The Passenger pigeon was highly gregarious and social, feeding, breeding and migrating in huge flocks. Its food included a variety of fruits and seeds and also invertebrate animals, birds feeding both on the ground and in trees. A considerable amount of damage was done not only to trees but also to cultivated crops. The birds apparently flew considerable distances to feed: the crops from a number of birds killed in New York state containing undigested rice grains which must have been eaten in Georgia or South Carolina. It seems that they also had a technique for catching earthworms by stalking them and seizing the head.

The nests were in dense colonies in trees, and were like those of other pigeons which nest in trees—a few loosely-arranged twigs. Only one egg was laid, as in some other bird colonies with enormous numbers of individuals. The incubation period was 13 days and the young were in the nest for another 14 days. There appears to have been a considerable amount of desertion of the young as a result of human interference towards the latter end of the species' existence and this may have been a significant factor in its extinction. Other factors were the enormous toll taken by man for food and the millions of birds simply destroyed as pests and not even used for food. It appears

that intense gregariousness had become an essential part of the Passenger pigeon's life and when its numbers were reduced below a certain level it no longer had the degree of mutual social stimulation necessary for successful reproduction. FAMILY: Columbidae, ORDER: Columbiformes, CLASS: Aves.
P.M.D.

PASSERIFORMES, the great order of perching birds, containing more than ½ the species and more than ⅓ of the families of the class Aves, the rest sometimes being lumped together as 'non-passerines'. By far the most successful order of birds, it contains all the most accomplished songsters, including many mimics. There is a great deal of adaptive radiation to be seen in the group, which is cosmopolitan, members being absent only from the highest latitudes and the least hospitable islands. Alternative names are Passeres or passerines. The largest suborder is Oscines, the songbirds.

All passerines are land birds, with feet adapted for perching and walking, with four toes joined at the same level and the big toe—the hallux—directed backwards. The feet are never webbed—even in the few species, such as the dippers (Cinclidae) that make forays underwater. Passerines of various kinds are found near water, obtaining their food around the edges of ponds, streams, lakes, rivers and the sea, but no species is fully aquatic and none is found out to sea, except during migration, or *wreck. There is considerable variation in the shape of the bill correlated with a wide variety of feeding habits. Passerine young are nidicolous, being confined to a nest by their helpless condition and cared for by their parents. A few species are *brood parasites.

The variety of types found in the Passeriformes, their distribution, and the number of species, are indicated by the list of families which follows. In some cases the number of species in a family may vary slightly according to the authority.

Suborder Eurylaimi:
Eurylaimidae. Broadbills. 14 species. Found in Africa and through Asia to Malaysia.

Suborder Tyranni:
Superfamily Furnarioidea:
Dendrocolaptidae. Woodcreepers. 48 species. Found in Mexico and Central and South America.
Furnariidae. Ovenbirds. 215 species. Found in southern Mexico and Central and South America.
Formicariidae. Antbirds. 222 species. Found in southern Mexico and Central and South America.
Conopophagidae. Antpipits. 11 species. Found in South America.
Rhinocryptidae. Tapaculos. 26 species. Found in Central and South America.

Superfamily Tyrannoidea:
Pittidae. Pittas. 23 species. Found in Africa, Asia and Australasia.
Philepittidae. Asitys. Four species. Restricted to Madagascar.
Xenicidae. New Zealand wrens. Four species. Confined to New Zealand.
Tyrannidae. Tyrant-flycatchers. 365 species. Found through North and South America.
Pipridae. Manakins. 59 species. Found through Central America and in South America.
Cotingidae. Cotingas. 90 species. Found in southern USA, Mexico, Central and South America and Jamaica.
Phytotomidae. Plantcutters. Three species. Found in South America.

Suborder Menurae:
Menuridae. Lyrebirds. Two species. Found in southeastern Australia.
Atrichornithidae. Scrub-birds. Two species. Found in Australia.

Suborder Oscines ('songbirds'):
Alaudidae. Larks. 75 species. Found in the Americas, Africa, Eurasia and Australasia.
Hirundinidae. Swallows. 75 species. Cosmopolitan.
Motacillidae. Wagtails and pipits. 48 species. Cosmopolitan.
Campephagidae. Cuckoo-shrikes. 71 species. Found through Africa, Asia and Australasia.
Pycnonotidae. Bulbuls. 109 species. Found in Africa, southern Asia and Malaysia.
Irenidae. Fairy bluebirds or leafbirds. 15 species. Found through Asia and Malaysia.
Laniidae. Shrikes. 72 species. Found in Africa, Eurasia and North America.
Vangidae. Vanga-shrikes. 12 species. Restricted to Madagascar.
Bombycillidae. Waxwings and silky-flycatchers. Three and four species, respectively. Discontinuously subarctic and temperate; and southern USA, Mexico and Central America, respectively.
Dulidae. Palmchat. One species only. Restricted to the West Indies.
Cinclidae. Dippers. Five species. Found in Eurasia and the Americas.
Troglodytidae. Wrens. 63 species. Northwest Africa, Eurasia and the Americas.
Mimidae. Mockingbirds. 30 species. The Americas and the West Indies.
Prunellidae. Accentors. 11 species. North Africa and Eurasia.
Muscicapidae. A very important family of over 1,300 species, including the former families of Old World flycatchers, Muscicapidae; Old World warblers, Sylviidae; thrushes, Turdidae; and babblers, Timaliidae. The family is represented over the whole world.

Paridae. Titmice. 65 species. Found through much of the Old World and North and Central America.
Sittidae. Nuthatches. 23 species. North America, Eurasia, Australasia and Malaysia.
Certhiidae. Treecreepers. Five species. Discontinuously distributed in the northern hemisphere, particularly in the Old World.
Climacteridae. Australian treecreepers. Nine species, convergent with the Certhiidae. Found in Australia and New Guinea.
Dicaeidae. Flowerpeckers. 54 species. Found through Asia, Malaysia and Australia and east to the Solomon Islands.
Nectariniidae. Sunbirds. 104 species. Found in Africa, Asia, Malaysia and Australasia.
Zosteropidae. White-eyes. 80 species. Found in Africa, Asia, Malaysia and Australasia.
Meliphagidae. Honey-eaters. 160 species. Found in southern Africa, the East Indies, Australasia, Samoa, Hawaii and the Marianas.
Emberizidae. As presently constituted contains more than 440 species of buntings, cardinal-grosbeaks, tanagers and swallow-tanagers, distributed severally over the whole world. Previously these various groups have been included in other families or have been given family status of their own, but the classification of most of the finch-like birds is in a state of considerable uncertainty and the classification given here follows the most recent authoritative opinion.
Parulidae. American wood-warblers. 119 species. The Americas and the West Indies.
Drepanididae. Hawaiian honeycreepers. 22 species. Found only in the Hawaiian Islands.
Vireonidae. Vireos, shrike-vireos, and peppershrikes. 42 species. Found in the Americas and the West Indies.
Icteridae. American orioles or troupials. 94 species. Found through the Americas and in the West Indies.
Fringillidae. Finches. Around 130 species, including the 14 species of Darwin's finches on the Galapagos. Found otherwise through Eurasia, Africa and much of the Americas.
Estrildidae. Weaver-finches and, possibly, the viduine wydahs. 108 and 11(?) species, respectively. Found in Africa, Asia, the East Indies, Australasia and many Pacific Islands.
Ploceidae. Weavers and sparrows. 129 species. The weavers are African, and the sparrows are widely distributed in the Old World, with recent introductions into the New World and Australasia.

The Painted bunting *Passerina ciris* of North America, a typical member of the Perching birds.

rodents look like long-legged rabbits or hares, the hindlimbs being long each with three toes bearing hoof-like claws. *D. patagonum* is much larger than *D. salinicolum* having a head and body length of 27–29½ in (69–75 cm) with large individuals weighing 20–35 lb (9–16 kg). The coat is dense, the upperparts greyish and the underparts whitish, with some yellow-brown on the legs and feet. Patagonian hares are diurnal, sleeping during the night in burrows where their 2–5 young are also born. They are fond of basking in the sun and feed on any available vegetation. FAMILY: Caviidae, ORDER: Rodentia, CLASS: Mammalia.

PATAS MONKEY *Erythrocebus patas,* a tall monkey living in open country in West Africa. See guenon.

PAUROPODA, little known arthropods, related to millipedes, 1 mm long at most, living under bark, among dead leaves and in rotten wood, in temperate and tropical regions. The 60 or more species are similar. The head is followed by a body of 11 segments, sometimes 12, with nine pairs of functional legs and one vestigial pair, each leg having five joints. Pauropods have no eyes but there are numerous tactile bristles on the sides of the body and the antennae are branched. The newly hatched larvae have three pairs of legs. CLASS: Pauropoda, PHYLUM: Arthropoda.

Sturnidae. Starlings, including the ox-peckers. 104 species. Found through Africa, Eurasia, Malaysia, Australasia and Oceania.

Oriolidae. Orioles. 26 species. Found in Africa, Eurasia, the East Indies, Australasia and the Philippines.

Dicruridae. Drongos. 20 species. Found in Africa, Asia, Malaysia, Australia and on a number of Pacific Islands.

Calleidae. Wattlebirds. Three species (one extinct). Restricted to New Zealand.

Grallinidae. Mudnest-builders. Four species. Found in Australia and New Guinea.

Artamidae. Wood-swallows. Ten species. Found through Asia, the East Indies, Australia and a number of Pacific Islands.

Cracticidae. Bell-magpies. Ten species. Found in Australasia.

Ptilinorhynchidae. Bowerbirds. 18 species. Found in Australasia.

Paradisaeidae. Birds of paradise. 43 species. Also Australasian.

Corvidae. Crows. 103 species. Cosmopolitan except for New Zealand and some Pacific Islands. P.M.D.

PASTEUR, L., 1822–1895, French scientist and microbiologist who disproved the theory of spontaneous generation in which animals were supposed to arise from inorganic matter.

Hindered in his education by privation and sickness, and intending to make teaching his career, Louis Pasteur became one of the great scientific benefactors of mankind. Originally interested in the structure of the organic acids for which he was later awarded the Ribbon of the Legion of Honour, he was Professor of Physics at Dijon and Professor of Chemistry at Strasburg before becoming Professor and Dean at Lille in 1854. Here he started his detailed studies of the processes of fermentation which he continued after his removal to Paris four years later. He showed that fermentation, and many diseases, are caused by minute organisms present in the air. He improved the brewing of beer and the fermentation of wine; he solved the problem of the infection of the silkworm stocks of the French silk industry; and in particular he worked out the responsible agents and remedies for certain diseases of man and his domesticated animals. These included chicken cholera, anthrax and rabies. His discoveries also induced Lister to find a way of reducing infection in operating theatres. Pasteur Institutes throughout the world bear tribute to his great work.

PATAGONIAN HARE, or Patagonian cavy, two species of which *Dolichotis patagonum* and *D. salinicolum* are found in Argentina and Patagonia. These short-tailed

PAULING, L. C., born 1901, American physical chemist and worker for peace. Joining the staff of the California Institute of Technology in 1922, Pauling's first important discovery was the nature of the chemical bond between atoms. Other findings followed and from 1936 he applied his knowledge of physical chemistry to biological systems. With a research team he was able to work out the angles at which lie the bonds between two atoms in a protein molecule, and the spacing between these atoms. The arrangement he discovered indicated that protein molecules have a coiled, or helical, structure.

Pauling's other biological work has included the detection of the chemical abnormality in the structure of the haemoglobin in patients suffering from sickle cell anaemia; the first connection between a mutation and an observable chemical change. His work earned him the Nobel Prize for Chemistry in 1954.

Of recent years Pauling has been increasingly concerned with the cause of peace among men, and his efforts to promote that peace have been such that he was awarded the Nobel Peace Prize for both 1962 and 1963.

PAVLOV, I. P., 1849–1936, Russian physiologist. Born in central Russia, the son of a poor priest, Pavlov was left-handed but taught himself to be ambidextrous, gained

Common mussel gaping, exposing a Pea crab living within its mantle cavity.

wiped across the mouthparts, and these work the food backwards into the mouth.

Other Pea crabs have somewhat bizarre associations with other animals. One species lives inside the rectum of a Sea urchin and another lives inside the respiratory trees of Sea cucumbers.

The larval development of Pea crabs is often shorter than that of other crabs. One of the tropical species *Pinnotheres moseri*, which lives in a Sea squirt *Ascidia nigra*, has only a single zoea stage (see crustacean larvae), and reaches the megalopa stage in 36 hours. The species from temperate waters may take between three and six weeks to reach the megalopa stage. FAMILY: Pinnotheridae, SUBORDER: Brachyura, ORDER: Decapoda, CLASS: Crustacea.   Ja.G.

PEAFOWL, relatives of pheasants, the males having a long train of up to 150 feathers formed from the tail coverts, which can be erected to make a showy fan. For centuries peacocks have figured in mythology and folklore. They have been admired for their beauty and hunted for their flesh, while in more recent times they have become a popular and graceful addition to parks and gardens. There are two species, the Indian peafowl *Pavo cristatus* which comes from Ceylon and India and the Green peafowl *Pavo muticus* which has a more easterly distribution and occurs in Burma, Thailand, Indo-China, the Malay Peninsula and Java.

The Congo peacock belongs to the genus *Afropavo* and is the only pheasant originating outside Asia, being found in the rain-forests of the east-central Congo Basin in Africa. FAMILY: Phasianidae, ORDER: Galliformes, CLASS: Aves.

degrees in both science and medicine, and for many years led a team of workers concerned with digestive physiology. He was responsible for considerable progress in our knowledge of digestive gland secretions and their actions; and only latterly did he become interested in conditioned reflexes—as a result of his interest in blood pressure changes during digestion. He is perhaps best known for this last area of work but in fact he never actually conditioned an animal himself. He was made a Nobel Laureate for his work on the physiology of digestion, and was elected a Fellow of the Royal Society of London in 1907.

PEACOCK, large exotic ground birds of the genera *Pavo* and *Afropavo*, well-known as ornamental birds. The term may refer to the male alone or, collectively, to both sexes. The proper collective term is 'peafowl', where it is described more fully.

PEA CRABS, so called for their smooth rounded bodies and because the males of many species are no larger than a pea. They readily form associations with other animals, and the best known species are those that live inside the mantle cavities of bivalve molluscs. The female of such a species may grow to such a size that she can no longer escape from the interior of the mollusc shell, but the males remain small and so can enter the shells and mate with the trapped females.

Peacock displaying to a peahen.

Pinnotheres pisum, which lives inside the mantle cavities of the mussels *Mytilus* and *Modiolus,* obtains its food from that collected by the host. The crab positions itself at the edge of the gills where a large ciliary tract conveys food towards the bivalve's mouth. The pincers of the crab are hairy, and are used to remove mucus and entrapped food from the ciliary current. The pincers are then

PEARLFISHES, an alternative name for *cucumberfishes.

PEARLS, white spherical gems produced by bivalve molluscs, especially by Pearl oysters, in response to an irritation of the mantle. Under natural conditions small sand particles often form the necessary nucleus and stimulation for pearl formation, the animal surrounding it with an organic matrix embedded with numerous flat plates of calcium carbonate, called nacre. This process leads to the development of a natural pearl. A cultured pearl is produced by inserting a tiny bead between the valves of the oyster and then collecting it after a number of years, after it has become coated with nacre.

Pearls are very variable and the most valuable are black, although many people prefer the rose coloured types. Cream or yellow coloured forms are far less prized.

In Roman times, before the growth of the Far-Eastern pearl fishing industry, the European, and especially the British, pearl industry was famous, the pearls being collected from the freshwater Pearl mussel, *Margaritifera margaritifera*.

PEARLS FROM DEW. It was once thought that pearls were conceived in shellfish from dew, the quality and size of the pearl depending on the type of dew; if pure and clear, the pearls were white and fine. Pliny describes the hazards of pearl-fishing: 'let the fisher look well to his fingers' for the 'mother of pearl' was well aware what groping fingers are seeking for. Also, the molluscs are found among craggy rocks where lurk 'curst Sea-dogs'. However, as Pliny finishes, 'and yet all this will not serve to scare men away from fishing after them: for why? our dames and gentlewomen must have their ears behanged with them'.

PEARLY NAUTILUS, a shelled member of the Cephalopoda, the group of molluscs that includes octopuses, squids and cuttlefishes. It is the sole surviving representative of a group of molluscs that dominated the seas in Paleozoic and Mesozoic times (see ammonites). There are six living species, all placed in the genus *Nautilus*, the best known being *N. pompilius*. All are found in deep water around coasts in the southwestern Pacific and Indian oceans.

The shell is coiled, chambered and 6–8 in (15–20 cm) in diameter in adult specimens. The animal lives in the last chamber, further partitions being laid down behind it as it grows. The partitions are never quite complete and a long thin prolongation of the abdomen connects through to earlier sections of the shell. This is known as the siphuncle and is richly supplied with blood vessels, and

it has the capacity of absorbing salt from the fluid—mostly sea water—that is left in the abandoned chambers as the animal grows. Removal of the salt creates an osmotic gradient between the blood of the animal and the water in the shell chambers, with the result that much of the water is drawn out, to be replaced by gas coming out of solution in the bloodstream. As a result, the partially gas-filled shell counterbalances the weight of the animal, so that this otherwise rather bulky creature is able to float delicately just above the bottom, propelling itself with jets from a funnel slung below the main part of the body.

Very little is known about the habits of *Nautilus*. In aquaria, they are mainly active at night. The eyes are large but simple, lacking the lens and cornea of more recent cephalopods, and although the animals are plainly able to see a little (they will, for example, approach the light of an electric torch shone through the walls of their aquarium) they do not appear to recognize their surroundings or their food by sight. Their chemical sense, in contrast, is obviously very acute. The Pearly nautilus appears to be a scavenger and if food, such as dead fish or crustaceans, is placed in a tank with a *Nautilus* the cephalopod extends its many tentacles and circles to search the area. Having found the source of the smell the food is grasped by the cephalic tentacles, which are very mobile and extensible, and transferred to the mouth to be bitten off in chunks by the massive beak.

Structurally, *Nautilus* differs from other living cephalopods in a number of ways besides the possession of a shell. The arms are numerous and each consists of a leathery

sheath and a slender tentacle that can extend far beyond the sheath. These bear no hooks or suckers. The top of the head is developed into a tough shield that closes the mouth of the shell when it has been disturbed. The digestive and excretory systems are similar to those in other *cephalopods but the circulatory system is unusual in having not one but two pairs of gills, a feature that has sometimes been cited in support of the view that the ancestors of the molluscs were segmented animals with serially repeated structures, like the annelid worms. See also *Neopilina*. The nervous system is concentrated into a ring around the gut between the eyes, and although quite large by molluscan standards, it is rather poorly developed compared with other cephalopods. The sexes are separate, but nothing is known of the sex life of the adults or about the development of the young animals. ORDER: Tetrabranchia. CLASS: Cephalopoda, PHYLUM: Mollusca. M.J.W.

PECCARY, a pig-like mammal with long slender legs. The Collared peccary *Pecari tajacu* is greyish to black, paler underneath than on the back, and with white annulations on the bristles. An erectile mane extends from the head to the scent gland on the rump at the dorsal midline. An incomplete whitish collar crosses the neck and extends obliquely upward and backward. The young are reddish brown with a lighter collar and usually a blackish dorsal band. There is a puffy scent gland, devoid of hair and about 4 in (10 cm) in front of the base of the abortive tail which is only about 1–1·5 in (2·5–3·8 cm) long. Males and females are of a similar

The Collared peccary, of tropical and subtropical America, is so named for its white neck band.

size the length of the head and body of the male averaging 36·9 in (93·7 cm) and of the female 36·1 in (91·7 cm). The height at shoulders of 20 males measured averaged 19·8 in (50·3 cm). For females this height was 20·5 in (52 cm). Large samples showed no significant difference in the weights of the two sexes. The 25 adult males weighed, averaged 44 lb (20 kg) and the same number of females averaged 45 lb (20·6 kg).

The middle metacarpals and metatarsals are fused into a cannon-bone. There are four toes on the front feet and three on the hind feet. The dental formula is as follows: incisors $\frac{2}{3}$; canines $\frac{1}{1}$; premolars $\frac{3}{3}$; molars $\frac{3}{3}$=38.

Collared peccaries range throughout southwestern USA in the states of Arizona, New Mexico and Texas and southwards to include most of Mexico, except the high mountains, Central America, all except the high mountainous areas of northern South America and as far south as Rio Platte in Argentina.

Some breeding takes place throughout the year but at the northern edge of the range most of the young are born in July and August. The gestation period is 142–148 days and there are usually two in each litter. The young are precocial and weigh about 1 lb (0·45 kg).

They inhabit mountainous canyons and brushy thickets and are vegetarian, eating fruits, green plants, acorns, cactus pads, cactus fruit and roots. Peccaries are highly social animals, travelling in bands of up to 20 individuals. Mothers with their young follow the herd, which remains in a home range area of about $\frac{1}{2}$ sq mile (about 1·3 km²). When alarmed the animals exude musk from their dorsal gland, causing a strong odour. When friendly animals meet, each rubs its cheek over the scent gland of the other. They also mark rocks, trees and other landmarks within their home range.

The only other living member of the family Tayassuidae is the White-lipped peccary *Tayassu pecari* which is larger than the Collared peccary having a head and body length of 43–47 in (109–120 cm). This species has long bristly hair and a scent gland on its back like the Collared peccary but unlike the latter its cheeks, nose and lips are

white. It inhabits dense forests of southern Mexico, Central America and South America. It is a highly social animal, travelling in large bands and living off nuts, fruits, green vegetation and roots. Little is known of its breeding, and it has a reputation for ferocity when cornered or wounded. FAMILY: Tayassuidae, ORDER: Artiodactyla, CLASS: Mammalia.   L.K.S.

PECK ORDER, the hierarchy among a group of birds in which the top bird can peck all others, the second peck all but the top bird and so on to the bottom bird who is pecked by all but can peck none. See dominance hierarchy.

The marine worm *Pectinaria koreni*, of northwest Europe, removed from its sandy tube.

PECTINARIA, short-bodied polychaete worms with delicate bodies which they protect by a tube which they build. The tubes are slightly tapered and slenderly conical in shape, perhaps 1 in (25 mm) or even 3 in (75 mm) in length. The worms build them from sand grains or very small pieces of shell neatly cemented together with a hardening mucus which they secrete from a 'building organ' just beneath the mouth. These are the most elegantly constructed of all polychaete tubes, thin but strong, and remarkable for the precise way in which the tiny fragments of which they are composed are fitted together. They are reminiscent of some freshwater caddis cases. The worm lies wholly within the tube, the slightly wider end of the tube downwards, the narrow end just projecting from the surface of the sand, which the worm eats, casting its sandy faeces from the narrow

chimney-like end of the tube onto the surface. The head is provided with numerous short tentacles with which it feeds and these have cilia and also mucous cells. On each side of the head is a comb-like row of very strong, usually golden, iridescent chaetae. These are used for digging and surrounding the tentacles which work within their grasp.

Different species of *Pectinaria* are found all over the world in sandy beaches near low water mark or are found in material dredged offshore. CLASS: Polychaeta, PHYLUM: Annelida.   R.P.D.

PEDOGENESIS, is sexual maturity and reproduction in the otherwise immature condition, that is, by animals which retain larval or other pre-adult features. See pedomorphosis and neoteny.

PEDOMORPHOSIS (Gk *pais*-child; *morphosis*-shaping), the term given by W. Garstang in 1894 to a mode of evolution in which the adult form of the descendant resembles the young form of the ancestor. This is precisely the opposite of E. Haeckel's 'biogenetic law' or 'theory of recapitulation' in which he insisted that during its embryonic development (ontogeny) the descendant recapitulated the sequence of adult stages of the evolutionary series of its lineage (phylogeny). This would have meant that the young descendant resembled the adult ancestor and that evolutionary novelties could only be inserted at the end of successive life-histories, to become compressed so that their abbreviated 'chapter-headings' (which is what recapitulation means) were pressed back into increasingly early stages of embryonic development.

Garstang showed that it was from the free-swimming larval forms of echinoderms that the evolution of *chordates and hence vertebrates, could be most satisfactorily traced, a conclusion which has since been confirmed from paleontological research. This principle was generalized by Gavin de Beer who showed that 'successful' groups of animals (as measured by their prevalence, breakthroughs into new ecological vacua, and consequent adaptive radiation) exhibited pedomorphosis (which is also found in plants). Insects, the most successful inverte-

The skulls of juvenile (above) and adult (below) ape and man to illustrate pedomorphosis, a mode of evolution in which adults resemble the juvenile stages of their ancestors. From left to right: *Pan troglodytes* (chimpanzee), *Australopithecus*, *Pithecanthropus*, *Homo neanderthalensis* and modern man *Homo sapiens*.

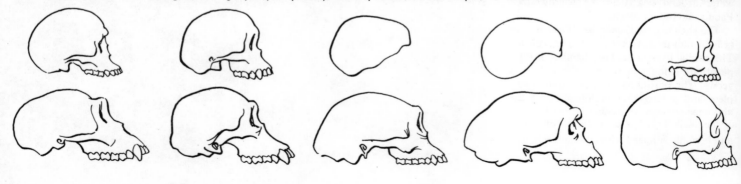

brates, can be derived from larval centipedes; modern man evolved from youthful australopithecines by greatly delayed development, which not only 'dropped' the ancestral adult stage with its specializations off the end of the life-history altogether, but also ensured a childhood so helpless and so prolonged that the parents were biologically indispensable for keeping children alive, and thereby able to bring about psycho-social evolution through instruction, resulting in humanization and civilization in a family unit. See neoteny.

G.deB.

PELICANS, large or very large aquatic birds highly adapted for swimming but ungainly on land. The order, Pelicaniformes, is one of very diverse forms including cormorants and gannets, but all have all four toes webbed. Pelicans themselves have long bills provided with an expansible pouch attached to the flexible lower mandible. The short powerful legs are set far back on the body, ideally suited to rapid swimming, but making the traversing of land difficult. Oddly enough, all are magnificent fliers, capable of sustained soaring flight over great distances. The whole body, beneath the skin, and even in the bones, is permeated with air spaces, probably assisting buoyant flight.

Pelicans weigh 10–25 lb (4½–11 kg), the larger species being among the largest flying birds, with wing-spans of 9 ft (2·7 m). They are usually white or mainly white, with areas of grey, brown or black plumage. The

White pelicans roosting in East Africa.

Brown pelican preening.

A flock of Pelicans taking off from an East African lake.

American brown pelican *Pelecanus occidentalis* is mainly brown. In the breeding season the colours of areas of bare skin, beak, pouch and legs, are intensified and several species grow crests at this time. In the American white pelican *P. erythrorynchos* a strange horn-like growth develops on the bill and in the Great white pelican *P. onocrotalus* the forehead becomes swollen. Males are considerably larger, and can also be distinguished from the smaller females by the colour of bare skin and other features such as the length of the crest. Despite their somewhat grotesque shape pelicans in breeding dress are often beautifully coloured; in *P. onocrotalus,* for instance, a rosy flush derived from a preen gland above the tail tinges all the silky-white plumage. Brown and yellow colours in this plumage are derived from staining in the waters in which the pelicans swim.

All seven species of pelicans belong to one genus, *Pelecanus,* which divides conveniently into two, perhaps three, superspecies or groups. In the first group there are four very large species, the American white pelican, the Great white pelican, the Dalmatian pelican *P. crispus* and the Australian pelican *P. conspicillatus.* All these breed in large colonies on the ground, roost on the ground and rarely perch in trees or bushes. The second group consists of three smaller species, the Brown pelican, the African pink-backed pelican *P. rufescens* and the Asian spotted-billed pelican *P.*

philippensis. These all breed in smaller, looser colonies in trees, but occasionally on the ground. They readily perch and roost in trees. The Brown pelican is rather different from the other two, and should perhaps be placed in a superspecies or group of its own, because of its more specialized fishing habits.

The basic adaptation for fishing of all pelicans is the bill. Contrary to general belief this is not used for storage or holding fish, but is simply a catching apparatus, resembling a scoop-net in function. The pouch is not permeable like a net, but is highly expansible and elastic. When the pelican plunges its bill into the water the flexible lower mandible automatically expands to a broad oval shape. As the pelican raises its head again fishes are scooped into the extensible pouch, the lower mandible contracts again and the upper mandible closes over the pouch like a lid so that entrapped fishes cannot escape. They are then swallowed whole at once, but can be transported long distances in the bird's gullet in a nearly undigested state.

This basic fishing method is varied and elaborated in several ways. The Brown pelican is unique in being the only species which regularly dives. Flying above the water it sights a fish and at once plunges vertically. Just before striking the surface of the water the neck, which is doubled up in flight, is shot straight out and the pelican penetrates the surface with neck at full stretch. The

fishes are caught underwater and swallowed when the pelican returns to the surface.

Pink-backed and Spotted-billed pelicans usually fish singly, when swimming; they do not dive. They swim slowly along, or often remain stationary for some moments. On sighting a fish they dart out the head and neck and catch it in the pouch. These species are coloured a neutral grey. Occasionally they fish in groups, using the 'scare line' technique perfected by larger pelicans. This is rare, however, and is usually only used in deeper water.

The 'scare line' method is perfectly demonstrated by the Great white pelican. A group of 8–12 swim rapidly forward in a horseshoe formation, with the open end of the horseshoe pointing forwards. At intervals of half a minute or so, as if at a given signal, all plunge their bills into the open centre of the horseshoe, where presumably fishes have collected. At the same time they part-open their wings, perhaps intensifying the shadow effect of the 'scare line'. This technique is often used by human fishermen to confine fishes to small areas whence they can be scooped out. Some fishes do not attempt to swim past the shadow of the scare line, but remain bemused in the centre. Great white pelicans habitually fish in this way, but occasionally fish singly, like Pink-backed pelicans. Probably the particular method adopted is connected with a relative abundance of fishes.

Naturally, pelicans have been suspected of damaging fishery interests. They probably eat from 5–10% of their own bodyweight a day, that is between $\frac{1}{2}$–$2\frac{1}{2}$ lb (0·2–1·2 kg) and estimates of greater quantities, such as their own weight of fish a day, are probably unfounded. If necessary they can starve for several days, for instance when on migration. While it is undeniable that a large number of pelicans eat great quantities of fish in a year recent work in the Danube Delta has shown that they take a higher proportion of diseased fishes than occurs in the fish population as a whole. In this way they help to keep the fish population healthy and may actually be beneficial, though appearing harmful.

In many areas pelicans are sedentary, but all northern populations migrate in winter and even tropical pelicans undertake long local movements. Pelicans are not well insulated and avoid cold, though they survive hard winters in zoos. When travelling they fly superbly. They take off in flocks when thermals begin to form, usually about nine or ten o'clock in the tropics, locate a rising current and mount spirally upon it for several thousand feet. Having gained the necessary height they 'peel off' from the thermal, forming into long lines and V form-

White pelicans at the nest.

ations, alternately flapping and gliding until they reach their destination or find another thermal on which to gain more height. In this way they are able to cover hundreds of miles with little effort, and will often breed in localities far from any source of fish, travelling 50 miles (80 km) or more each day to feed.

All pelicans breed gregariously, in colonies varying from about 50 to tens of thousands. The largest colonies reported in recent times have been of the Great white pelican in southern Tanzania, where up to 40,000 pairs have been sighted. The smaller pelicans normally breed in trees, making stick nests barely large enough to sit on. The four larger species breed on the ground, making a very simple nest. In the Great white pelican the male collects nesting material and carries it to the female in his pouch. She then places it around and beneath her. The same nesting colonies are used year after year for centuries, and in the tropics breeding may be protracted, sometimes even continuing throughout the year. Inaccessibility of the nesting area, for example the summits of some of the large rocks used for breeding in Chad, is apparently more important than any other factor in determining breeding season, but pelicans tend to breed in dry warm times when the site is permanently inaccessible. Pelicans, especially the ground-breeders, are very shy and will desert *en masse* if disturbed; they must always be approached with caution when breeding.

Courtship is usually short and not spectacular. In some, pair formation apparently immediately precedes egg-laying. Two to three, occasionally more, eggs are laid and are large, rather elongated and chalky white. The yolk is often red. Both sexes incubate, one remaining on the nest night or day while the other is away fishing. Incubation takes about 35–37 days.

Newly-hatched young are ugly, being naked and pink at first, turning black or grey, then growing a coat of grey or blackish down. In ground-breeding species they collect in groups or 'pods' when they can walk after about three weeks. Even so each parent recognizes and feeds only its own young in these pods. Feeding is by regurgitation at all times. The newly hatched young is fed small quantities of liquid matter dribbled down the parent's bill, and the young of the Great white pelican peck feebly at the red nail on the end of the bird's bill at this time—perhaps the origin of the mediaeval belief that the pelican fed her young on drops of blood from her own breast. Larger chicks reach into the parent's bill and gullet to obtain food and feathered chicks recognize their own parent and run to meet it on arrival. A parent feeding a large chick must face a violent struggle, the chick's head being thrust far down the parental gullet, and the chick struggling and

gyrating in its efforts to obtain the food.

Young pelicans take wing when 60–70 days old. Before flying they become larger, fatter and heavier than their parents. They are fed less, or even perhaps deserted at this time, and grow lighter before flying. If nesting close to water they usually learn to fish before they can fly and can immediately become independent of their parents once they have left the nesting colony.

In America the Brown pelican is threatened with extinction through ingestion of agricultural chemicals (DDT, dieldrin etc) found in fishes. In Europe the Dalmatian and Great white pelicans have been greatly reduced by direct persecution and destruction of habitat by drainage and development. Pelicans as a group were formerly very much more abundant than they are today, for instance in the period of the shallow warm Cretaceous seas. However, they are still relatively common in many warmer parts of the world, and provide a spectacular example of a highly specialized group of large birds.
FAMILY: Pelicanidae, ORDER: Pelicaniformes, CLASS: Aves.   L.B.

PELICAN'S PIETY. In heraldry the pelican is displayed 'in its piety', that is standing on the nest pecking its breast so that the young can feed on their parents' blood. This unusual form of parental care led to the pelican becoming the symbol of charity or piety and it is frequently found on the coats of arms of churchmen. The origin of the story probably lies in the Scriptures rather than with classical Greek or Roman authors. According to the 12th century bestiary translated by T. H. White, the young pelicans flap their wings in their parents' faces and the latter kill them, but three days later the mother revives them by sprinkling their bodies with her blood. In another version the young are killed by a serpent and the mother returns three days later to revive them.

PELLET, compacted mass of hard material, especially bones, regurgitated by many birds. Pellet formation is well-known in birds of prey, especially owls, but many other types of birds, including insect eaters and even honey-eaters, eject pellets. The habit would seem to be an adaptation for the efficient elimination of hard, indigestible items by wrapping up bones, teeth, insect cuticle and other hard objects in a soft substance such as fur or feathers. Birds which regularly eject pellets deliberately eat soft material. When fur or feathers are not eaten with the food, they may be deliberately sought, or paper, plastic and rubber bands used as an alternative. Grebes deliberately swallow feathers, and even present them to their young, presumably because of the difficulty of regurgitating

sharp fish bones without a soft wrapping. The collection of pellets from below a nest or feeding post is a good way of investigating a bird's diet.

PELOBATIDAE, a family of frogs belonging to the suborder Anomocoela, intermediate in structure between the more primitive Amphicoela, Opisthocoela and Procoela and the more advanced Diplasiocoela. Like the more primitive Discoglossidae and Pipidae the vertebrae are stegochordal. This means that during development the ring of tissue around the notochord ossifies only in a small arc over the notochord which then degenerates. In the other families the ring of tissue ossifies completely and replaces the notochord to form a solid bony centrum. Like the more advanced families, however, some of the muscles of the hindlimb of the Pelobatidae are separate while in the more primitive forms they are still fused together.

The genus *Pelodytes* contains two species which are found in Europe. They are sometimes placed in a separate family, the Pelodytidae. *P. punctatus* is called the *Mud diver.

Some members of the Pelobatidae are known as Spadefoot toads. The name refers to the hard tubercle on the edge of each foot which is used for digging. The animal shuffles backwards into the ground, pushing the soil to either side with the scraper-like tubercles.

The European Spadefoot toads belong to the genus *Pelobates*. *P. fuscus* is found throughout Europe, usually in areas with light, sandy soil in which it can dig easily. As it burrows the soil falls over it and it takes less than a minute to disappear from sight. They are stout frogs, about $2\frac{1}{2}$ in (63 mm) long and are sometimes mistaken for toads. They can, however, be distinguished from the true toads (*Bufo*) by their smoother skin and the fact that the pupil of the eye is vertical instead of horizontal.

When disturbed the skin exudes an irritant fluid which smells strongly of garlic and in Germany these frogs are known as 'Garlic toads'. Besides this poisonous secretion they have another defence mechanism. They can sometimes be roused to what looks like a fit of rage; the frog inflates its body to a round ball and jumps repeatedly at its aggressor with gaping mouth as though to bite, while screaming loudly.

Spadefoot toads spend the day underground, emerging to hunt for food a few hours after sunset. In the breeding season the male calls underwater and during mating the large string of eggs is twisted round the stems of water plants. The tadpoles are large, sometimes reaching a length of 5 in (12·5 cm). The time which they take to develop into adults varies; occasionally the tadpoles hibernate and metamorphose the next year.

The Spadefoot toads of America belong to the genus *Scaphiopus*. Most species are found in the southwestern States in arid or semi-arid conditions. The Eastern spadefoot, *S. holbrooki* is found in the wetter east and southeast, but even here it seems to prefer the drier, sandier parts.

Spadefoot toads show several adaptations to the dry conditions in which they live. Primarily, they burrow, so avoiding the hot dry air, and remain in the soil where there is some moisture. They may bury themselves as much as 6 ft (1·8 m) below the surface. During the period of the year in which they are active they keep the entrances to their burrows clear but during the winter or in times of drought they allow the earth to collapse around them and may remain buried for several months until the conditions are right for emergence. When Couch's spadefoot *S. couchi* emerges from *aestivation it is covered with a hard layer like dried skin which forms a 'cocoon' around the frog and probably helps prevent loss of moisture in the burrow.

Spadefoots are also adapted to their dry habitat by being 'explosive' breeders. They appear in large numbers after heavy rain and breed in temporary pools. The Eastern spadefoot has the unusual habit of sometimes beginning to call while still buried. Early in the evening a muffled chorus is heard around pools although no frogs are visible. After a while the males emerge from their burrows and continue to call while floating in the water. Most species of spadefoots have a loud voice which can be heard more than ½ ml (0·8 km) away.

The eggs of spadefoots develop rapidly. In the Western spadefoot *S. hammondi* the eggs, which are attached to water plants, hatch after only 1½–2 days. The tadpoles also develop rapidly and may change into frogs after about 2 weeks. This time varies, however, and the conditions which affect it are not fully understood. It may be connected with the drying up of the pools. Tadpoles removed from a drying pool and placed in water remain as tadpoles for several weeks while those left in the pool change into frogs just before the pool dries up. The availability of food is also probably an important factor in governing the rate of metamorphosis. In some species of spadefoot, when food is scarce, the tadpoles become cannabalistic. This ensures that at least some of them are able to survive.

Megophrys nasuta belongs to a genus of Pelobatidae found in South Asia. It has a curious appearance which forms an effective camouflage. It has a triangular projection of skin on the snout and a similar projection over each eye. It lives on the floor of rain forests and its mottled brown colour blends with the dead leaves. From above, the skin projections hide the eyes and disguise the outline of the frog.

The tadpoles of *M. montana* and several

Dwarf pencilfishes, of the Guianas, kept as aquarium fishes tend to eat their newly-spawned eggs.

other species of the genus have greatly enlarged lips which form a large funnel around the mouth. This floats on the surface of the water with the tadpole hanging vertically beneath it. The inside of the funnel has rows of horny teeth which are used to scrape food particles off the undersides of floating leaves. ORDER: Anura, CLASS: Amphibia.   M.E.D.

PELODYTIDAE, frogs of the genus *Pelodytes,* sometimes placed in a separate family, the Pelodytidae. They are more usually included in the *Pelobatidae. ORDER: Anura, CLASS: Amphibia.

PELYCOSAURS, extinct reptiles that flourished during the Upper Carboniferous and Permian periods, 300–225 million years ago. They were up to 12 ft (4 m) long and they had massive jaws. *Elaphasaurus* had crushing plates on its palate, possibly indicating that it fed on coarse, fibrous vegetation. The most remarkable feature of the pelycosaurs is the long neural spine on each vertebra, up to 3 ft (1 m) high, often with cross bones on them. It is supposed that these spines supported a web of skin, like a sail over the animal's back, possibly serving to take in heat from the sun, or for radiating body heat to the atmosphere. ORDER: Pelycosauria, SUBCLASS: Synapsida, CLASS: Reptilia.

PENCILFISHES, a family of slim, pencil-like fishes from the Amazon basin, belonging to the suborder of characin-like fishes, the Characoidei. A small fleshy adipose fin is sometimes present behind the rayed dorsal fin, but some authorities would prefer to place all the pencilfishes in the single genus *Nannostomus*. These fishes live in slow-flowing and weedy waters and many feed from the surface. In aquaria they tend to swim in an

oblique position with the head directed upwards. Almost all the species not only have a characteristic colour-pattern but also develop a differing pattern at night, the nocturnal colouration being darker than that of the day.

The Dwarf pencilfish *N. marginatus* is less slender than most of this genus. The back is olive, the flanks silvery with three longitudinal dark bands (the middle one edged with red) and the dorsal fin has a crimson blotch. At night the blotch darkens and a small dot appears on the gill cover. This species grows to 1½ in (4 cm) and is easy to keep in an aquarium. The Two-banded pencilfish *N. bifasciatus* is similar but has only two longitudinal stripes; at night there is only one faint band and three blotches.

If kept in an aquarium, these fishes should be provided with a heavily planted area and the water should be kept at 77–82°F (25–28°C). FAMILY: Lebiasinidae, ORDER: Cypriniformes, CLASS: Pisces.

PENDULINE TITS, about eight species of small birds of the tit family, Paridae, in the subfamily Remizinae. All but one of these occur in the Old World, but the rather distinct verdin *Auriparus flaviceps* from North America is normally included also. See tits. FAMILY: Paridae, ORDER: Passeriformes, CLASS: Aves.

PENGUINS, the most highly specialized of all aquatic birds, with 17 species restricted to the southern hemisphere. It is now generally accepted that their nearest relatives are the *tubenosed birds, Procellariiformes.

The word penguin is probably derived from 'pin-wing', a name given in the 16th century to certain seabirds found near Newfoundland. It has subsequently been established that the 'pin-wings' were Great auks and the name was later transferred to the penguins of the southern seas. The external appearance of the Great auk was very similar indeed to that of a medium-sized penguin such as the Gentoo penguin *Pygoscelis papua*, being of similar shape, with a length of 30 in (75 cm), black above, white beneath and flightless, using the wings as flippers for swimming under water.

In 1868 a French encyclopedia contained the statement 'Thanks to the many descriptive documents furnished by ancient as well as modern navigators, the natural history of penguins may be considered complete'. Since then four more species have been described, the breeding grounds of others have been discovered and some fossils have been found. In the 1960's very detailed work has been started on the population dynamics of penguins and on certain aspects of their behaviour such as breeding and migration. On the whole we may say that we are beginning to have a reasonable understanding of the biology of the family. We can now be fairly sure we know all the living representatives.

Penguins are fairly large and bulky, 16–48 in (40–120 cm) long, and quite conspicuous in their natural surroundings, particularly in the breeding season when they come to land. They are among the most distinctive of birds. Indeed, as Conor O'Brien wrote: 'Who would believe in penguins, unless he had seen them?' In some ways they are the most specialized of living animals, yet their extreme specialization has not led them into the insuperable difficulties which are often the case with ultra-specialization. This is probably due to the fact that their specialization is non-restrictive. They have as much freedom of movement in the aquatic medium as many birds have in the air and they may have fewer competitors, particularly in the case of the high antarctic species.

A useful series of fossil discoveries shows us that after the early Eocene in New Zealand, some 60 million years ago, penguins increased in size; two Miocene species, living around 20 million years ago stood, respectively, rather more and rather less than 5 ft (150 cm) high. The largest living species is the Emperor penguin *Aptenodytes forsteri*, standing up to 3 ft 6 in (105 cm) high, and the smallest the Little blue penguin *Eudyptula minor* which stands only about 14 in (35 cm).

There has been a considerable amount of discussion as to the relationships of the penguins with other groups. They have been given equivalent rank to all the rest of the modern birds put together; they have been placed in the exclusive superorder Impennae; and recently they have been shown to be related to the albatrosses and shearwaters, sharing a number of structural and behavioural features and possibly being derived from an oceanic, flying, shearwater-like ancestor.

Lowe, however, tried to show that penguins are primitively and primarily aquatic, not being descended from flying ancestors but from a reptilian or pre-avian stock, but this we now know not to be true. Penguins show their ancestry with other birds in a number of features. The pectoral girdle, for example, shows a convincing similarity to those of carinate birds—birds with a keel on the breastbone for the attachment of wing muscles. The penguin's breastbone still has the keel, but the pectoral muscles are now used for 'flying' underwater.

The skeleton of the flipper also shows that it is derived from the wing of a flying bird. The carpal (wrist) and metacarpal (hand) bones are fused, as in flying birds, to form the carpo-metacarpus, a special modification connected with the attachment of flight feathers. Although the bones of the penguin flipper are shortened and flattened, they are the same bones in the same basic arrangement as the bones of a flying bird's wing. If penguins had not been derived from a flying stock there would have been no reason at all

for such an arrangement of bones in the flipper.

The penguin skull is certainly that of a typical bird, having the avian palate and a cranial structure developed to contain a well-developed cerebellum—the part of the brain highly developed in birds for the elaborate co-ordination of muscular activity necessary for efficient flight.

Perhaps the most significant clue to the penguins' aerial past is the pygostyle or plough-share bone—the structure formed by the fusion of the terminal vertebrae of the tail for the purpose of supporting a fan of tail feathers used in flight. Also as in flying birds, the penguin's remaining tail vertebrae are flexibly arranged and the main tail feathers (rectrices) are equivalent in number to the tail-coverts.

It is likely that penguins arose from an oceanic flying bird such as an early shearwater, a member of the order to which penguins are now generally thought to be most closely related. The shearwaters and other tubenosed birds are some of the most accomplished of soaring birds, but they are also perfectly at home in the open ocean—like the penguins only coming to land to breed—and some of them obtain their food by 'flying' underwater. The family of Diving petrels could well represent a stage through which the developing penguin stock passed on their way to true penguin-hood. The present Diving petrels are rather small, up to 10 in (25 cm) long, but they are gregarious oceanic birds which feed on fish, Crustacea, etc., which they catch by 'flying' underwater. They are very much at home in the water, and when they moult their flight feathers, which, as in a number of other groups of aquatic birds, are all moulted at the same time, they are flightless. But this does not prevent them from using the wings as efficient paddles for underwater swimming, and at this stage they are, in effect, pseudo-penguins. They even breed colonially in burrows and crevices on subantarctic islands, and feed the young at night, as in certain penguins.

This does not mean that Diving petrels are the ancestors of penguins; it merely indicates the possibility of deriving a penguin from a tubenosed-type ancestor, Support for this idea is lent by certain tubenosed characteristics, particularly in the skull, of the early Eocene penguin fossil and by considerable similarities between the breeding displays of penguins and albatrosses. On the other hand, a close relationship between penguins and tubenoses is not indicated by recent studies on their egg-white proteins.

Penguins can propel themselves through the water at a steady 10 knots, and can reach twice that speed in bursts. Their normal method of travel, when they are not pursuing prey or being pursued, is by 'porpoising', that is by leaping from the water at intervals to

Penguins are essentially birds of the southern hemisphere and live mainly in the southern latitudes, but one species reaches as far north as the Galapagos Islands on the equator.

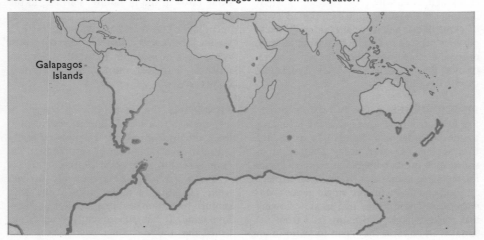

Galapagos Islands

King penguins on Grace Glacier, South Georgia.

King penguin chicks on South Georgia in their crèche.

breathe and re-entering in a smooth curve. The plumage of penguins is very dense and compact. In most birds the feathers grow in tracts, known as pterylae, with featherless areas, or apteria, in between (see feathers). For a number of reasons this is the most efficient arrangement for an aerial bird. But in penguins it would be a disadvantage as it would be difficult to keep such a plumage waterproof. Penguins, therefore, do not have apteria but have a continuous covering of densely-packed feathers. In the Emperor penguin, for example, there are 38 rows of scale-like feathers from the anterior to the posterior borders of the wing. This would give about 3,800 feathers on the dorsal surface of the forearm alone. The number of feathers on the whole bird is going to be far in excess of that found in other groups. Another example of this is given by a count made on the Gentoo penguin. In a 25 mm square of the back of this species there were approximately 300 feathers. Pressures to evolve such an extreme adaptation must have been considerable and waterproofing and insulation without continuous preening has been one of the main problems with which penguins have had to cope.

The density of the penguin's feather covering is enough to ensure a continuous covering over the surface of the body, but it would not serve efficiently for temperature regulation purposes in an animal spending much of its time in water below freezing point. Its heat conservation is achieved partly by a thick layer of blubber—in the breeding Emperor it may amount to one third of the body weight. Also, the feathers have a fluffy accessory

Adélie penguins on Michelson Island.

shaft—the aftershaft—growing from the base. When the aftershafts are held close to the body by the main part of the feathers which cover them they add to the insulating properties of the outer feather covering and the blubber. Furthermore the blood flow through the blubber can be modified according to the general temperature situation. When heat loss is necessary these vessels allow more blood through to the skin and heat is thus lost from the surface. At other times the blood flow through the blubber is kept low.

Most penguins live in regions where, for part of the year at least, temperatures are above freezing point. With their efficient insulation penguins then have an overheating problem; and like the problem of heat conservation this is solved in a number of ways. In addition to increasing the blood flow to the skin, the feathers can be raised to a certain extent to allow for radiation. Also the flippers can be held out from the body to increase the effective radiating surfaces, and bare patches on the face, flippers and feet of certain species can be flushed with blood with a consequent increase in loss of heat to the air.

The plumage pattern of penguins is, throughout the group, dark above and light beneath, any colours shown being entirely confined to the head and neck. In 1907 E. A. Wilson, the first biologist to see a breeding colony of Emperor penguins, noted that this colour distribution is correlated with the low floating position of the group. With their heads removed it would be very difficult to distinguish between many species of pen-

guins. Thus, generic as well as specific distinctions have been developed in head characters, shown by strong differences in bill colour and shape, the pattern of markings on head and throat, and the development of bright plumes over the eyes and ear patches.

The basic black and white body pattern is a positive adaptation to the aquatic mode of life. The white undersurface is less easily seen from below than a dark one and the penguin is thus camouflaged from both prey and predators when it is above them. In this, it is similar to many other marine fish-eating birds, such as terns, divers and auks.

An ever-present problem for diving birds is the reduction of buoyancy, and penguins, as with other groups of diving birds, show a decrease in the pneumatization of bones typical of flying birds. Penguins have been able to take this further than most diving birds because of their surrender of the powers of flight. Also, the taking of stones into the crop may be a ballasting device as well as an aid to grinding hard food. A total of 10 lb (4·5 kg) of stones have been taken from the crop of a single Emperor, which must be more than is needed for the grinding of food. There are disadvantages in diving deeply (see diving animals) and penguins must also have structural and physiological devices for dealing with increases in pressure and energy loss at greater depths, but these are as yet little understood.

The distribution of penguins is by no means limited to the Antarctic. In fact, only two of the 17 species actually cross the Antarctic Circle. Five more nest in regions with a varying ice cover; six species belong to the south-temperate zone; and four species are tropical or subtropical. The distribution of some of the species is circumpolar, so that around the Cape Horn-Antarctic region can be found seven species; in the South Indian Ocean four species; and around the New Zealand region eight species. This distribution has been achieved by dispersal from the Antarctic region of origin by means of ocean currents, the birds either swimming or being carried by ice floes. Thus they are now found not only in the Antarctic and subantarctic but also around the south coasts of Australia, Africa, and South America, and north along the west coast of South America as far as the Galapagos on the equator.

The size of penguins seems to have become reduced the farther they have spread from their original centre of dispersal. Thus the largest species is the Emperor of Antarctica and the smallest the Galapagos penguin *Spheniscus mendiculus* and the Little blue penguin of Australia. The Peruvian penguin *Spheniscus humboldti*, which extends northwards along the coast of Peru seems to be an exception for it is larger than the Little blue penguin but extends farther north. However, it is the exception which proves the rule, for

the major factor influencing penguin size has probably been heat loss—the larger the animal the smaller its surface area relative to bulk and the smaller its heat loss. The Peruvian penguin seems to have pushed northwards up the west coast of South America together with the cold Humboldt Current. This current even influences the Galapagos and must have been the means of transport of the Galapagos penguin. This species, with a very small population of possibly under 2,000 individuals, would probably not be able to survive on the Galapagos if it were not for this current.

The fact that penguins are so unafraid of man and their nests are so accessible had led to the wanton destruction of colonies. Such is the case with the King penguin *Aptenodytes patagonica* which was wiped out in many places for the sake of the oil obtained from its blubber. On Macquarie Island, south of New Zealand, in 1834 individual colonies covered 35 acres (14 ha), and up to 60,000 individuals could be seen entering or leaving the sea at any hour of the day or night. Less than a century later the whole island contained no more than 7,000 individuals. This is only one of many similar examples covering populations of several species, but protection has generally been an effective remedy and species are on the increase again.

Penguins nest on the ground, usually on the surface but some, such as the Little blue penguin, nest in burrows or crevices. An exception is the Emperor which breeds on floating sea ice and is, therefore, the only bird never to touch land. The nest is usually made of pebbles, grass, sticks or bones, depending on what is available. The Emperor and King penguin make no nest but carry their single eggs on their feet, covered with a flap of skin. Most species nest in colonies or 'rookeries', sometimes with hundreds of thousands of nests packed together, each sitting bird being just out of pecking range of its neighbours. The clutch consists of two, sometimes three, eggs, except in the King and Emperor penguins which lay a single egg.

Penguins are long-lived and they are usually faithful to mate and nest site throughout life. The more southerly species undergo a long fast during the incubation period. The Adélie penguin *Pygoscelis adeliae,* for example, fasts for $2\frac{1}{2}$–$3\frac{1}{2}$ weeks while establishing its territory and nest, and the male then continues to fast for another 2–$2\frac{1}{2}$ weeks while incubating, until relieved by the female who has been to sea to feed. In the Emperor penguin, the male incubates, and fasts, for 64 days. Both parents collect food for the chicks and even when half-grown chicks have collected in 'crèches' the parents still pick out

The Emperor penguin, the largest of living penguins, 3 ft (1 m) or more high, with chick.

The Gentoo penguin lives on the South Shetlands and other antarctic islands.

and feed only their own chicks. Their food consists of crustaceans, such as krill, fish and squid.

Most rookeries are near the sea but rookeries of the Emperor penguin and Adélie penguin may be many miles from the open sea when the birds take up territory, for unbroken sea ice extends a considerable distance from the land. As the ice breaks away later in the season it would be unsafe for the birds to nest on it. Thus, Adélies may travel 30–40 miles (50–65 km) or more over the ice to reach their nests, and the Emperor perhaps twice as much. The tracks of an Emperor have been found 186 miles (300 km) from open water, and those of a Chinstrap penguin *Pygoscelis antarctica* 250 miles (400 km) inland. It is possible that these birds wandered off course during overcast weather, for it is known that penguins can navigate using celestial clues, as other birds can.

Although penguins can navigate successfully over land as well as through the sea, there is a certain rigidity in their behaviour which can lead to wasted effort. Adélies displaced laterally from their colonies—even for some hundreds of miles—return by marching to the sea on a fixed bearing and then swimming around the coast to their normal landfall. This doubtless is an efficient system for a penguin which only has to find a traditional nest site. But Adélies will walk along an 'inherited' route rather than swim more quickly round another way. And this fixity of behaviour is also shown by the regular occurrence of Adélies passing unfilled colony sites on their way to set up territories at more distant sites .where they had been reared. The penguins are undoubtedly a successful group, but it would seem that a little more adaptability would be a considerable value to them.

The breeding habits of the Adélie penguin have been studied in the greatest detail and can be considered as typical of penguins as a whole. The penguins arrive at the rookery in spring, sometimes travelling over the frozen sea from their winter feeding grounds farther north. They immediately occupy their nest sites and commence courtship. Nest-building starts as pebbles are exposed by the melting of the snow. Both sexes assist in building the nest, collecting the pebbles or small stones from near the rookery or stealing them from neighbouring nests. After laying two eggs the female goes back to the sea to feed, leaving the male to incubate. By the time he is relieved he will have lost about 40% of his body weight, but he returns to the nest just before the eggs hatch. At first the chicks are brooded but they later gather in crèches of 100 or so.

The problem facing the two large species, the King and Emperor penguins is to raise a very large chick within the short space of the Antarctic summer. The Emperor penguin has overcome this problem by laying during the winter so that the egg hatches in early spring. The male incubates the egg for 64 days and feeds the young chick on a secretion from its crop. The King penguin has a different solution. Eggs are laid in the summer and the chicks lay down a large supply of fat then stay in the nest throughout the winter, when they lose about half their weight. The following spring brings plentiful food and their development is completed. It is then too late for their parents to lay again that season, so King penguins lay only in alternate years.

Another species which differs from the more 'typical' penguins in a number of ways is the Yellow-eyed penguin *Megadyptes antipodes* which breeds only in New Zealand and neighbouring islands. Firstly, it is sedentary and may be found in the breeding area at any time of the year; secondly, it does not breed in large colonies and the nests are somewhat isolated from each other; and thirdly, it breeds in forest areas. Detailed studies of this species showed that chick mortality was principally in the first week after hatching. A percentage of chicks were crushed by the parents but other factors such as flooding and predation also took their toll. Further, of 1,073 eggs laid only 15% were known to result in breeding adults.

One of the problems which penguins have to face is the moult, which in these birds is unusual in that sizeable patches of feathers come away in one piece, rather as in a reptile sloughing its skin. During this period, which may last for a month or more, the birds are very lethargic. As they are no longer waterproof they cannot feed, and they therefore may lose 40% of their body weight.

The lengthiness of many of the penguins' activities—including incubation, rearing of young, and moulting—is reflected in their longevity. The Yellow-eyed penguin will live 20 years or more, and the Emperor 10 years longer. Clearly, in creatures whose breeding season may last 18 months as in the King penguin, and only one chick is reared by the most successful pairs, a long life is necessary to maintain the population by successive breeding. However, the fact remains that penguins, when not destroyed by man, are successful animals, having evolved adaptations to extremes of environmental conditions which have been too much for most other groups. FAMILY: Spheniscidae, ORDER: Sphenisciformes, CLASS: Aves.   P.M.D.

PENGUINS STAY SOUTH. Although penguins are popularly regarded as birds of ice and snow, only two, the Adélie and Emperor penguins, are limited to the Antarctic and only three or four more enter antarctic regions. Nevertheless, the penguin family is restricted to the southern hemisphere and penguins have never colonized the North Pacific or Atlantic Oceans, having been unable to cross the warm tropical seas. There seems to be little against their living in the northern hemisphere apart from competition with the ecologically similar auks and predation by Polar bears and Arctic foxes. In 1936 and 1938 King, Jackass and Macaroni penguins were liberated in northern Norway but failed to survive. Many fell foul of the local people, a King penguin was caught on a fishing line in 1944 and a bird of unknown species was last seen in 1954. On the other hand penguins have become acclimatized in zoos and in some places (Edinburgh), at the same latitude as Norway, they breed successfully.

PEPPERSHRIKES, sparrow-sized insect-eating birds of the New World. There are two species in the genus *Cyclarhis* of the family Vireonidae, which has 43 species. Before being merged with this family the peppershrikes were considered to be a family of their own, the Cyclarhidae. The Rufous-browed peppershrike *Cyclarhis gujanensis* has a wide distribution ranging from Mexico south through Central and South America as far as Argentina, while the Black-billed peppershrike *Cyclarhis nigrirostris* is confined to Colombia and Ecuador.

These small birds have a strong hooked bill and the sexes are alike. The Rufous-browed peppershrike is the best known of the two. Its back, wings and tail are bright green, its crown and the sides of the face are grey with a broad rufous brown streak across the sides of the face to the nape. The throat is yellow, the breast grey and the lower underparts white. The eyes are red, the upper mandible pinkish and the lower one blue-grey. The legs are a pinkish grey.

Peppershrikes live in pairs in light forests, scrub and in cultivated land. They live in trees and although their song, consisting of a short but quite melodious phrase, is uttered for long periods, especially in the early morning, the singing bird is difficult to locate among the green foliage.

The nest is an open cup hanging in the fork of two horizontal twigs. Two or three eggs are laid which are pale creamish with brown spots and blotches. Both sexes incubate and it is reported that the male sings loudly all the time it sits on the eggs. The incubation period is still unknown. The nestlings are naked when hatched and both parents feed them on insects while they remain in the nest. The nestling period is also unknown. FAMILY: Vireonidae, ORDER: Passeriformes, CLASS: Aves. F.H.

PERCEPTION, involves three processes: firstly, the detection of changes in the environment by a sense organ, secondly the transmission of messages in the form of nerve impulses from the sense organ to the central nervous system and finally the co-ordination and analysis of the information from the sense organ by the nervous system.

The distinction between these processes can be illustrated using the example of human vision. When we perceive an object close at hand each eye records a slightly different picture of the object; these images are both transmitted to the brain but we are aware of only a single three-dimensional image of the object. Thus the image of which we are aware is essentially a 'brain image' derived, but differing from, the images recorded by the eyes and co-ordinated by the brain. Our knowledge of the structure and behaviour of other animals leads us to believe that many of them possess a system of perception analogous to our own.

Perception depends upon the senses and some of them are common to a wide diversity of animals. Vision, olfaction (the senses of smell and taste), hearing and responses to electric shock, gravity and heat occur together in many animals, but the elaboration of these senses differs greatly from one species to another. In addition, some animals can detect environmental stimuli which are not perceptible to human beings. The honeybee can detect ultra-violet light which is invisible to man. Certain fish, for example *Gymnarchus niloticus,* can perceive objects in their vicinity by producing an electric field. Bats and porpoises hunt their prey and detect obstacles by echolocation whilst the fish *Aphelocheirus lineatus* has pressure receptors on its head which enable it to detect the ripples on the surface of the water made by its prey. Pit vipers such as the rattlesnake *Crotalus horridus* possess a pair of temperature sensitive organs on the snout which enable them to detect warm-blooded prey at a distance.

Even individuals of the same species may differ in their powers of perception, for example, 7½% of the British male population is colourblind. However, there is some evidence that the mechanism of perception may be fundamentally similar in widely differing animals. The sense of taste in man and Water beetles *Dytiscus marginalis* enables both to recognize four main categories of substances which we term sweet, sour, bitter and salt.

Although human beings learn to perceive the world through experience in the early months of their lives, many animals such as the cow or sheep are born with a perceptual system which operates without experience.

An important psychological aspect of perception is that of alertness for what an animal perceives depends upon the concentration and selectivity with which its observations are made. Motivation also influences perception for a hungry animal shows particular alertness for stimuli which may be associated with food.

Animals may have similar sensory systems but frequently their powers of perception differ radically. A turkey (*Meleagris gallopavo*), for example, which has good colour vision and hearing but a poor sense of smell resembles a human being in these respects. Yet a male turkey will court the decapitated head of a female showing that its interpretation of the sensory information which it receives differs vastly from our own.

The German biologist, Jacob von Uexküll, expressed this idea clearly in 1909 when he stated that each species of animal lives in its own unique *Umwelt* or 'perceptual world'.

T.B.P.

PERCHES, a family of spiny-finned fishes that have been considered central to the great radiation of perch-like fishes that comprise the order Perciformes. This order contains nearly 150 different families, ranging from the diminutive blennies to the large tunas, from the ragfishes to the surgeonfishes, and the icefishes to the archerfishes. The many thousand species of perch-like fish vary widely in their general form but all share with the common perch the development of spiny rays in the fins, a protrusile upper jaw and, at least originally, sharp-edged scales.

The family Percidae contains the darters, the Pike perches and the true perches (the name perch is often used, however, for fishes of other perch-like families, e.g. the Nile perch, family Centropomidae).

The European perch *Perca fluviatilis* is widespread in England and Ireland but rare in Scotland and Norway. It is common throughout the rest of Europe as far as the Soviet Union. It is a deep-bodied fish with two barely separated dorsal fins, the first spiny with a prominent black spot near the rear. The back

The European perch has given its name to a large order of spiny-finned fishes.

The distribution of the perch-like fishes of the family Percidae.

is olive brown, the flanks yellowish (often brassy) with about six, dark vertical bars, and the belly white. The tail and the lower fins are often tinged with red. The perch prefers slow and sluggish waters but can live almost everywhere. When in fairly fast streams, these fishes form small shoals in the eddies. Perches are predators, feeding throughout life on small fishes and invertebrates. Beloved of anglers, because of the ease with which they take the bait, perches have been caught up to 6 lb (2·7 kg) in England and up to 10 lb (4·5 kg) on the continent of Europe. They spawn amongst weeds in shallow waters in late spring. The males first congregate at the spawning grounds and when the females arrive several males will accompany one female as she lays long strings of eggs entwined in weeds. Perches make excellent eating.

The American perch *P. flavescens* is closely allied to the European species and is found over large parts of central and southern United States, in some regions reaching as far north as 60°N. The body is greenish-yellow and it is slightly smaller than its European counterpart, attaining a weight of 4 lb (1·8 kg).

Related to the perch is the ruffe or pope of Europe, which has been described elsewhere.

In the Danube basin there are other related but rather rare species. They include the schratzer *Gymnocephalus schraetser*, a species allied to the ruffe, the streber *Aspro streber* and its relative the zingel.

The multitude of perch-like fishes show that the basic body plan has been highly adaptable and has enabled fishes of this type to conquer an enormous range of habitats. FAMILY: Percidae, ORDER: Perciformes, CLASS: Pisces.

PÈRE DAVID'S DEER *Elaphurus davidianus,* the most remarkable of all the Chinese *deer which has never been recorded as being seen in the wild state.

PEREGRINE FALCON *Falco peregrinus,* the most widespread of the large falcons, being found on all continents but Antarctica and on many oceanic islands. About 16 races are recognized. The largest, Peale's

falcon *F. p. pealei* comes from coastal British Columbia, the smallest and palest, the desert shaheens *F. p. pelegrinoides* and *F. p. babylonicus* from North African and Asian deserts. Northern peregrines migrate south in winter, but those living in warmer climates are sedentary.

Peregrine falcons are the most valued of all falcons used in falconry. Relatively easily obtained and trained, they are docile but large enough to kill gamebirds in spectacular style. Their speed in the diving attack (stoop), variously estimated at 100–275 mph (160–440 kph), coupled with their readiness to 'wait on' above the falconer until he flushes the quarry, makes them superior to larger falcons such as gyrs or sakers. Peregrine eyries were jealously guarded in the Middle Ages, and records show that some are still in use.

Peregrines usually inhabit mountains or sea cliffs, but some live in tundras or in boggy areas among conifer forests. Cliffs are usually necessary for nesting, and peregrines sometimes make use of man-made 'cliffs' in cities. The most famous of these, the Sun-Life falcon of Montreal, bred on the building of that name for 16 years.

Peregrines normally feed on birds up to the size of wild duck, caught in the air and, either struck dead with the foot, or seized and carried to the ground. Their favourite prey is pigeons but in smaller races smaller birds are more usually taken. They eat an

occasional small mammal and in Alaska one has been known to catch a fish.

Peregrines probably pair for life and return annually to the same cliff to breed. They lay between three and six eggs in a scrape on a ledge, or sometimes in an old nest of a crow or other raptor. Some north European peregrines breed on the ground, and nesting in trees is known. The smaller male (tiercel) feeds the female (falcon) during courtship and incubation and provides for the whole brood until they are half-grown. Thereafter the female assists him in catching prey.

Usually the female incubates the rich red brown eggs alone for about 28 days, but males may play some part. The new-hatched young are covered in white woolly down. They are feathered and can fly at six to seven weeks, but are still fed by the parents near the nest site for some time after their first flight.

Since 1950 peregrine populations have declined drastically all over Europe and North America. Even north European migratory races that only winter in developed areas have declined. In Britain the population is about halved, the worst losses being observed near agricultural land. The drop is attributed to the effects of certain agricultural chemicals, DDT, dieldrin etc, acquired through the peregrine's food, either birds feeding in agricultural areas or seabirds that ingest these substances with fish. The effect

Hen peregrine on its eyrie with a chick. The peregrine is the most famous bird in falconry.

is to reduce the thickness of the eggshell so that the peregrines cannot breed successfully. The decline has been aggravated by increased human persecution. There seems little doubt that the peregrine is a sensitive indicator of contamination of the whole environment. FAMILY: Falconidae. ORDER: Falconiformes. CLASS: Aves.   L.B.

PERIPATUS, the most well known genus belonging to the *Onychophora, its species occurring in Australasia. There is so little superficial difference between onychophoran species that the word 'Peripatus' is used colloquially to mean any onychophoran, because there is no other common name for them. As these animals have become better known, however, new genera have been recognised, and the genus *Peripatus* consequently has become more restricted.

PERISSODACTYLA or Mesaxonia, an order of mammals comprising the odd-toed ungulates with two suborders; the Hippomorpha, the horse and its relatives; and the Tapiromorpha, the tapirs and rhinoceroses. They have in common that the middle toe in each foot has become the main support for the body. During evolution the other toes have become more or less reduced. However, their number on one foot is not necessarily an odd one: tapirs have four toes on their front feet, of which the second, the original middle one, is the strongest. The Perissodactyla are non-ruminating specialized plant-eaters with simple stomachs but with large caeca. At the present time the order is only represented by a few species: there are six species of horses, five of rhinoceroses and four of tapirs. In the Tertiary era, however, this group was abundant with many species and no fewer than twelve families are recognized the common ancestry of which is dated to the Palaeocene. The fossil history of the Perissodactyla is comparatively well known, and that of the Hippomorpha is particularly suited to illustrate the process of evolution.

The earliest mammal that may be definitely regarded as a forerunner of the horses appeared at the beginning of the Eocene, 60 million years ago, in North America and Eurasia which were then connected by a land bridge from Siberia and Alaska, the Bering bridge. It is commonly referred to as eohippus, but because of priority rights, its correct scientific name is *Hyracotherium*. Several species of this genus are recognized and they measured from 10–20 in (25–50 cm) at the shoulder. Unlike modern horses they had arched backs and their hindlegs were considerably longer than their front legs. This made them particularly suited for living in dense, shrubby vegetation. Compared with the five-toed Condylarthra, the basic, primitive stock of Palaeocene mam-

mals, from which the Perissodactyla and probably the other ungulates have developed, the number of toes in eohippus was already reduced to four in front and three behind, each ending in a small, separate hoof. On the forefoot, the original first (inner) toe had become lost, the fifth was small but still functional, the second and fourth were larger, but smaller than the third, which was the longest and strongest. On the hindfoot, the first and fifth toes were absent, the others were as in front. The animal was not standing on the hoofs, i.e. the tips of its toes, but on a pad of connective tissue which formed a cushion on the underside of the foot, similar to that of dogs. The skull of eohippus was still quite unlike that of a horse: the eyes were much farther forward, in the middle of the skull, like those of the Condylarthra, and the brain was still at the same low level as in that group. Eohippus had the original mammalian dentition of 44 teeth, 11 in each half of each jaw: three incisors, one canine, four premolars and three molars. This pattern has only slightly changed during evolution (see Equidae). The diastema, the gap between the incisors and the cheekteeth, was already present. The structure of the cheekteeth indicates that eohippus was a browser: their crowns were short and covered with an unfolded layer of enamel and they would not have stood up to the grinding of grasses for the lifetime of the animal.

In the later Eocene Eurasia and North America became separated. The European stock of horse ancestors developed into forms which later perished, whereas the further evolution of the Equidae took place in North America. Still in the Eocene, two forms, at first *Orohippus* and later *Epihippus*, arose from eohippus, from which they differ mainly in the increasing molarization of their premolars, i.e. the process of premolars taking the shape of molars.

In the Oligocene a horse-like animal, the *Mesohippus*, appeared, which had three toes only on each foot, the original second, third and fourth. Another remarkable step in evolution was the development of a more horse-like head and brain, indicating a higher level of equine intelligence. The molarization of the premolars was completed and, judging from the structure of the teeth, the animal was still a browser. Its legs were long and slender: an adaptation for fast running.

In the middle Oligocene *Mesohippus* developed into the larger *Miohippus*, the ancestor of several horse-like animals of which all but one perished later. One of these, the *Anchitherium*, appeared in the early Miocene and spread from North America via the Bering bridge to Asia and Europe, but did not survive the Miocene. In North America, *Hypohippus* arose from

Anchitherium and this also migrated to the Old World. Another descendant of *Anchitherium*, the *Megahippus*, was restricted to North America. All three died out in the early Pliocene.

Another line of Miocene horses, *Parahippus* and *Merychippus*, deriving from *Miohippus* as well, had long tooth crowns with enamel folds which formed, when the tooth was worn, rough surfaces with hard ridges. These teeth were suitable for grinding even hard, mineral containing grasses: these forms are the first grazers in the ancestry of the horses. In *Merychippus* the pad of the foot became reduced and a spring mechanism developed which allowed these forms, and all the later ones, to run much faster.

By the end of the Miocene there were six different lines of three-toed horses developing from *Merychippus*, of which five are considered to be side developments as they did not survive to the present day. They are mainly distinguished by the shape of their teeth. One of them was the *Hipparion*, the Pliocene horse which evolved in North America and spread to Asia and Europe as well as to Africa, where it survived until the Pleistocene, the period during which the present horses of Africa, the zebras and the ass, came to that continent.

In the main line, during the late Miocene, *Merychippus* developed into *Pliohippus*, the first one-toed horse, which differed in details only from our present day horse and its relatives. One more side branch should be mentioned, that is *Pliohippus*. It was the first horse to reach South America, which, in the late Pliocene, was connected to North America by a land bridge. It developed there into the *Hippidion* and other genera which survived until the Pleistocene.

The main line leads to the genus *Equus* which comprises all living Equidae. *Equus* most probably arose in North America as did all its ancestors and spread from there, via the Bering bridge, to Asia, Europe and Africa, and via the Panama bridge to South America. The horses disappeared from the American continent after the Ice Age, i.e. only a few thousand years ago, and for reasons unknown.

After the separation of North America and Eurasia in the Eocene, the European stock of eohippus developed into the three-toed palaeotheres, some of which became as large as a rhinoceros. They survived only until the Oligocene.

Closely related to the horse ancestors and also included in the Hippomorpha are the Titanotheriidae and the Chalicotheriidae. The titanotheres lived, during the Eocene and Oligocene, in North America, Asia and Eastern Europe. Some were huge, measuring 8 ft (2·4 m) at the shoulders, and having a pair of large, horn-like processes on their noses. The chalicotheres of the Eocene to

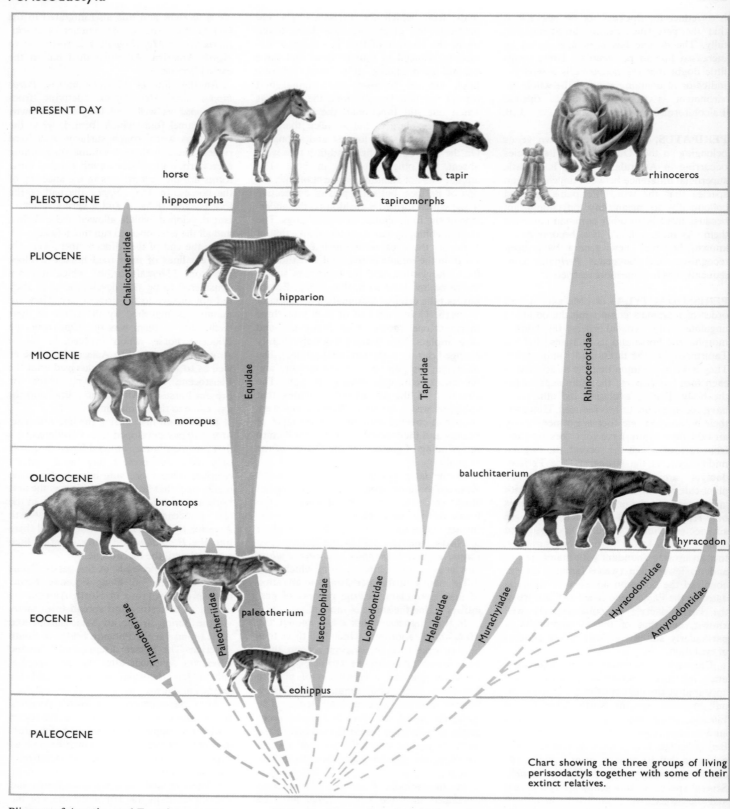

PRESENT DAY

horse

tapir

rhinoceros

PLEISTOCENE — hippomorphs — tapiromorphs

PLIOCENE

Chalicotheriidae

hipparion

MIOCENE

Equidae

Tapiridae

Rhinocerotidae

moropus

OLIGOCENE

baluchitaerium

brontops

hyracodon

Titanotheriidae

Paleotheriidae

Isectolophidae

Lophodontidae

Helaletidae

Murachyiadae

Hyracodontidae

Amynodontidae

EOCENE

paleotherium

eohippus

PALEOCENE

Chart showing the three groups of living perissodactyls together with some of their extinct relatives.

Pliocene of America and Eurasia were more horse-like in general appearance, but their front legs were longer than their hindlegs. Some of them, in contrast to all other Perissodactyla, had claws which were probably used for digging up roots and tubers for food.

Of the Tapiromorpha, which all have the same basic tooth structure, two of the eight lines of evolution were to be successful and have representatives in the present day, the Tapiridae and the Rhinocerotidae. The tapirs have not changed very much from the early Eocene: they still have the same number of toes as had the eohippus (four in front and three behind) and their teeth are good for browsing only, as in the early horses. True tapirs (genus *Protapirus*) appeared in the Oligocene in Eurasia and North America, where they persisted until the beginning of the Pleistocene, the Ice Age, when they

Flat periwinkles, small sea snails common on European shores. They derive their name from the obliquely flattened apex of the spiral shell.

became restricted to South America and to the Malayan region. Other tapir-like forms of the Eocene were the Lophiodontidae, some of which were the size and proportions of a rhinoceros, but others were more horse-like.

The Eocene ancestors of the rhinoceroses were similar in build to those of horses and tapirs, and some had the same numbers of toes as these. They are the 'running rhinoceroses' of Eurasia and North America, the Hyrachyidae and the Hyracodontidae, the latter surviving until the Oligocene. An early side branch is the Amynodontidae, hippopotamus-like forms that lived in America in the Eocene and Oligocene, and in Eurasia until the Miocene. The main line of rhinoceroses probably arose from the early 'running rhinoceroses'. They appeared in the late Eocene and early Oligocene and were large, like the present day forms. Some of them already had the three-toed foot of the modern rhinoceroses, but they had no horns. This remarkable feature was first developed by a member of another side branch, the *Diceatherium* of the American Miocene, which had, in the male sex, two horns placed side by side on the tip of the nose.

In the Oligocene and early Miocene giant rhinoceroses evolved in Asia. One of them, the *Baluchitherium* had a head of 4 ft (1·2 m) in length and a shoulder height of 18 ft

(5·7 m). It had a long neck and was thus able to browse from high trees. *Baluchitherium* is the largest land mammal known.

During the Pliocene the rhinoceroses died out in America, but they were common in Eurasia, and from this stock arose the modern forms, the direct ancestry of which is, however, not quite clear. They are, with the exception of the Indian and the Javan rhinoceros, less closely related than are the equids and the tapirs.   H.K.

PERIWINKLES, small sea snails living mainly on the shore and possessing a horny operculum (characteristic of prosobranch snails) and breathing by means of a single gill which has leaflets along one side only (the 'pectinibranch' condition—which occurs in all mesogastropods). They feed on seaweeds, rasping these with their horny tongue, or radula.

Common species include the crevice-dwelling Small periwinkle *Littorina neritoides* which occurs at high tide mark on exposed rocky coasts in northwest Europe (but not in the southeast of England) and in the Mediterranean. The shell rarely exceeds $\frac{1}{5}$ in (5 mm) in length and is dark black-brown in colour. Apart from living in crevices, large numbers are often aggregated amongst lichens and in dead barnacle shells on the upper shore. A larger species is the Rough

periwinkle *Littorina saxatilis* which occurs from the middle to the upper shore throughout much of northwest Europe and on both east and west coasts of North America. Its shell commonly reaches $\frac{1}{2}$ in (12·5 mm) in length and is marked with fine spiral lines. The sutures between each whorl of the shell are deep. This winkle is easily confused with small specimens of the Common or Edible periwinkle *Littorina littorea* but may be distinguished by the tentacles having longitudinal dark stripes in the Rough periwinkle and transverse concentric stripes in the Edible periwinkle. The latter is a widespread intertidal and estuarine winkle which is commonest on the middle shore and below but may extend much higher than this in some areas. It occurs throughout northwest Europe and on the east coast of North America. The final European species is the Flat periwinkle *Littorina littoralis* (or *obtusata*)—so called because the apex of the spire is obliquely flattened. It occurs predominantly on the Bladder wrack *Fucus vesiculosus* but can also occur on other seaweeds such as the Knotted wrack *Ascophyllum nodosum*. The Flat periwinkle is an active animal found browsing when uncovered by the tide; the shell may be brown-orange, black or yellowish and is commonly $\frac{1}{2}$ in (12·5 mm) long. Other littorinids include *Littorina punctata* which occurs in West Africa and *Littorina knys-*

naënsis which occurs on rocky shores in South Africa. Closely related to these periwinkles are the Chink shells, the commonest of which is the Banded chink shell *Lacuna vincta* which occurs on *Fucus* covered rocks near the low water mark in northwest Europe.

There are differences in the breeding biology of the periwinkles. The lower shore Common periwinkle liberates egg capsules freely into the plankton and pelagic larvae hatch after about six days. The upper shore Rough periwinkle broods the young in an enlarged duct of the genital system, transverse folds in the wall of which allow embryos of different ages to be separated. The youngest embryos are near the upper end of the pouch which may contain as many as 900 young. Finally, the high level Small periwinkle sheds its eggs freely into the sea—a curious feature in an animal which is only immersed at the highest of spring tides.

The behaviour of several species of periwinkles has been investigated and the snails have been found to be capable of responding to light and to gravity. The Flat periwinkle always crawls away from light and upwards; it is capable of orientating to the presence of Bladder wrack but at least dim light is necessary for this response. In the Common periwinkle, specimens living on vertical surfaces tend to make feeding excursions first by crawling downwards when uncovered by the tide and then crawling upwards along a different path. When living on a flat surface it crawls first towards the sun and then away from it, leaving a U-shaped trail. In each case this reversal of response to gravity or light tends to prevent dispersal of the animals from their optimal zone on the shore. Some winkles are apparently able to respond to the topography of their habitat. The periwinkle *Littorina punctata* of Ghana responds to the topography of the shoreline and certain other winkles such as the Rough periwinkle and the Small periwinkle may achieve their normal zonation under experimental conditions by the use of form-vision. The eye of the Common periwinkle would be expected to allow form-vision although the acuity is probably poor. All four of the European periwinkles are also capable of responding to plane polarized light; winkles that normally crawl away from light orientate parallel to the plane of vibration of the polarized light whilst winkles that normally crawl towards light orientate at right angles to the plane of vibration. Both of these responses to the plane of polarization of light are probably associated with the structure of the periwinkle eye which allows more light to enter by refraction when the head is at right angles to the plane of vibration of the light. Conversely, when the head of the periwinkle is parallel to the plane of polarization of the light, the minimum amount of light is refracted into the eyes.

Much work has been carried out on the resistance of periwinkles to environmental stresses such as heat and cold, anaerobic conditions, low salinities, and desiccation. In general, the resistance of the snails to such conditions follows their distribution on the shore, high level species such as the Small periwinkle being more resistant than the lower shore species such as the Common periwinkle. FAMILY: Littorinidae, ORDER: Mesogastropoda, CLASS: Gastropoda, PHYLUM: Mollusca.   R.C.N.

PESTS AND PESTICIDES. The vast majority of animal pests are insects. The grubs or caterpillars of beetles, flies and moths especially do an immense amount of direct damage to crops and forestry. Some insects are important mainly as carriers of plant disease, for example the aphid vector of virus yellows in sugar-beet and the beetle that transmits Dutch elm disease. Important among the pests of livestock are Warble (or Bot) flies *Hypoderma* spp and Screw worms *Cochliomyia hominivorax* of cattle and sheep, as well as a variety of lice which attack pigs and poultry. In public health, flies and mosquitoes are the chief culprits in the spread of the diseases malaria, yellow fever, filariasis, sleeping sickness and dysentry while fleas and lice are responsible for the spread of two other scourges: plague and typhus.

Pest species occur in many other groups of animals, from the humble earthworm which can be a nuisance in bowling greens and golf courses, to the introduced deer in New Zealand which do much damage to woodland. Several species of birds are pests notably the woodpigeon *Columba palumbus* in Britain, the Red-winged blackbird *Agelaius phoeniceus* in America and the quelea in Africa. Even among fishes there are pests, like the Sea lamprey *Petromyzon marinus,* which has done serious damage to the lake trout fishing industry in Lake Michigan.

The term pesticide covers a wide range of chemicals used to control plant or animal pests; it includes herbicides (weed-killers), fungicides, insecticides, molluscicides, rodenticides and others. Some pesticides, like pyrethrum, nicotine and rotenone (derris), are obtained from plants and have been known for over 100 years as potent insecticides. A number are based on the metals copper, arsenic, lead, mercury, zinc and tin: copper arsenite (Paris green) was successfully in 1867 against the Colorado beetle *Leptinotarsa decemlineata* on potatoes in the United States and mercury compounds, now in general use to control fungal diseases on grain, were introduced in the 1930's. The great majority of pesticides, however, are synthetic organic compounds developed since 1945. Today there are about 300 pesticides in general use marketed in more than 10,000 different formulations. Approximately 35% of the world's harvest is lost each year; 14% destroyed by insect pests, 12% by diseases and 9% due to losses from weed competition. This represents $70,000–90,000 million per year. The present annual world production of insecticides, fungicides and herbicides is worth about $1,000 million while the saving due to control measures against insect pests of cotton in the United States is alone worth about $1,700 million.

Two of the most important groups of insecticides are the organophosphorus compounds such as TEPP, malathion, parathion, schradan, diazinon and dimethoate, and the organochlorine (chlorinated hydrocarbon) compounds, including DDT, aldrin, endrin, BHC, endosulphan and toxaphene. Many of the organophosphorus compounds are systemic, that is they are absorbed into plants and kill insects like aphids which feed on the sap. Some, though highly toxic, are used on vegetable and fruit crops close to harvest because of their short persistence; mevinphos (phosdrin) breaks down so rapidly that it is safe for most animals to enter a treated crop one day after spraying. Other compounds with low mammalian toxicities, like trichlorphon, are used to control insects that attack livestock. The organochlorines have been extremely successful insecticides because of their low cost and broad spectrum of use. The best known of these, DDT, was first synthesized in 1874 but its insecticidal properties were not discovered until 1939. It has since proved extremely successful in public health, agriculture, and forestry against a very large number of pests. One of the main features of the organochlorine insecticides is their high stability which makes them particularly suitable for combating soil pests. Their use, however, appears to have reached its peak, at least in the United States and Britain. while the use of organophosphorus chemicals is still increasing rapidly and there appears to be no limit to the number of insecticidal compounds in this class that can be synthesized.

Before a new pesticide is put on the market it is screened against a wide range of pests and its physical properties such as solubility and persistence are examined. Toxicological data are also obtained from laboratory tests on rats and nowadays often also on hens, fishes and honeybees to assess the dangers to humans, domestic animals and wild life. Feeding trials with low doses are sometimes continued for two years to look for long term effects, and other tests are done to detect carcinogenic or other dangerous properties. The acute toxicity of a compound is measured by the dose which would on average kill half of the animals in a group exposed to the chemical within a given time. This is called the 50% lethal dose or LD_{50}

and is expressed in milligrams of chemical per kilogram of body weight. Examples of LD_{50} figures for insecticides given in single doses to rats are, in descending order of toxicities: TEPP 0·5, parathion and endrin 5, aldrin 50, nicotine 70, DDT 400, derris 1,500 and malathion 1,600 mg/kg. These indicate, for instance, that parathion is ten times as toxic to rats as aldrin and about 80 times as toxic as DDT. For comparison, the rodenticide, fluoroacetamide, (similar to the compound 1080 used against rabbits and deer in Australia) has an acute oral LD_{50} value of 15 mg/kg.

Birds are often more sensitive to pesticides than mammals but wide differences occur among different species and raptors appear to be more sensitive than the domestic hen or the House sparrow *Passer domesticus*. Derris, endrin and toxaphene are particularly toxic to fishes, the first of these being widely used in the tropics as a fish-poison before its use as an insecticide. It is impossible to generalize about the effects of pesticides on invertebrates. Most arthropods are suscep-

tible to insecticides to a greater or lesser extent while there is as yet no satisfactory chemical for controlling nematodes on a field scale. Molluscicides have been specially developed to kill the snails which transmit bilharzia in Africa.

Chemical control of pests has produced some new problems. Resurgence of Spider mite, aphid and caterpillar pests has occurred as a result of the reduction of their natural enemies by the pesticide. This is particularly likely with a persistent compound like DDT which prevents recovery of insect predators. Serious outbreaks of other insects or mites, hitherto unimportant in the crop, have also sometimes followed from the reduced predator control or reduced competition resulting in 'man-made' pests. Many insects, notably flies, have developed resistance to insecticides and this is one reason for the continuing need for new compounds.

There have been numerous instances in which wild animals have suffered extensive casualties as a result of insecticidal applications and many of these are graphically

described in Rachel Carson's book *Silent Spring*. Mass control measures in the United States against forestry and soil pests with DDT, dieldrin or heptachlor, have affected millions of acres. In Britain the incidents have been on a much smaller scale but noteworthy cases have arisen from the use of schradan and DNOC in the early 1950's and from organochlorine seed-dressings in the early 1960's which severely affected the populations of Peregrine falcon *Falco peregrinus* and sparrowhawk *Accipiter nisus*. Industrial accidents are also a hazard. In 1964 endrin was responsible for deaths of many millions of fishes in the lower Mississippi river and in 1969 endosulphan was similarly implicated in the river Rhine fish deaths.

Less obvious but disturbing effects have resulted from the persistence of the organochlorine insecticides. They can be transmitted from one organism to another in food chains and are transported by wind and water sometimes to remote areas. As a result residues are now widely disseminated in the world; traces have even been found in

When a pesticide goes wrong. Dead fish being taken from the lower reaches of the Rhine in 1969, the result of pollution.

samples of fishes from the mid-Pacific and in penguins and seals from the Antarctic. There is also evidence that residues of DDT and dieldrin well below lethal levels can impair breeding success in birds by upsetting their hormone balance and this could be responsible for the very slow recovery of Peregrine falcon and sparrowhawk populations.

Few of the herbicides are very toxic to animals but their indirect effects have undoubtedly been very great. The use of weedkillers on cereal crops has reduced insect populations just as effectively as any insecticide and similarly the alteration of the sagebrush *ecosystem in Wyoming with brushwood killers affects the grouse and deer which depend on it. Pesticides are indeed powerful new tools for controlling nature and they will play an increasing role against pests and disease. Care must, however, be taken to ensure that they are used only to improve the environment and do not degrade it (see also biological control).   N.K.D.

PETRELS, seabirds of the order of tubenosed birds, Procellariiformes, particularly the typical petrels and shearwaters of the family Procellariidae, the Storm petrels of the Hydrobatidae and the Diving petrels of the Pelecanoididae. The term may be used as a general name for the order or may be used in the English name of many of the species. It is derived from the habit of some of the smaller species of fluttering so close to the surface of the water that they appear to be walking on it—as St. Peter is said to have done.

The petrels all have the webbed feet and

White-faced storm petrel *Pelagadroma marina*, of the southern oceans, near its nesting burrow.

hooked bill with nostrils opening through horny tubes characteristic of the order. They have a strong, characteristic musty smell and well-developed olfactory organs which suggest that, unusual for birds, they have a well-developed sense of smell. Their plumage is thick and strongly waterproof and they swim and fly expertly—though the smaller species in particular are not infrequently driven ashore in 'wrecks' during long periods of severe weather.

All petrels are marine, feeding, according

to species, on a variety of marine organisms including plankton, fish, squids, and offal. Normally they go ashore only to breed, in holes, crevices, or other concealed places on islands or remote cliffs and headlands, laying one egg only per year. Over the breeding grounds they commonly perform display flights and produce complex vocalizations both in the air and on the ground—particularly in their burrows. These calls include various screaming, churring, choking and wailing sounds and as many of the species are nocturnal these may assist in individual recognition. The young are fed by both parents regurgitating partially-digested food. The fledging period is very long, from two months in the smallest species to five months in the largest. Most of the medium and larger petrels are members of the Procellariidae, which contains over 50 species. There are six species of fulmars, including the Northern *fulmar *Fulmarus glacialis* which feeds basically on large plankton but has increased enormously in numbers as a result of the supply of offal from fisheries activities. The fulmars are rather large birds with strong bills. They spit oil defensively.

There are 15 species of *shearwaters, the one which has been most studied being the Manx shearwater *Puffinus puffinus*. It is dark above and light beneath, with long narrow wings on which it glides over the surface of the ocean 'shearing the water' as it tilts from side to side. The shearwaters are not so bulky as the fulmars.

There are some 12 species of *prions in the genus *Pachyptila;* small birds of the southern oceans which have fringed bills for filtering the plankton from the sea. There are also some 24 species of Gadfly petrels of the genera *Bulweria* and *Pterodroma;* medium-sized birds of the open ocean which seem to feed nocturnally on squid.

The family Hydrobatidae contains over 20 species of small birds which feed on individual planktonic animals which they take at the surface of the water. Like the shearwaters

they breed colonially. A typical species is Wilson's Storm petrel *Oceanites oceanicus* which breeds all round the Antarctic.

The Diving petrels of the family Pelecanoididae form an unusual group of small to medium-sized birds of the southern hemisphere which show convergent similarities to the auks. They have a compact form and fly with rapidly-whirring wings, the latter also being used as flippers for swimming underwater. There are five species, in the genus *Pelecanoides*. ORDER: Procellariiformes, CLASS: Aves.   P.M.D.

PETRELS AND ST PETER. The name 'petrel' is derived from Peter in allusion to the Storm petrel's common habit of pattering over the surface of the water with outstretched wings, like St Peter walking on water. Another name for Storm petrels was sea-stamper and, like other seabirds, petrels were supposed to be harbingers of bad weather. Other beliefs are that Storm petrels are the reincarnations of drowned sailors or are devil-birds searching for their bodies. These ideas are retained in some of the vernacular names, such as waterwitch, oiseau du diable, âmes damnées and diablotin. In the eastern Mediterranean it is the shearwaters that are thought to be carriers of lost souls.

PHALANGERS (Possums), Australian herbivorous marsupials often called possums or, more rarely, opossums because of their superficial resemblance to the true opossums of North and South America. The group, collectively the family Phalangeridae, includes the cuscuses, Flying phalangers and Pigmy possums as well as the animals treated below. The Phalangeridae is one of four families of living marsupials included in the superfamily Phalangeroidea (the diprotodont *marsupials) which are characterized by having the anterior pair of lower incisor teeth enlarged and pointing forwards. The phal-

Giant petrel *Macronectes giganteus* and chick, of South Georgia. The Giant petrel, 3 ft (1 m) long, has two colour phases.

Sugar glider *Petaurus breviceps*, one of the Flying phalangers, feeds on insects and sweet things.

angeroids also differ from all other marsupials in possessing an extra bundle of connecting fibres, the fasciculus aberrans, in the brain.

The most common phalanger is the Australian brush possum *Trichosurus vulpecula* which is about the size of a domestic cat. It is arboreal, grey or black, with a fox-like face and a long prehensile tail, bushy above and hairless beneath. It occurs in coastal eastern, southern and southwestern Australia, and Tasmania and on many offshore islands but not in New Guinea. Its range extends into inland and central Australia along river systems where river Red gums *Eucalyptus camaldulensis,* and other trees, provide food and suitable home sites in hollow limbs. It is a grass and herb eater as well as a leaf eater and sometimes eats garden plants including rose petals and leaves.

The Brush possum was introduced into New Zealand in 1837, and on numerous later occasions, where it rapidly reached pest proportions and now maintains its hold in spite of an active eradication campaign. In Australia it had been extensively exploited for the fur trade and over one million pelts were sold from the island of Tasmania (26,000 square miles) in the years 1923 to 1955. In spite of past exploitation, and recent destruction because of its nuisance value in suburban and agricultural areas, the Brush possum remains one of Australia's most common marsupials. It occurs in all large towns and cities where suitable trees exist. The rate of reproduction is slow there being but one young per litter born after a gestation period of 17 days and reared in the pouch for about four months. Sometimes two successive young are raised in the one year but in many areas but one young is raised each year.

The Short-eared mountain possum *Trichosurus caninus* inhabits mountainous districts and rain-forest in coastal southeastern Australia. The Scaly-tailed possum *Wyulda squamicaudata* has a naked prehensile tail and occurs only in the Kimberly district of northwestern Australia. It is intermediate between the cuscuses and Brush possums.

The Ringtail possums *Pseudocheirus* include about 15 species of arboreal animals distributed in coastal Australia, New Guinea and Tasmania. Ringtails are smaller than Brush possums and have a long tapering prehensile tail lacking the brush but usually clothed in white hairs at the end. They have short ears and soft grey to black fur on the dorsal surface and are whitish beneath. The first and second toes of the forefeet are, like those of the koala, opposable to the remainder. The litter size is two to three and the pouch has four teats. FAMILY: Phalangeridae, ORDER: Marsupialia, CLASS: Mammalia.

G.B.S.

PHALAROPES, three species of fairly small semi-aquatic wading birds, similar in build to the sandpipers and stints, that is with thinnish, though rather long, necks and small heads. Since all three species swim a great deal, their morphology shows several adaptations which parallel those found in water birds—dense plumage on their breast, belly and underparts, to provide both waterproofing and buoyancy; legs with an oval cross-section so that the width of bone is much smaller in the direction of movement than at right angles to it, thereby cutting down resistance to the water flow without losing leg strength; and toes broadened or lobed and slightly webbed at the base. They have different plumages in summer and winter. In the breeding plumage females are more brightly coloured than males, an unusual feature found also in the dotterel, a mountain plover.

In their grey and white winter plumage the Grey phalarope *Phalaropus fulicarius* and the Red-necked phalarope *P. lobatus* are very similar, and both resemble the sanderling in general colouration. The Grey phalarope is slightly larger than the Red-necked, but the main difference in winter is in bill proportions, that of the Red-necked being fine and delicate while that of the Grey is shorter and broader. In summer plumage the Grey phalarope is, confusingly, the more richly coloured of the two. This is reflected in its American common name, Red phalarope. The Red-necked phalarope is known as the Northern phalarope in North America, and this also is confusing, as the Red-necked has the more southerly distribution of the two. The third species in the family, Wilson's phalarope *Steganopus tricolor,* is placed in a different genus. It is slightly larger than the other two, with longer legs and a long needle-like bill (of the same shape but longer than the Red-necked's). It differs at all seasons in plumage from the Grey and Red-necked in the possession, among other features, of a white rump. It is a rare vagrant to Europe.

Two of the species are of arctic origin. The Grey has a patchy circumpolar breeding distribution in the tundra zone, while the Red-necked is found usually to the south of the Grey, in both tundra and boreal climatic zones between about 60° and 70°N. However, in several parts of Canada the two species breed alongside each other. It is not yet known whether they have any differences in food preference in these areas. In Britain, the Red-necked phalarope breeds in small, but decreasing, numbers to the south of its normal range, while it is reported to be extending its breeding range northwards in other parts of the world. Both species reach their arctic breeding grounds in June, but stay there only a few months. After breeding they move first to coastal waters close to the breeding areas, where they gather in large concentrations on the sea to moult, in the same way as many ducks. Later, they migrate to tropical and sub-tropical oceanic regions where 'upwellings' occur, i.e. where persistent offshore winds bring cold water, laden with nutrients, to the sea surface, so that phytoplankton, and consequently zooplankton, are abundant. While both species are often found together outside the breeding season, the chief wintering areas of the Grey phalarope are believed to be off the coasts of northern Chile and West Africa, whereas concentrations of Red-necked phalaropes have been recorded chiefly in more tropical waters, off Peru, to the north of New Guinea and off the coasts of Arabia. Wilson's phalarope is restricted as a breeding bird to the North American continent, where it is found between the latitudes of California (about 35°N) and northern Alberta (about 55°N). Both males in full reproductive condition and females, not yet ready to lay, reach the northern part of their breeding range in Canada in mid-May. Females leave the actual breeding grounds about a month later, and males and juveniles follow some two months after them. They move south to Central and South America, where they winter inland on and around freshwater.

Phalaropes normally nest on the grassy margins of shallow freshwater pools. Wilson's may, however, nest in meadows up to 330 ft (100 m) from the water's edge. Usually several pairs nest around the same pool, and in some parts of the Canadian Arctic, Wilson's phalarope may be described almost as colonial nesters, since they are so common. While it is possible that a small area around the nest may be defended against other phalaropes, breeding phalaropes do not have well-defined feeding territories, but rather feed communally. The nest consists of a scrape made by the female, to which some lining may be added later, either during the laying period, or during incubation, which is done entirely by the male. Often several scrapes are made before the female chooses one for laying the three, or more usually, four eggs. Incubation lasts about three weeks, and the chicks take to the water soon after hatching. Many females, particularly of Red-necked and Wilson's phalaropes, leave the breeding area before the young hatch, so that the male has sole responsibility for the chicks, and it is he who performs the distraction displays to lure away potential predators.

The hormonal control of the phenomenon of sex-reversal (a term sometimes used for the partial reversal of roles of male and female in the breeding activities) has received considerable attention, particularly in Wilson's phalarope. Associated with the brighter breeding plumage of the female, it is found that she is more aggressive than the male. Pair-formation takes place by the female selecting and chasing the male of her choice, and driving off other females. There is apparently no fighting between males. (In spite of repeated claims, there is no strong evidence that females mate with more than one male; they certainly do not in Wilson's phalarope.) In accord with the male's sole responsibility for incubation, females do not develop brood-patches. Brood-patches can be induced outside the breeding season by

Wilson's phalarope, of North America, a species of wader in which the hen 'does the courting'.

injecting birds with the hormones prolactin and testosterone (an androgen), but not with prolactin plus oestradiol (an oestrogen). In the wild, only males produce prolactin, and so only they develop brood-patches and incubate. The bright nuptial plumage can be induced in captive birds of non-breeding condition by injections of testosterone, which in most bird species is produced in quantity in the wild only in the males. Oestrogen injections are ineffective in inducing nuptial plumage in phalaropes. Surprisingly, it is found that female phalaropes in the wild secrete quite high concentrations of testosterone (relative to the amounts of oestrogen) from their ovaries; hence it is they who develop the brighter plumage. The evolution of such a system of altered levels of hormone production is difficult to envisage. One suggestion is that both sexes of phalarope ancestors shared incubation, as found in most other species of wading birds, but that a mutant line of females arose which were deficient in prolactin production, and so did not incubate. There would then be selection against bright plumage in the sex that did incubate, the males, and so the females

would retain brighter plumage than the males. This assumes that the broods raised by the pairs in which the female had faulty incubation behaviour survived better than other broods.

Phalaropes spend more time swimming than any other species of waders, both in the breeding season, when they are found on shallow freshwater lakes and pools, and outside this period, when the Grey and Red-necked phalaropes are pelagic, spending many months on the open sea. In freshwater habitats, they take aquatic insect larvae (chiefly mosquitoes) and small crustaceans from the surface layers of the water. They stir up these food items from lower levels, or at least cause them to move so that they become conspicuous, by rapid swimming movements with their feet. At the same time they spin their bodies round and round on the water, making many revolutions per minute. This behaviour marks off the phalaropes from other wading birds, as also does their occasional up-ending (like a Dabbling duck). Wilson's phalarope spins less than the other two species and often swims directly or wades. It also sometimes feeds on land. In addition, all three species pick flying insects from the surface of the water. It is thought that the Red-necked phalarope may do this more than the other two. At sea, the Grey and Red-necked feed on zooplankton, again taken from the surface layers of the water. During their months spent at sea, and also on their long over-sea migrations, phalaropes are particularly susceptible to prolonged gales, which, since the birds are so light and buoyant, may lift them from the surface of the water and drive them inshore. Only under such conditions do they normally occur on the coast. FAMILY: Phalaropididae, ORDER: Charadriiformes, CLASS: Aves.   P.R.E.

The Grey phalarope is richly coloured in its summer plumage; and is known in America as the Red phalarope.

PHARYNGEAL TEETH, grinding, crushing or combing teeth found in the throat in certain fishes. They are developed on the bones of posterior gill arches, so that they lie within the gill cavity and immediately before the opening of the pharynx. In some fishes the lower set of pharyngeal teeth are fused forming a triangular plate on which the teeth are set. In the wrasses (Labridae) the teeth are blunt and used for grinding, as is also the case in some of the cichlid fishes. In others the pharyngeal teeth are adapted to grinding vegetable foods and in those fishes that live on micro-organisms (e.g. some species of *Tilapia*) the upper and lower sets of pharyngeal teeth may shuffle back and forth over each other to 'comb out' the food. In the carp-like fishes the pharyngeal teeth lie on sickle-shaped bones and take the place of jaw teeth, which are lacking in this group. The pharyngeal teeth not only offer a good indication of an animal's food and feeding habits but are also of great importance in the identification and classification of fishes.

The pharyngeal teeth appear to be intimately linked with diet and feeding habits so that it seems as if the size and shape of the teeth are actually dependent on the food. A noteworthy example is a cichlid fish *Astatoreochromis* living in Lake Victoria, in Africa. This fish feeds almost entirely on water snails and when dead its stomach is found to contain an appreciable amount of

The Common pheasant was taken across Europe, and has since been taken to other parts of the world, as a sporting bird.

Below (top): Vertical section of skull of bowfin; (bottom): Ventral view of skull on left, dorsal view of lower jaw and gill arches of a wrasse on right. P= pharyngeal teeth.

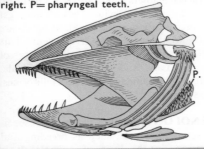

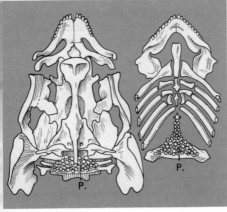

crushed shells. The teeth in the jaws are unlikely to be responsible for this crushing, which is presumably done by the pharyngeal teeth that are large and blunt. In other lakes in the region in which this same species lives, the food is mainly insects, small fishes and plant food, very few molluscs being taken. The pharyngeal teeth are considerably smaller. Some years ago individuals of this species were kept and bred in aquaria in the United States and these were given very few molluscs to eat. After they had been bred for several generations their descendants were examined and shown to have pharyngeal teeth quite unlike their immediate ancestors

brought from Lake Victoria and more like those in the African lakes where the cichlids eat few molluscs.

It has been noted that the orfe *Idus* fed with pieces of earthworm makes vigorous gasping movements with its mouth for some minutes after it has swallowed food. Orfe have been experimentally killed and dissected immediately after feeding. Their stomach contents were made up of pieces of worm thoroughly lacerated.

The Chinese grass carp *Ctenopharyngodon* which feeds on leaves of aquatic plants is almost entirely vegetarian. Its pharyngeal teeth are saw-like. The contents of its stomach are made up of plant material scraped to fragments. Fishes cannot break down and digest cell walls of plants but the Chinese grass carp, by ripping the plant food to pieces, is able to obtain about half the protein contained in it.   M.B.

PHEASANTS, game birds forming a well-defined group of the subfamily Phasianinae which also includes such other closely related birds as snowcocks, francolins, spurfowls, partridges and quail. There are 16 genera of pheasants comprising 48 species in existence

today and in some cases there are numerous races or subspecies, bringing the total number of forms to 150. All the world's pheasants, including peafowl, junglefowl and tragopans originated in Asia with one exception, the rare Congo peacock.

In nearly all pheasants the male is far more brightly coloured than the female. This is one of the characteristics which helps to distinguish them from other members of the Phasianidae, particularly from their close relatives the partridges, francolins and quail. The more sombre, cryptic colouration of the females must have considerable survival value during the long weeks of incubation and brooding when they are especially vulnerable to predators.

All pheasants spend a great deal of their time on the ground searching for food. They scratch the earth with their feet like domestic chickens in search of seeds, worms and insects. They have long and powerful legs and can run far and fast, so much so that many pheasants prefer to run into cover rather than take to the air when alarmed. When they do fly up, they rise almost vertically on their short but broad wings.

Most pheasants nest on the ground, making a scrape under cover of a bush, tussock of grass, or even among dead leaves on the forest floor. A few species prefer to lay their eggs in an elevated position and in these cases they usually take over an old nest of some other bird such as a pigeon. The tragopans and the Congo peacock adopt this method but it may well occur among other species. Some pheasants are polygamous or even promiscuous but in at least seven of the 16 genera this is not the case.

No group of birds can claim to have made such an impact on the social and economic history of mankind as have the pheasants. As sporting birds they have been widely introduced throughout the Old and New Worlds and they have often indirectly affected the lives of other creatures, for whenever the pheasant is regarded as an important game bird, legislation has been passed to protect it. In his concern for the introduced pheasant man has often needlessly destroyed other forms of wildlife. The pheasants' impact upon the economic scene has been even greater since all breeds of Domestic fowl are descended from one or more of the four species of junglefowl, themselves members of the pheasant family.

It is probable that the first pheasants to arrive in Britain were brought by the Romans during their 400 years' occupation but the first historical evidence does not appear until the 11th century when pheasant figured on the menu at various banquets and monastic feasts. By the 12th century pheasant was a regular item on the bill of fare and by the 16th century it was established as a wild bird. This pheasant was almost certainly the Southern Caucasus pheasant or what is more popularly, if inaccurately, called the Old English black-neck. It is the only pheasant whose range just overlaps from Asia into Europe, being found in the extreme southeast, on both sides of the Caucasus.

The Blood pheasant *Ithaginis cruentus* resembles a partridge in shape and size and is among the most delicately coloured game birds. The general colour of the male is bluish-grey with pale greenish below and crimson markings on the throat and beneath the tail. Blood pheasants live at a higher altitude than any other in the mountains of Central Asia from Nepal through Tibet to northwest China. They always live near the snow line, usually between 9,000 and 15,000 ft (2,750–4,500 m) according to the season.

Koklass *Pucrasia macrolopha* are medium-sized pheasants of fairly dull colouration. The male has a long crest of dark green and rufous brown feathers, glossy green-black head and upperparts of silvery grey streaked with brown. The female is brownish. It is found in the Himalayas from Afghanistan to central Nepal and in northeastern Tibet and eastern China and is confined to mountain forests between 4,000 and 13,000 ft (1,200–4,000 m).

Large and powerfully built the males of the three species of monals *Lophophorus* are the most brilliantly coloured of all pheasants. The iridescent metallic hue of their plumage is rivalled only by the hummingbirds. Monals are mountain birds whose distribution extends from eastern Afghanistan along the Himalayan Range to the mountains of western China. They spend a great deal of time searching for grubs, insects and roots, digging with their powerful bills and never scratching with their feet.

The ten gallopheasants *Lophura* are upright in stature and have longish legs armed with sharp spurs. The tail is compressed and ridge-shaped. There are large wattles of bare skin covering the face round the eye, blue in two species and red in all the others. Gallopheasants are forest birds living at low or moderate altitude from the Himalayas through Southeast Asia to Taiwan (Formosa) and Borneo. The Silver pheasant is the most well-known member of this genus and the most frequently kept in captivity. Swinhoe's pheasant is also popular as an aviary bird though rare in its native land of Taiwan where it is threatened with extinction. In 1967 the Pheasant Trust sent 15 pairs of Swinhoe's pheasants that had been bred in captivity back to Taiwan for release to help build up the depleted wild population.

Other pheasants in this genus include the kalij, Edwards's (from Vietnam and neighbouring Laos), Salvadori's, the Crestless firebacks, the Crested firebacks, the Siamese fireback and Bulwer's wattled pheasant from Borneo.

There are three distinct species of Eared pheasants *Crossoptilon*; the White-eared, Brown-eared and Blue-eared. All are large distinctive birds adapted to life at high altitudes and obtaining much of their food by digging with their powerful bills. The general colour of both sexes is implied by the name of the species, and the so-called 'ears' refer to the elongated white ear coverts common to all of them. The Eared pheasants are confined to China, Tibet and Mongolia.

The sexes of the Cheer pheasant *Catreus wallichi* are rather similar in colouration, both being dull grey and brown. The Cheer pheasant inhabits the western Himalayas as far east as Nepal, living in forests and scrub at 4,000–10,000 ft (1,200–3,000 m).

There are five well-defined species of Long-tailed pheasants *Syrmaticus* including Elliot's pheasant from eastern China, the Bar-tailed pheasant from Burma, the Mikado pheasant from Taiwan, the Copper pheasant from Japan and Reeves' pheasant from China. The last named is the best known and most often kept in captivity. The Mikado pheasant is confined to Taiwan and is in danger of extinction in the wild. The Pheasant Trust is engaged in a project to reinforce the wild population with young birds of which no Trust's less than 140 were bred in the collection in 1969.

There are numerous races of the Common pheasant *Phasianus colchicus* stretching across Asia from Transcaucasia in the west to Taiwan in the east. A number of different forms have been introduced as sporting birds to Britain and elsewhere in the world so that the so called 'Common pheasant' is a mixture of several races. The Green pheasant *Phasianus versicolor* is similar in form but is confined to the Islands of Japan.

The two species of the Ruffed pheasant *Chrysolophus,* the Golden and the Lady Amherst's pheasants, are among the most beautiful and certainly the most popular of all game birds. They get the name of Ruffed pheasant from the males' large ruff of wide feathers which are spread like a fan across either side of the head and neck during display. Both species come from the mountains of central China.

Peacock pheasants *Polyplectron* are small dainty birds with loose plumage of intricate design. They are related to the Argus pheasants and, like them, lay only two eggs in a clutch. There are six species all inhabiting the tropical forests of Southeast Asia from the eastern Himalayas south to Sumatra and east to Borneo and Palawan.

The Great argus *Argusianus argus* is one of the most highly specialized of the pheasants and though the male's plumage may look less colourful than that of some species, his display, which is one of the most remarkable in the bird world, more than compensates. The secondary wing feathers are very broad and of tremendous length with a line of beautiful ocelli running the length of each feather while the two central tail feathers are even longer and twisted towards the tip. During his display the male argus faces the hen, bends forwards and spreads his wings, twisting them so that they meet in front of his head. The tips of the two central tail feathers project above the circle of feathers.

The Great argus lives in the tropical forests of the Malay Peninsula, Sumatra and Borneo. The male makes a display or dancing area to which he attracts the hens by his loud calling.

The male of the Crested argus *Rheinartia ocellata,* also called Rheinart's crested argus, is remarkable for the length and breadth of its central tail feathers which are over 5 ft ($1\frac{1}{2}$ m) long and 6 in (15 cm) wide. They are amongst the largest feathers in the world. Its habits are similar to those of the Great argus. This species inhabits the tropical forests of Vietnam, Laos and the Malay Peninsula. FAMILY: Phasianidae, ORDER: Galliformes, CLASS: Aves. P.W.

PHENOLOGY, the study of periodic, especially seasonal, events, such as breeding and migration, in the lives of animals. It is particularly concerned with the manner in which these activities are initiated and synchronized and the part played in the isolation of species.

PHENOTYPE, the characteristics actually shown by an organism as opposed to the *genotype, which refers to the genetic constitution. Organisms with the same phenotype may have different genotypes.

PHEROMONES, chemicals produced by one individual of a species that affect the

The Golden pheasant *Chrysolophus pictus* is one of the most handsome pheasants.

behaviour, and possibly the development, of other individuals. They may not directly change the behaviour but may sensitize other animals to certain kinds of stimuli. They are the means of chemical communication between one individual and another.

A good example of such chemicals are those concerned with recognition. Colonies of bees have distinctive odours which can be recognized by all members of the colony and the absence of which marks out intruders attempting to force an entrance into the colony. This common scent seems to be derived from shared food; nectar collected by foragers, for example, is very rapidly shared among the workers in the hive giving them a common odour. Many mammals mark their territory with secretions of various sorts, thus ungulates may use glands in the face or the hoof for this purpose, while hippopotamuses employ a mixture of faeces and urine.

Woodlice seem to have an odour which encourages other individuals of the same species to aggregate with them. This reinforces the grouping which is brought about by the common reactions to light and humidity, in themselves tending to make these animals gather in crevices and dark, damp places generally.

A number of pheromones act as alarm substances. Thus a minnow *Phoxinus laevis,* when wounded by a predator, releases a substance from special cells in the epidermis which causes other minnows in the school to swim rapidly away. A similar response to broken skin can be shown in tadpoles. The substance produced by glands of the ant *Pogonomyrmex* is attractive to fellow-ants in low concentration and at this level it acts as a trail marking substance, but at higher intensities produces an alarm response.

Pheromones may influence development, thus, a group of male locusts will mature more quickly than one on its own. This is due to a chemical produced by the integument which, as well as speeding up maturation, can also be seen to induce some behavioural effects such as twitching of the antennae.

Many animals, including insects, crustaceans, fishes and mammals employ pheromones to attract mating partners. Thus, male moths may be attracted to females over distances of 6,550 ft (2,000 m) or even farther when conditions are favourable. Compounds of the same sort produced artificially are used to attract Gypsy moths to traps as a method of control of this pest insect. It might be expected that such attractants would be species-specific but it has been found, for example, that a number of male pyralid moths respond to the sex attractants of females of other species. In nature, however, confusion of this sort is prevented as the two species are active at

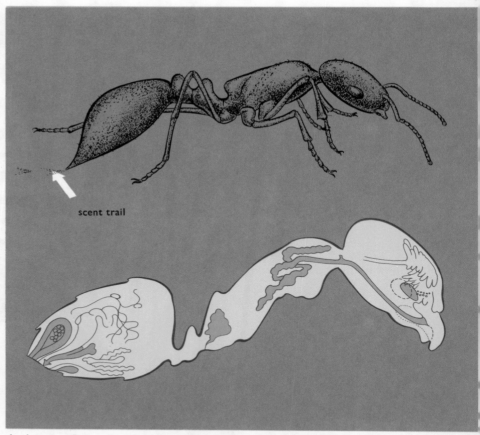

scent trail

An American Fire ant leaves a scent trail which leads other ants to food objects too bulky for one ant to retrieve. The scent markings are arrow-shaped as a result of initial pressure on the sting; this enables other ants to recognize the direction of the trail. Lower picture shows the scent glands, each producing a different pheromone, from which a combination of meanings may be expressed.

different times. Queen substance is produced by an active queen honeybee from her mandibular glands. This is 9-oxodec-2-enoic acid which she licks on to her body. It is removed by the workers tending her and circulates through the hive by food-exchange between individuals and as long as the substance is being received by workers they are inhibited from making the larger cells in which new queens will be raised. But as soon as the queen is removed or dies, the pheromone is no longer available and royal cell production begins.

Most of the substances thus far isolated from insects have molecular weights of about 2–300, giving them a reasonable diffusibility and at the same time being small enough for their production not to be a burden on the metabolic system of the animal. Their study has been aided by the use of such special techniques as gas-chromatography which allows very small quantities of complex chemicals to be analyzed.   J.D.C.

PHOCIDS, earless seals or true seals of the pinniped family Phocidae. Included in this group are the smallest seals—the little Ringed seals and Baikal seals of under 5 ft (1·5 m), and also the largest seals—the

Elephant seals which may reach 20 ft (6 m) in total length.

Phocids are streamlined for efficient swimming, and their outline is smooth with no unnecessary protuberances. Their ears are not visible externally except as small holes on the sides of the head. The forelimbs and hindlimbs are short and almost completely within the body outline, only the flippers protruding. All the digits of the foreflipper are bound within the skin like a fur mitten. The hind digits are separated by a webbing of thin skin. Claws of varying sizes are present, long and strong on all digits in the Common seal for instance, but reduced to small nodules on a specialized animal like the Ross seal. The hindflippers project backwards and cannot be brought forwards under the body so they cannot be used on land and the animals progress in a series of caterpillar-like 'hitches'. In the water the hindflippers make alternate strokes, assisted by side to side movements of the hind end of the body while the foreflippers help in steering.

All phocids have a short coat of flattened guard hairs with very sparse underfur. Phocids are plentiful in the cooler parts of the world: in the Arctic and Antarctic and along coasts and estuaries that are cooled by ocean currents. Only the Monk seals live in tropical seas.

Although predominantly marine, two forms of Ringed seal occur in freshwater lakes in Finland, and some landlocked Common seals live in Seal Lakes, Hudson Bay. The only other non-marine phocids are the Baikal and Caspian seals which live in the inland seas from which they take their names. Both are related to the Ringed seal *Pusa hispida*. Miocene fossils of the same genus have been found in Russia and Hungary and it is likely that this Arctic genus was widespread at one time, the two inland sea forms having been isolated from their immediate ancestors since the Miocene. Most phocids eat squid, fish and small crustaceans; the Crab-eater seal feeds almost exclusively on krill which it sieves through its complicated teeth, while the Leopard seal feeds on penguins in addition to fish and squid. FAMILY: Phocidae, ORDER: Pinnipedia, CLASS: Mammalia.　　　J.E.K.

PHOENIX, a mythical bird. First mention of the story of the phoenix is by Herodotus the Greek scholar (484–425 BC). It was elaborated by later writers as follows. The phoenix is a bird that comes from the East every 500 years to the land of Phoenicia where it makes a nest in a palm tree and then sets the nest on fire, being itself consumed in the flames. Three days later the phoenix is reborn from its ashes. It then takes the ashes of its father, wraps them in myrrh and aromatic leaves in an egg-shaped mass, flies with this in its claws to the Temple of the Sun at Heliopolis in Egypt, places it on the altar, crows and bows to the sun, flies east and is not seen again for another 500 years. Herodotus said the phoenix had a plumage of red and gold.

For centuries scholars have debated whether the phoenix was the golden pheasant or a Bird of paradise. In 1957 Australian anthropologists found that since time immemorial Birds of paradise skins have been traded by New Guinea aboriginals and taken across the trade routes of southern Asia to the Mediterranean. To protect the skins from moth and other destructive agents on the journey each was wrapped in myrrh surrounded by scorched banana leaves in an egg-shaped mass. See also 'anting' for False phoenix.　　M.B.

PHORESY (Gk *phorein* – to carry), a term applied to an association between two animals, usually of different species, one carrying the other which is either permanently or temporarily sedentary. The huge queen of the South African ant *Carebara vidua* carries a number of tiny workers attached to her body during her mating flight. These help her found the new colony in the termite nest which this ant parasitizes. This is an unusual example of phoresis between members of the same species.

The female of the 'Warble' fly *Dermatobia hominis* catches female mosquitos of the species *Janthinosoma lutzii* and cements her eggs to the mosquito's abdomen. These hatch out when the mosquito lands on the human host to take a blood meal and the skin heat stimulates the emergence of the larvae which immediately bore into the human skin. The larvae of the Spanish fly wait in flowers and attach themselves to bumblebees who carry them to the bee colony where they feed on pollen, honey and bee larvae.

Many examples of phoresis are known in freshwater where protozoans of the class Ciliophora attach themselves to crustaceans or insect larvae. There is often a close relationship between the two species involved as the passenger will not survive experimental transplantation to another host. In other cases it has been shown that the passenger species will attach to mechanical models with the same frequency of vibration as the normal carrier species.

In the Irish sea the ciliate protozoan *Rhabdostyla* may be found on the gills and body of the terebellid worm *Nicolea*. The Mediterranean fish fierasfer is found inside the hind intestine of the Sea cucumber. The fish feeds only at night when it emerges for short periods from its host.

These inter-relationships between species are not easy to divide into clearcut categories as can be seen from the varying definitions given by different authors. Clearly phoresis may, in time, lead on to parasitism or, on the other hand, to mutual interdependence, or symbiosis, between the two species. F.J.O'R.

PHORONIDA, or Horseshoe worms, are marine, tube-living worm-like animals generally less than 8 in (20·4 cm) long. Each individual lives in a chitinous tube which is buried in sand or attached to a rock or shell in shallow water in temperate and tropical seas. Chitin is a tough but flexible substance which also occurs in the external covering of insects. When first secreted it is transparent and sticky, but it soon hardens and in phoronids often becomes covered with sand grains, shell fragments and other detritus. *Phoronis architecta* produces separate vertical tubes coated with fine sand, whereas *P. hippocrepia* forms a complex mass of fine intertwining tubes either on the surfaces of rocks or shells or embedded in burrows in the substratum. Most species are colonial. Although the animal is free within its tube only the anterior end normally emerges from it.

The body is cylindrical, but slightly enlarged at the hind or basal end. It bears no appendages except at the front end on which is situated the lophophore. This consists of two parallel ridges curved into a crescent, the ends of which may be highly coiled. The centre of the crescent is so arranged that one ridge passes above the mouth and the other below it. Both the ridges of the lophophore bear hollow tentacles, which are slender and ciliated. These may number as few as 20 or 500 or more. They have a relatively thick membranous layer, the basement membrane, which underlies the epidermis, and which allows only a little movement of these rather stiff appendages. A crescent-shaped fold of tissue, the epistome, overhangs the mouth between the inner and outer ridges of the lophophore. The anal opening is situated above the mouth and outside the upper lophophoral ridge. An opening (the nephridiopore) of the excretory organs (nephridia) occurs on each side of the anus.

The body wall of phoronids consists of an outer, glandular epithelium which is adjacent to a rather thick basement membrane, a thin layer of circularly arranged muscle fibres and an inner layer of longitudinal muscle which is covered internally by a layer of cells known as the peritoneum. The epithelial gland cells are particularly abundant at the front end of the animal, especially on the lophophore. The body cavity of *Phoronis,* a true coelom, is divided into two main portions, the mesocoel in the anterior of the body, lophophore and tentacles, and the metacoel in the trunk of the body.

The digestive system of *Phoronis* is a slender U-shaped tube with the mouth and anus both placed anteriorly and the bend of the U at or near the basal end of the animal. The part of the gut immediately before the bend is swollen to form a stomach.

The blood system includes a dorsal vessel lying between the lengths of the gut. It carries blood forwards and a ventral vessel which lies to the left of the foregut transports blood posteriorly. The dorsal vessel divides into a crescent-shaped afferent vessel in the lophophore which supplies each tentacle with a single, blindly ending blood vessel. Each lophophoral afferent blood vessel connects with a lophophoral efferent vessel which drains blood away from the lophophoral region into the ventral vessel. The posterior ends of the dorsal and ventral blood vessels are linked by a complex of blood spaces or sinuses in the stomach wall. Blood circulation is accomplished by contraction of the walls of the dorsal and ventral vessels. The blood is a colourless fluid in which are red blood corpuscles, containing the respiratory pigment haemoglobin. The relatively simple nervous system consists of a nerve ring in the epidermis, at the base of the lophophore, from which nerves are given off to the tentacles and longitudinal muscles. The nerve ring is also linked with a nervous layer under the epidermis which innervates the body wall musculature and the sensory cells of the epidermis. A single giant motor fibre given off from the nerve ring passes through the epidermis on the left side and facilitates very rapid contraction of the trunk into the protective chitinous tube when the animal is disturbed.

Most species of phoronids are hermaphroditic, that is both male and female sex cells are produced by the same individual. The sex cells arise from a cell layer covering the ventral blood vessel and are released into the sea via the excretory pores. The eggs are fertilized in the sea and develop into ciliated larvae which are either free drifting (planktonic) or are brooded between the arms of the lophophore. The larvae are termed actinotrochs and are similar to the trochophore larvae of annelids and molluscs. After some weeks the actinotroch undergoes a rapid metamorphosis, sinks to the sea bed and secretes a tube.

Feeding in phoronids is accomplished through the action of cilia on the tentacles which create a water current which flows downwards and along the lophophoral groove towards the mouth. Plankton and suspended detritus trapped in the current become entangled in mucus on the tentacles and are transported into the mouth.

The 15 species of the phylum Phoronida seem to be distantly related to the *Bryozoa (Moss animals) and Brachiopods (*lampshells). All three phyla have in common the mode of development of the embryonic foregut (stomodaeum) which originates from the anterior end of the blastopore, an important site of infolding of embryonic tissue which results in the establishment of the main layers of the adult body.   M.J.P.

Red-banded frogs of Africa, of the family Phrynomeridae, are unusual in losing their bright colours in strong sunlight. Another special feature is that they walk or run rather than jump.

PHYLOGENY, the evolutionary history of an animal or group of animals. It is customary to express this in the form of 'trees', or genealogies showing probable descent of one group or of several groups from an original ancestral group.

PHRYNOMERIDAE, a small family of frogs, members of which are distinguished from the Microhylidae only in the possession of an extra cartilaginous element in each digit and they are sometimes included in that family. There is only one genus, *Phrynomerus,* which is found in Africa.

Phrynomerus bifasciatus is known as the Red-banded frog. It is about 2 in (5 cm) long, black with a band of scarlet along each side and a similar coloured patch on the back. It burrows into the ground and usually emerges only at night. When placed in the light for a few hours the red stripes fade, first to orange and then to pink. In stronger light all the colour fades and the frog becomes a uniform grey. It is the skin itself and not the eyes which is sensitive to the light; if part of the back is shaded this part remains coloured.

Red-banded frogs walk or run rather than jump. Although the tips of their fingers and toes are expanded into discs they are not strictly arboreal in habits. They clamber over logs and small bushes while searching for food which consists mainly of ants and termites. They are sometimes found in the chambers of termite nests.

Breeding occurs only after rains and large numbers of frogs congregate in shallow pools. The calls of the males can be heard more than $\frac{1}{2}$ ml (0·8 km) away. About 600 eggs are laid and hatch after four days. The tadpoles resemble those of Microhylidae in that, unlike most other frogs, the mouth does not have a cornified beak or rows of teeth. It is, instead, a simple aperture at the tip of the head through which the food particles suspended in the water are sucked. Metamorphosis into frogs occurs after about a month.

The habits of other species of *Phrynomerus* are not so well known as for the Red-banded frog. *P. annectens* is smaller and is found in open scrub country in Southwest Africa and Angola. It has patches of red-brown and yellow spots rather than red bands and is better adapted to running than the Red-banded frog. The front legs are longer and the toes point forward rather than outwards. It runs very quickly, more like a mouse than a frog. It is very flattened and probably lives under stones and leaves. ORDER: Anura, CLASS: Amphibia.   M.E.D.

PHYLLOSOMA, the larva of the *Spiny lobster, one of the most beautiful of small marine animals. The flattened, leaf-like glassily transparent body may be almost 2 in (5 cm) long and the legs with which it rows itself through the water span about 6–8 in (15–20 cm).

PHYSIOLOGY, the study of the physical and chemical processes that occur in living animals and plants. It is mainly concerned with function as opposed to structure.

PHYTOFLAGELLATES, pigmented single-celled organisms which swim by lashing a flagellum or flagella. They are the only organisms that photosynthesize like plants but are classified by zoologists amongst the animals. The phytoflagellates form the class Phytomastigophorea of the superclass Mastigophora (flagellates) of the phylum *Protozoa. A recent classification divides the class into ten orders. Some of these include colourless forms which are clearly related to the pigmented ones and are assumed to have lost their chloroplasts (organelles of photosynthesis) secondarily. A few orders include amoeboid or filamentous forms which are clearly related to the flagellated ones. The main characters used to separate the orders are types of pigments, whether these are chlorophylls, carotenes or xanthophylls, the chemistry of storage products, structure and chemistry of the cell wall, number and form of the flagella, methods of reproduction and any special morphological peculiarities. Some of the important taxonomic features, such as flagellar hairs and body scales, can be seen only by electron microscopy.

The detailed characteristics of the ten orders are as follows:

1. **Chrysomonadida.** Golden-brown flagellates with chlorophyll *a*, *β*-carotene, lutein and fucoxanthin; storage products leucosin (a soluble carbohydrate composed of *β*-1:3 linked glucose residues) and fat; some forms naked and capable of ingesting solid food by pseudopodia, others with a wall of pectin and/or cellulose, often impregnated with silica or lime, others with a covering of silicified scales or a lorica; one or two flagella, one directed anteriorly and bearing a bilateral array of submicroscopic hairs, the other shorter, smooth, directed posteriorly (typical heterokont flagellation); reproduction by fission or sexually by fusion of equal-sized motile gametes; small monads (less than 20*μ*), sessile forms and colonies; important constituent of both marine and freshwater phytoplankton; the genus *Ochromonas* is used in research on nutrition and as an assay organism for vitamin B$_{12}$; the silicoflagellates, marine forms with an internal tubular skeleton of silica and only one flagellum, are sometimes separated as an order, the Silicoflagellida.

2. **Haptomonadida.** Golden flagellates with the same pigments and storage products as the chrysomonads: two equal length smooth flagella and a third appendage, the haptonema, which coils and uncoils and may function as an attachment organelle; cells covered with delicately patterned organic scales which never become silicified but may become calcified; in the coccolithophorids, lime is deposited on scales as minute discs or rings, the coccoliths, and these calcareous ornaments are known in many varieties as fossils in chalk; some non-motile coccolithophorids and filamentous forms have haptomonads as an alternative phase in their life cycle; very important organisms in the economy of the sea, especially in warm waters where coccoliths form deep sediments on the sea floor; the monad *Prymnesium parvum* produces a fish toxin and has caused mass fish poisoning in Norwegian fjords and in fish culture ponds in Israel.

3. **Heterochlorida.** Rare yellow-green flagellates of freshwater, related to the yellow-green algae; thought to have chlorophyll *a*, heterokont flagellation and fat as the main storage product.

4. **Cryptomonadida.** Brown, green, red or blue flagellates with chlorophylls *a* and *c*, *α*- and Σ-carotene, zeaxanthin, and the accessory pigments phycoerythrin and phycocyanin which cause reddish and bluish colouration respectively; storage products fat and a form of starch; two flagella, one with bilateral sub-microscopic hairs, the other probably unilateral; cells small (10–30*μ*), flattened and typically with a lateral groove lined with projectile bodies called trichocysts, thought to be a defence mechanism; reproduction by fission only; freshwater and marine, some species forming symbiotic pigmented cells in various sea animals such as radiolarians, corals, anemones, clams and mussels.

5. **Dinoflagellida.** The *dinoflagellates.

6. **Euglenida.** The euglenoid flagellates, with chlorophylls *a* and *b*, *β*-carotene, antheraxanthin and neoxanthin; storage products paramylon (an insoluble carbohydrate composed of *β*-1:3 linked glucose residues) and fat; cell naked but with a flexible or rigid pellicle with helical organization, some forms with an envelope of ferric hydroxide precipitated on mucilage; two flagella, one or both emerging from an anterior invagination of the cell, the emergent portions bearing a unilateral array of sub-microscopic hairs; reproduction by fission only; eyespot independent of the chloroplasts; cells fairly large (20–300*μ*), elongated as in the best known green genus *Euglena*, flattened in *Phacus*, ovoid in an envelope in *Trachelomonas*; several non-pigmented genera, including saprophytes (*Astasia*, virtually a colourless form of *Euglena*) and active phagotrophs (*Peranema*); widespread and common organisms in most freshwater habitats, only a few species marine.

7. **Choanoflagellida.** The collar flagellates; yellow, pigments and storage products not studied by modern techniques, but no chlorophyll *b* or leucosin present; one flagellum at anterior end of cell, surrounded at its base by a single or double collar which electron microscopy shows to be a tight ring of fine tentacles; some forms attach to the substrate by their posterior end and form a lorica reminiscent of the chrysomonads; most species are colourless and are thought to be a link with the sponges which have cells with a similar collar.

8. **Chloromonadida.** Small group of green flagellates with chlorophyll *a*, *β*-carotene, lutein and antheraxanthin; storage product fat; large naked cells (50*μ* or more) with many trichocysts just beneath the plasma membrane or scattered through the cell; two anteriorly placed flagella of unequal length (structure not studied); mostly freshwater.

9. **Volvocida.** Green flagellates with chlorophylls *a* and *b*, *α*- and *β*-carotene, lutein, astaxanthin and other xanthophylls; storage products starch (an insoluble carbohydrate composed of *α*-1:4 linked glucose residues) and fat; cell wall of cellulose and pectin; two or four flagella, equal in length, smooth, inserted anteriorly on a small papilla; reproduction by fission within the mother cell wall, or sexually by fusion of equal or unequal motile gametes, or by fusion of a sperm with an egg; monads and colonies; many species, nearly all freshwater; *Chlamydomonas* is a well known monad, *Volvox* a beautiful colonial form.

10. **Prasinomonadida.** Green flagellates with the same pigments and storage products as the Volvocida; one, two, four or eight flagella, covered by layers of submicroscopic organic scales; cell also covered by several layers of organic scales (with different patterning from the flagellar scales) or by a non-cellulosic wall formed by fusion of scale-like particles; reproduction by fission; all known species small and marine; one genus has been identified as the green symbiont of the marine worm *Convoluta*.   G.F.L.

The subclass Phytomastigina, or phytoflagellates, contains ten orders, six of which are shown here. They are distinguished by the colour of the chromatophores as well as by the number of flagella and the presence or absence of a gullet, stigma and cellulose membrane.

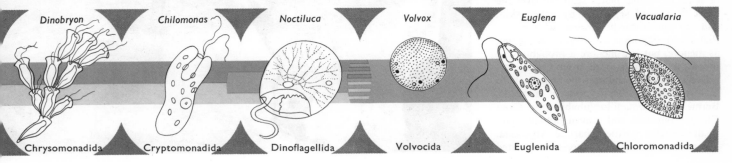

Dinobryon   Chilomonas   Noctiluca   Volvox   Euglena   Vacualaria

Chrysomonadida   Cryptomonadida   Dinoflagellida   Volvocida   Euglenida   Chloromonadida

PICHICIAGO, the smallest armadillo and the smallest member of the mammalian order Edentata to which belong not only the armadillos but the sloths and anteaters as well. There are two genera of pichiciago and only two species.

Pichiciago menore or the Fairy armadillo *Chlamyphorus truncatus* measures 6 in (15 cm) at the most in length and its spatula-shaped tail is less than 1 in (25 mm) long. In this smallest armadillo the many-banded head and body armour is scanty and is anchored only in two places, on the skull over the eyes and by a narrow ridge of flesh down the animal's back. Pichiciago menore is the only armadillo in which the dorsal armour is almost separate from the body. The squared-off rump, however, is covered securely with a large anal plate attached firmly to the pelvic bones. Pichiciagos are said to use this rear plate to plug their burrow entrances. The tail projects from a notch at the bottom of the anal plate and cannot be raised because of it. The shell in Pichiciago menore is pale pink (hence they are sometimes called Pink fairy armadillos), and the rest of the body is covered with soft, fine white hair that hangs down over the legs and feet. Supposedly the babies are hidden beneath this protective curtain when they are very young.

Fairy armadillos are found only in the sandy arid plains of west-central Argentina where they burrow in the hot dry earth where cactus and thorn bushes grow in abundance. Pichiciago menore is a very rapid digger, supporting itself with the stiff tail and using all four feet. In soft soil it is reported to be able to disappear from sight before a man can dismount from his horse. At dusk Fairy armadillos emerge from their burrows to feed principally on ants and occasionally on worms, plant tops and roots.

Burmeister's armadillo or Pichiciago mayore *Burmeisteria retusa* closely resembles the Fairy armadillo and is only slightly larger. The head and body length of Pichiciago mayore is 5·5–6·8 in (14–17·5 cm), and the tail is about 1·4 in (3·5 cm). In this species the shell is whitish and yellowish-brown in colour, and it is completely attached to the skin of the back. The woolly under-hair is white. The anal shield in Burmeister's armadillo differs in being made up of small individual plates scattered over the blunt rump and separated by naked skin, and the tail is partly covered with plates. Pichiciago mayore is not as good at digging as menore, but like menore it probably also presses itself against hard ground when surprised in the open and uses the anal shield to seal its burrow like a cork in a bottle. Burmeister's armadillo inhabits the Gran Chaco from west and central Bolivia south to the extreme northern part of Argentina. The cries of Pichiciago mayore are reported

to be almost like that of a human infant.

Much is still to be learned about the habits and natural history of pichiciagos, but unfortunately they are very difficult to keep alive in captivity, and they are now extremely rare. Their decline in numbers is attributed mainly to the expansion of agriculture and to domestic animals, namely dogs. FAMILY: Dasypodidae, ORDER: Edentata, CLASS: Mammalia. M.M.W.

PIDDOCKS, marine bivalve molluscs which bore either into soft rock or into wood; those boring into wood are distinguished from the shipworms by the absence of calcareous tubes and long extensions of the siphons. The piddock's shell is cut away anteriorly leaving

a permanent gape through which the rounded foot projects. The end of the foot forms a sucker which anchors the piddock to the end of the burrow whilst rasping movements are made. Such movements of the shell valves are brought about by the alternate contraction and relaxation of the anterior and posterior adductor muscles which rock the valves about a central area of articulation or fulcrum. There is one such area in all the rock-boring piddocks belonging to the family Pholadidae but in the Wood piddock *Xylophaga dorsalis* there are two fulcra (a dorsal and a ventral one as in the shipworm). A common feature of all the true piddocks is the presence of accessory shell plates which lie between the valves on the upper surface.

Above: details of structure of a piddock. Below: piddock exposed in its tunnel in rock.

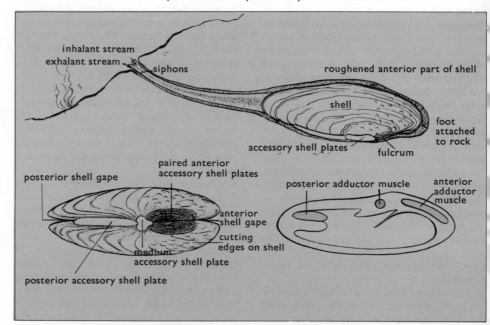

This distinguishes them from the unrelated but superficially similar American piddock *Petricola pholadiformis,* a boring bivalve belonging to the family Veneracea (see Venus shells) which has no accessory shell plates and its inhalant and exhalant siphons, connecting the animal with the surface, are separate, whereas in the true piddocks they are united and covered for half their length by a horny sheath.

The largest European species is the Common piddock *Pholas dactylus* the shell of which reaches 3 in (7·7 cm) in length; there are four accessory plates, three anterior and one longer posterior one. The Oval piddock *Zirphaea crispata,* as its common name suggests, is much less elongated. The shell reaches only 2 in (5·1 cm) in length but the siphons are very long and connect the piddock with the surface of the clay or shale into which it has bored. There is only one small accessory shell plate. Other piddocks are much smaller than these two; the Little piddock *Barnea parva* is always less than 1½ in (3·8 cm) and is slender whilst the thin-shelled White piddock *Barnea candida* scarcely reaches 2 in (5·1 cm) in length. The final European species of true rock-boring piddocks is the Paper piddock *Pholadidea loscombiana* which has a pronounced oblique furrow running across the surface of the shell. The base of the siphons is protected by a characteristic membranous cup-like structure. A distinctive feature of the Paper piddock is that the foot degenerates and the gape between the front of the shell valves closes when the animal becomes adult and ceases to bore into the rock. Other 'piddocks' include the Wood piddock *Xylophaga dorsalis* (Family Xylophaginidae) which makes shallow borings in timber, and the American piddock *Petricola pholadiformis* (Family Veneracea) which has been mentioned above. This last is a remarkable example of convergent evolution in which two unrelated families of bivalve mollusc living in a similar environment have evolved a very similar overall shell form. The American piddock was probably introduced to the southeast of England in about 1890 along with relaid American oysters (*Crassostrea*) and has since spread around the North Sea to the western Baltic. FAMILY: Pholadidae, ORDER: Eulamellibranchia, CLASS: Bivalvia, PHYLUM: Mollusca.   R.C.N.

PIG, DOMESTIC, also known as hog or swine, has been used by man for the last 5,000 years, since the Neolithic Period. Probably Asiatic pigs were first domesticated and there is evidence that these were first brought to Europe, although the European wild boar was later domesticated. By the nature of its behaviour, the pig was unlikely to have been domesticated before human communities became agricultural. Nomadic tribes would

Young domestic pigs basking in their wallow.

have difficulty in moving about with a relatively slow and refractory animal, and it seems likely that the use of hogs spread from one settled village to another.

Although primarily a prolific source of meat and cooking fat, pigs were put to other uses. They have at times been employed as draught animals and in Ancient Egypt were used to tread the corn, their hoofs making an imprint in the ground of just the right depth at which wheat should be sown. Individual pigs have at various times been used for rounding up cattle, for retrieving game and for detecting truffles, the fungus delicacy which grows 1–2 ft (30–60 cm) below ground. Their main use, apart from being suppliers of meat, was in clearing the ground. Pigs root for food, turning over the soil with their snout, feeding on acorns, beechmast and other fallen fruits, roots and tubers, and in the process destroying seedlings, even uprooting small saplings as well as bushy undergrowth. Grass then covers the ground and from Neolithic times onwards they seem to have been used for ground clearance by the farmer, to convert open woodland into arable and pasture land.

The swineherd was then an important member of the community.

There are a number of explanations for the pig having been branded filthy or unclean, and for the taboos arising from this. One is that people eating partially cooked pork are liable to *trichiniasis. Pigs are also apt to be infected with tapeworms. Another explanation suggested is that pig's fat readily goes rancid in hot climates. Probably the explanation most favoured by archaeologists is that hunting tribes looked with contempt on the settled farmer and came to despise also the pig he bred, in time developing religious prohibitions against the animal.

There are two kinds of pigs: herd pigs and sty- or house-pigs. Herd pigs tend to be long-legged and long-snouted and these were the kind generally used in Europe until nearly 200 years ago when Chinese house-pigs were imported and crossed with the European to give the thick-set Berkshire. Indian breeds were also imported for further crosses, to give the sty-pigs selectively bred for their higher meat yield. FAMILY: Suidae, ORDER: Artiodactyla, CLASS: Mammalia.   M.B.

PIG TABOO. It is generally considered that the ban imposed on the eating of pig flesh by Jews and Moslems is based on hygiene. In hot countries pork is more likely to cause intestinal disturbances or poisoning than other meat and it is the carrier of the Pig *tapeworm. This parasite is nowadays controlled by curing or cooking pig products and infection by the Beef tapeworm is more likely through the eating of half-raw 'rare' steaks.

The bygone English custom of bringing in the Boar's Head at the Christmas Feast, is probably derived from a pagan sacrificial ritual. In the Viking Saga of King Heidrek the White a boar was sacrificed at Yule (the pagan festival at the same time of the year as Christmas) to the god Frey and boars were often portrayed on helmets as a symbol of the god and therefore acted as talismans.

PIGEONS, a family of some 255 species of birds spread over most of the world except for polar and subpolar regions and some oceanic islands. The term 'pigeon' is sometimes used to designate the larger species, in contrast to the smaller species which are known as 'doves', but the terms are not consistently used and are not based on any real biological distinction.

Pigeons have undergone a considerable degree of adaptive radiation and now vary in size from that of a lark to that of a hen turkey, from 6–33 in (15–84 cm) in length. They also vary considerably in plumage, some of them being amongst the most brightly coloured of birds, others rather drab. The most typical plumage is some pastel shade of grey, brown or pink, with contrasting patches of brighter colours. The feathers are soft and often loosely inserted in the skin, but are nevertheless strong and dense. The wings and tail show much variation in size and shape, but the legs are usually short, being rather long only in some of the terrestrial species. The body is compact, the neck rather short and the head small. The bill is usually small, soft at the base but hard at the tip, and at the base of the upper mandible is a fleshy 'cere', a naked area of skin which in some species is much swollen. This swelling is much more common in domesticated varieties. Some species have a noticeable crest. In most species the male is rather brighter than the female, but in a few species the sexes are similar and in others they are very different.

Most species of pigeons perch readily and regularly in trees, but some are terrestrial, others cliff-dwelling and some have taken to nesting on buildings in towns and cities. The feral pigeons which are so common in towns are all 'escapes', or descendants of such, from stocks of domestic pigeons. All domestic pigeons are derived from the Rock dove *Columba livia*, of Europe, which in the wild

Feral pigeons, descendants of the domesticated Rock dove, in Trafalgar Square, London.

form nests on rock ledges, so feral pigeons take naturally to breeding on buildings. Most species are gregarious, at least outside the breeding season, and some of them may be seen in large flocks. In the *Passenger pigeon *Ectopistes migratorius*, now extinct, flocks of literally countless millions were common at all times of the year. Most pigeons are very strong on the wing.

The food of pigeons is very varied, including berries, nuts, acorns, apples, seeds of many kinds, for example weed seeds and cultivated grain, and also buds and leaves. Many species also take animal food such as snails, worms and caterpillars. Food is stored temporarily in a crop which may be capacious. The distended crop of a Wood pigeon *Columba palumbus*, for example, after a

successful day's feeding may be seen clearly as the bird flies home to roost. Most pigeons have a large, muscular gizzard which, with the enclosed grit deliberately swallowed, grinds up even the most intractable food. In some of the Fruit pigeons, however, the gizzard does not have a crushing function and the rest of the gut is wider than in other species. These adaptations are connected with the habit of swallowing large fruits whole, digesting the flesh and ejecting the stones complete.

Pigeons drink in a manner unusual for a bird. They immerse the bill and then, instead of lifting the head and tipping the water down the throat, they suck, which means they must immerse the bill more deeply than most other birds. This habit of drinking by sucking is said to be shared with the sandgrouse (Pteroclidae) and buttonquail (Turnicidae) and for this and other reasons the pigeons and sandgrouse have been said to be closely related. This, however, has been disputed, as sandgrouse seem to drink in a manner rather intermediate between pigeons and other birds, and their various similarities may be due to convergence. Nevertheless, the pigeons, sandgrouse and the dodo and solitaires are united in the order Columbiformes.

Pigeons build a simple, rather unsubstantial and usually platform-like nest of twigs, stems or roots, in a tree or bush, on a cliff or building ledge, or sometimes on or in the ground or in a tree cavity. Two pale unmarked eggs form the usual clutch, and both sexes incubate. The young are helpless when first hatched and sparsely covered with a filamentous down. They are fed by both parents for the first few days on 'pigeons' milk', a curd-like material secreted by special cells lining the crop. This is scooped up by the broad, soft bill of the young inserted deeply into the parent's mouth to obtain the regurgitated material. Gradually it is supplemented with food partially digested by the parents.

Pigeon nestlings grow rapidly and in some of the smaller species the young can fly at two weeks of age. If eggs or young are lost through predation or other causes the female will usually lay again. In a successful season two or three broods may be produced. Such breeding habits must have contributed significantly to the success of pigeons as a group. Most species are highly palatable and are a favoured food of many animals including man. They are largely defenceless yet hold their own, even in competition with such successful groups as the parrots (Psittacidae).

The typical vocalization of pigeons is a cooing sound, usually produced while inflating the neck. Some species also produce harsher, sometimes whistling calls, without neck inflation. Cooing calls may be generally divided into two basic types: the advertising coo and the display coo. The display coo is usually given while the bird is performing its bowing display, which male pigeons direct towards females. In the bowing display the bird lowers its head and leans forward, thus exhibiting its display plumage to best advantage. In species which have brightly coloured neck patches the neck is inflated on production of the coo to show the patches. A considerable amount of variation in the bowing display may be seen in the family as a whole, and some species do not bow while uttering the display coo. In the Luzon bleeding heart dove *Gallicolumba luzonica*, which has a striking blood-red streak on the breast, the displaying bird throws its chest out and up to display the red patch, cooing as it returns to its normal posture.

The advertising coo is equivalent to the song of songbirds, usually being given by territory-owning males. It may, however, be uttered from the nest as well as from a perch well away from the nest. Males in breeding condition also perform display flights. Typically, these consist of a conspicuous flight with the wings beaten more slowly but over a wider arc, interspersed with glides, and the wings being clapped together from time to time. In several species the bird first flies up, clapping its wings above the body at the height of its climb, then gliding downwards to repeat the process. This places the displaying bird well above other pigeons in the vicinity, so that the display is more obvious. In other species, such as the Rock dove which breeds on cliffs, the display flight is straight, presumably because other pigeons in the vicinity are not likely to be below the displaying bird and will therefore view it from the side or above.

Derek Goodwin, in his recent monograph on the pigeons, has pointed out that the generalized type of pigeon, which spends at least some of its time in trees and shrubs but obtains a proportion of its food on the ground, is found in all geographical regions inhabited by pigeons. Many species of pigeons are involved, of great diversity of form, but the long-legged and short-winged rather terrestrial species are not found in the northern regions where considerable powers of flight are needed to avoid severe winters and other periods of food shortage. Treeless areas have become colonized by species adapted to nesting in caves, cliffs and rock cavities. These are ground feeders. Other ground-feeding forms are found in areas such as the Americas, Australasia and some Pacific islands, where there are plenty of trees, and these nest above ground level. Some of these species are quite bulky and highly terrestrial and live in regions (e.g. New Guinea) where there is little competition from game-birds. Australasia also has a number of species that normally nest on the ground, and this, like other aspects of Australasian zoology, is probably connected with the scarcity of carnivorous mammals in the region.

Pigeon species that are predominantly arboreal occur widely in tropical regions, but principally in Australasia and Indonesia. These include the Fruit pigeons. The abundance of such birds in these regions is probably correlated with the absence of monkeys which would be serious predators of eggs and young.

In the pigeon family as a whole Goodwin recognizes 43 genera, in four subfamilies. The subfamily Columbinae includes the typical pigeons and doves, and also the small South American doves as well as the Pheasant pigeon *Otidiphaps nobilis*, a highly terrestrial

The bizarre Nicobar pigeon *Caloenas nicobarica*, of the East Indies, most highly adorned of pigeons.

species of New Guinea, the Quail doves *Geotrygon* of South and Central America and the Australian Bronze-wing pigeons of a number of genera which in themselves show a high degree of adaptive radiation. This last group are largely ground-feeders, some of them being partridge-like, and two genera, *Ocyphaps* and *Locophaps*, are the only pigeons to have long pointed crests. Members of this subfamily are primarily seed-eaters.

The subfamily Treroninae contains the arboreal Fruit pigeons, in most of which the gut is specialized for digesting large fruits swallowed whole. The Green pigeons of the genus *Treron*, however, have a well-developed gizzard for crushing the seeds of the wild figs on which they feed. The Fruit doves of the genus *Ptilinopus* are brilliantly coloured species of the Indo-Malayan and Pacific regions, where the larger Imperial pigeons of the genus *Ducula* are also found. The Blue fruit pigeons of the genus *Alectroenas* are found on islands in the Indian

Ocean. Other genera are found in Australia, New Zealand and the Philippines.

The other subfamilies are much smaller. The Gourinae contains only the three species of Crowned pigeons of the genus *Goura* in New Guinea. These are rather terrestrial, forest-dwelling species, with an outstanding fan-shaped laterally-compressed crest on the top of the head.

The subfamily Didunculinae contains but the one species of Tooth-billed pigeon *Didunculus strigirostris* which lives in Samoa. This is a ground bird of wooded mountain sides, with a most unusual bill somewhat like that of a dodo. This large and strong tool is used to pick up food in the normal manner but is also used in an unique way for pigeons for breaking seeds and nuts into very small portions with an action rather like that seen in parrots. See Collared dove, doves, Fruit pigeons and Wood pigeon. FAMILY: Columbidae, ORDER: Columbiformes, CLASS: Aves.   P.M.D.

PIGEONS' MILK, a secretion from the lining of the crop of adult pigeons, on which the nestlings are fed for the first few days of their lives. Towards the end of the incubation period, part of the lining of the crop in both parents becomes enlarged and the cells are filled with the milk which is a curd-like substance similar in composition to mammalian milk. The cells are sloughed off and fed to the young by regurgitation, the baby pigeon, or squab, putting its bill into the parent's mouth to take the milk from its throat. As in mammals the activity of the milk-producing cells is controlled by the pituitary hormone prolactin.

PIGMENTS. The colours of animals are produced in two ways. Some have structural colours which are formed by reflection and diffraction at the surface of the animal. Such colours often vary according to the angle from which they are viewed, and they may have a metallic iridescence as the animal is

Above left: Rock dove and (above right) Wood pigeon. Below: some breeds of domesticated pigeons derived from the Rock dove: 1. Brunner cropper or Brunner pouter, 2. Single-crested priest, 3. runt, 4. Maltese, 5. barb, 6. Jacobin, 7. Dresden white-shield trumpeter, 8. Laced satinette, a subbreed of the Oriental fantail, 9. Danzig highflyer, a breed derived from the tumbler, 10. Racing or Homing pigeon.

rotated in the light. Such colours are found in many beetles and in the wings of some butterflies, for example the remarkable blue *Morpho* species from the Amazon. The other type of colouration is caused by pigments. These are substances which absorb some wavelengths of light and transmit others. Visible light can be considered as waves with varying lengths which correspond to different colours. The human eye can perceive light with wavelengths varying from about 400 mμ to 750 mμ (one mμ is equal to one millionth of a millimetre). This is known as the visible spectrum. Ordinary white light contains all these colours mixed together. Black colouration results when all wavelengths are absorbed.

One pigment which absorbs all wavelengths to a considerable extent is called melanin. This is the pigment in the dark skin of negroes, and the yellow and brown skins of other races of man. The colour depends on the concentration of pigment. The same pigment is present in hair. Most mammals have hair pigmented to a greater or lesser extent by melanin. Similar pigments are present in the feathers of many birds and in the skins of some Sea cucumbers.

Dark pigmentation can also be caused by ommochromes. These are present in the eyes of many insects and crustaceans and in squids and cuttlefish. In high concentrations some ommochromes are dark brown or black, but in lower concentrations they may be purple or reddish. The colour also depends on the state of oxidation of the pigment. Some ommochromes show a dramatic change in colour from dark red to yellow if treated with a mild oxidizing agent. The dark brown, or even black colouration of some insects is caused by the process known as sclerotization. This involves the tanning of proteins in the cuticle of the insect, the resulting tanned protein being brown. A similar process is involved in the formation of the egg cases of certain flatworms.

Striking red, orange and yellow colours are produced by the carotenoid pigments. These are so called because they are chemically similar to the orange pigments of carrots. As far as is known all animals obtain their carotenoids either directly or indirectly from plants. Animals cannot synthesize carotenoids, but once they have obtained them they can modify them. The pink colours of the feathers and legs of flamingos are the result of carotenoids taken in with the diet and then deposited in the skin and feathers. Similarly the yellow and red colouration of many crabs and shrimps is a result of carotenoid deposition, as is the dark blue of the uncooked lobster. In this crustacean the carotenoid is chemically linked to a protein, and the resulting compound is blue. When the lobster is cooked the link between the carotenoid and the protein is broken and

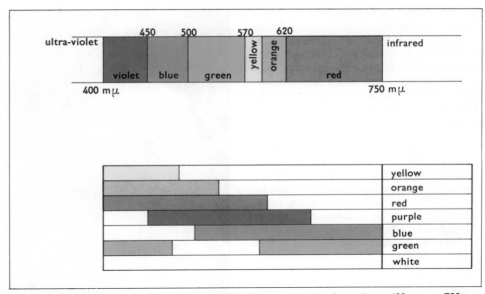

Top: the human eye can perceive light with wavelengths varying from about 400 mμ to 750 mμ (1 mμ= 1 millionth of 1 mm). This is known as the visible spectrum. The approximate range of colours is shown. Bottom: ordinary white light contains all these colours mixed together. Some of the colours produced by absorption of different parts of the spectrum are shown here.

the free carotenoid is bright red in colour. A whole range of colours can be produced by linking carotenoids to proteins, and these pigments are often deposited in eggs. Various crustaceans have been found with red, brown, blue, violet or green eggs. When all these various coloured eggs are boiled they turn pink, indicating that the original colour was due to a carotenoid linked to a protein.

A red colouration may also be produced by blood showing through the skin, as in red lips. The red colour of vertebrate blood is due to the pigment haemoglobin. This functions as a respiratory pigment, transporting oxygen around the body, so that its colour is incidental.

A similar pigment is found in some invertebrates, including some insects, most notably the larvae of chironomid midges, in many annelids, a few flatworms and some snails. A few annelids have a pigment similar in chemical composition and function, but bright green in colour. This pigment, chlorocruorin, is found particularly in fanworms, such as *Sabella*.

In the vertebrates haemoglobin is present in the blood only in certain cells, the red blood cells. These have a limited life, in man about 120 days, and at the end of this time the cells are destroyed, with a chemical breakdown of the haemoglobin. This results in the formation of bile pigments, which vary in colour from yellow through red to purple and green. The green bile pigments are known as biliverdins, and they may also be found in animals that do not have haemoglobin. The green colours of many insects are in part caused by bile pigments, as are the green colours of some polychaete worms. Under certain conditions biliverdin can appear to be blue and many birds' eggs, such

as those of the song thrush and starling, are coloured blue by this pigment.

Another series of pigments related to haemoglobin is formed by the porphyrins. These are similar to haemoglobin, but contain no iron and are not linked to a protein. Many different porphyrins have been extracted from animal tissues, and they are sometimes present in large enough quantities to cause conspicuous colouration. Perhaps the most interesting example is the feather pigment in turacos. Some of these tropical forest-dwelling birds have a bright red pigment which is formed by the linkage of a porphyrin with copper.

The red colouration of the shells of some Sea urchins is caused by a quinone pigment. Similar pigments are present in some other echinoderms, such as the Feather star *Antedon,* and allied pigments are found in a few insects. One of the most conspicuous is cochineal, extracted from a Scale insect.

Yet another red pigment is called erythropterin. This is present in the eyes and wings of certain insects, and in the skin of certain frogs. Other pigments of the same group, called the pterins, cause the bright yellow colour of the skin of the European salamander, and the bands around the body of a wasp. Yet other pterins are white, and were first discovered in the wings of butterflies. A common feature of pterins is that when they are exposed to ultra-violet light they give off a beautiful blue fluorescence.

From this brief survey it is clear that one cannot identify a pigment just from its colour. Redness may be due to ommochromes, carotenoids, haemoglobin, porphyrins, quinones or pterins. Green can be caused by structural colouration, bile pigments, or carotenoid proteins.   Ja.G.

Pigmy possums

PIGMY POSSUMS, dormouse-like marsupials with prehensile tails of the family Phalangeridae found in Australia, New Guinea and Tasmania. Unlike other phalangers the Pigmy possums have teeth adapted for an insectivorous diet, chromosomes alike in number and morphology to those of marsupial 'cats' and some American opossums and they give birth to up to six young at one time. These features indicate that the Pigmy possums are the most primitive of the phalangers and are perhaps like the stock from which the phalangers arose. Broom's pigmy possum *Burramys parvus,* previously known only as a Pleistocene fossil, was found alive in Victoria, Australia in 1966. FAMILY: Phalangeridae, ORDER: Marsupialia, CLASS: Mammalia.

PIG-TAILED MONKEY *Macaca nemestrina,* of Burma to Sumatra, largest of the *macaques, is heavily built, with a dog-like muzzle and short tail. It is trained to climb palms and throw down ripe coconuts.

PIKA, a member of the Lagomorpha, resembling a small, short-eared tailless rabbit and also known as Calling hare, coney, mousehare, haymaker, Slide rat.

It is the smallest of the lagomorphs, the adult weight of some species being only 5 oz (140 gm). The body is short and cylindrical, the ears short and rounded, the tail not apparent externally, and the hindlegs not much longer than the front ones, permitting a scampering run rather than the leaping-gallop typical of other lagomorphs. The colour of the 14 species, with many subspecies, varies from dark brown or dark slaty-grey to pale sandy or ash. 12 species are distributed from eastern Europe to Japan and from the Himalayas to Siberia. Two North American species range from Alaska southwards down the Rocky Mountains. Although predominantly a high altitude animal living above the tree line among the rocks and crevices of mountain slopes, a few species inhabit plateaux and open grasslands down to sea-level. All species live in a cold climate and all dig in the soil, but the forelimbs of the openland species, such as the Steppe pika *Ochotona pusilla,* of the steppes of eastern Europe, are specially adapted for this.

Breeding is dependent on seasonal changes in different habitats, and occurs from late spring to summer. Gestation lasts 30 days, and births are multiparous. The newborn are furred, with closed eyes and are dropped in burrows. Prenatal mortality followed by resorption of embryos, a characteristic of lagomorphs, is reported.

Pikas live in colonies which are spaced at distances from one another in accordance with the availability of food in different areas. There is evidence for the existence of a social hierarchy and territoriality. Defended

Pika *Ochotona pusilla,* one of the Mouse hares or Calling hares, a short-eared tailless rabbit.

territories are marked with the secretion from cheek glands. Pikas are sedentary, the range of movements for the American pika *O. princeps* and the Japanese pika *O. hyperborea* have been given as 100 ft (30 m) diameter. Co-operative defence against predators has been reported.

Unlike other lagomorphs pikas use characteristic sounds frequently and loudly, presumably for intraspecific communication, hence one of their common names, Calling hare.

Pikas occupy marginal areas where the supply of food is drastically reduced during severe winter conditions. They do not hibernate but have developed the habit of food-hoarding, involving not only storing it under rocky ledges but also preliminary drying and turning it as in haymaking. They feed on a variety of vegetation, the 'haypiles' often being brush piles consisting of grass, wood-twigs, and also pine cones, clumps of moss and sprigs of conifer needles. The stacks can be quite sizeable, reaching a few pounds in weight. In some countries the pikas' enterprise is exploited by herdsmen who feed their sheep on the 'haystacks' in winter.

The Mt Everest pika *Ochotona wollastoni,* occurring on Mt Everest and in northern Nepal is a member of the south Asian *roylei* group of pikas. It lives at altitudes up to 20,000 ft (6,000 m) thus having one of the highest vertical distributions among the mammals. The colour of the pelage is light

grey with a slightly drab tinge and the tips of the hairs are black. There are no conspicuous seasonal changes as in other species of the group, which show brilliant rufous colouration in summer. It inhabits rocky outcrops above the tree line, facing south or southwest. Crevices are utilized for nest sites and runs. Colonies are sometimes established in clearings under large rocks. It feeds on almost all available vegetation within reach and starts to harvest for the winter at the beginning of July. Reingestion of faeces, typical of all lagomorphs, adds to the efficiency with which available food is utilized. Depending on seasonal changes breeding takes place from April to August. Summer activity is diurnal with a peak at dusk. In general the *roylei* group are less vocal than other pikas. FAMILY: Ochotonidae, ORDER: Lagomorpha, CLASS: Mammalia. R.M.

PIKE, freshwater fishes of the northern hemisphere. The European pike *Esox lucius,* is a mottled yellow-green fish with an elongate body, the short and soft-rayed dorsal and anal fins being set far back towards the tail. The position of the dorsal and anal fins is characteristic of predatory species that lie in wait for their prey and then make a sudden dash. The head is long and the large jaws are armed with sharp teeth which are replaced at intervals during the life of the fish. Pike tend to lurk amongst weeds, blending well with their background, until the prey is sighted. The pike will then cruise very slowly forward, only the slightest movements of the fins indicating motion, until with an incredibly swift final lunge the victim is seized sideways in the jaws, juggled into position and swallowed. The pike swallows fishes such as the perch head first since the spiny fins and gill covers would otherwise stick in its throat.

The pike is the largest of the permanently freshwater British fishes, the record being a monster weighing 53 lb (24·5 kg) caught in Ireland. There are many legends of larger pike, some of which may well be true. The famous Kenmure pike, caught towards the end of the 18th century in Loch Ken, was said by one authority to have weighed 72 lb (32·6 kg), but by another to have weighed only 61 lb (27·6 kg). Most of the head of this noble fish is kept in Kenmure Castle and, although not complete, it was thought by Dr Tate Regan of the British Museum (Natural History) to be from a fish that might well, if in good condition, have weighed 72 lb.

Another legend associated with the pike is that, although voracious and even cannibalistic, it will not eat the *tench. The latter is called the Doctor fish by country people. The story goes that the pike, as well as other fishes, rub their wounds against the tench's slimy body, which heals the wounds and guarantees immunity to the tench. The legend is, however, unfounded since the pike, while not particularly fond of tench, is in some areas fished for with tench as the bait.

The pike is widely distributed all over Europe except on the Iberian Penninsula and across the northern parts of the Soviet Union. It is also found in North America, from the Great Lakes to Alaska. In North America it is referred to as the Northern pike to distinguish it from its American relatives. As in Europe, the pike has generated many legends in North America. The Canadian Eskimos relate stories of a Giant pike capable of swallowing canoes. The largest rod caught Northern pike, however, weighed only 46 lb (20·8 kg) and measured 52 in (132 cm).

The muskellunge or muskie, *Esox masquinongy,* from the north-east of North America is a rather different proposition. Muskies weighing 60 lb (27 kg) or more are by no means uncommon and the rod caught record is about 70 lb (about 32 kg). These large fishes have so far all proved to be

A pike catches its prey.

females, with ages ranging from 20 to 25 years. The muskie, whose predatory habits are similar to those of the Northern pike, can be distinguished by its rather smaller scales.

In addition to these giants, there are three smaller species of pike in North America which are usually referred to as pickerels. The Chain pickerel *Esox niger,* comes from the south and east of the United States. In color it resembles the European pike but the mottlings often have a brick-like appearance. The largest specimen caught weighed 9½ lb (4·3 kg) but a fish of 3 lb (1·4 kg) is usually considered a good size for an adult. The Red-fin pickerel and the Grass pickerel are very closely related and some authorities prefer to call them subspecies, respectively *Esox americanus americanus* and *E. a. vermiculatus.* Neither fish reaches more than 14 in (36 cm) in length. Both have shorter snouts than other pikes and the scales on the body are relatively large.

Pike make extremely good eating and in the past, both in England and on the Continent, these fishes were kept in ponds for culinary purposes.

Zoologically, the pikes occupy a rather isolated position, their nearest relatives being the Alaskan *blackfish and the European *mudminnows. FAMILY: Esocidae, ORDER: Salmoniformes, CLASS: Pisces.   K.B.

PIKE SIGHTS. When a pike strikes at its prey, it first poises for a moment, lines up its prey then strikes, darting up to 30 ft (10 m) in a straight line. To judge the position of the prey accurately, stereoscopic vision is needed. This is achieved by the presence of 'sighting grooves' in the long snout that run forwards from the eyes and allow stereoscopic vision at ranges down to about 5 in (13 cm). The pupil is also shaped to allow extra light in along the line of the sighting grooves. These grooves are found in other fish that hunt by sight, such as trout, and in reptiles such as Anole lizards.

A pike when swallowing its prey lifts its gill covers, exposing its blood-red gills.

PIKE PERCHES, fishes of the genus *Stizostedion* that are true members of the perch family but show a similarity in general form to the pike. The European Pike perch *S. lucioperca* is an elongated, pike-like fish widely distributed across Central Europe and introduced into southern England and southern Scandinavia. A population exists in the Baltic which migrates into the lagoons from the sea in winter. This species is also known as the zander. There are two dorsal

The European pike-perch, also known as the Zander, is a true perch that is pike-like.

fins, the first with stout spines. The mouth is armed with large canine-like teeth interspersed with many smaller ones. The back and flanks are greenish-grey with vertical dark bars in the young and there are longitudinal rows of dark spots on the two dorsal fins. The young feed on small aquatic animals but the adults are greedy predators feeding chiefly on fishes. The Pike perch grows to 4 ft (120 cm) and a weight of 22 lb (10 kg). The flesh is good to eat.

Closely related to the Pike perch of Europe is the walleye *S. vitreum* of the United States and Canada. Its name derives from the blind appearance of the eyes. In the last century some walleyes were introduced into a river in Cambridgeshire, England, in mistake for Black bass, but this population is now extinct and only a stuffed rod-caught specimen survives. All Pike perch in England are the European species. Commercial fisheries exist for the walleye in

North America and this industry has noted the great fluctuations in the size of populations from year to year. This appears to be due to the remarkable fecundity of the females, one female being able to lay up to half a million eggs, combined with the yearly variations in the conditions suitable for the survival of the eggs and fry. The average life-span is seven years but an 18-year-old female fish has been recorded. FAMILY: Percidae, ORDER: Perciformes, CLASS: Pisces.

PILCHARD *Sardina pilchardus,* a marine fish of the eastern North Atlantic and Mediterranean belonging to the herring family and widely known in its marketed form as both pilchard and sardine. The pilchard somewhat resembles the herring in its cylindrical body and fairly smooth belly, the series of small serrations along the belly (scutes) being poorly developed. It differs from the herring in having the last two anal rays longer than the rest, the colouring of the back rather greenish as opposed to bluish, and the presence of a dark spot behind the gill cover, followed by a series of small spots along the flanks (sometimes absent). The pilchard grows to 8 in (20 cm) in length and is found from North Africa to the southern coasts of Norway and also in the Mediterranean and adjoining seas. The fishes of the North African coasts and the Mediterranean have slightly more gillrakers and are considered to belong to a distinct subspecies *S. pilchardus sardina.* The species spawns in autumn and winter in the southern part of its range, but in late summer in the north.

The pilchard is of considerable economic importance to several European countries. Adult fishes are caught off the coasts of Cornwall, England, and although the fishery is rather small, the canned products are of excellent quality. Larger fisheries exist along the French coasts of Brittany and the Bay of Biscay. Off the coasts of Spain, southern France and in the Mediterranean, the juvenile fishes, of about a year and a half, are caught in enormous numbers and are referred to as sardines. In Basque country the sardines are caught by ring-nets, the fishes being enticed into compact shoals either by casting *rogue* (salted Norwegian cod's roe) onto the water or by the use of powerful incandescent lamps at night.

The name sardine, and derivatives of it, is used almost throughout the world for small and silvery herring-like fishes, often only distantly related to the pilchard. In England, only the young of the pilchard are recognized for trade purposes as sardines, the tinned young of other species being marketed under other names.

Elsewhere along temperate coasts (except the western Atlantic coasts) the pilchard is replaced by members of the genus *Sardinops.*

The species of *Sardinops* are outwardly very similar to the pilchard. In Japan, *S. melanosticta* forms the overwhelming bulk of the great Iwashi fisheries (the anchovy *Engraulis japonicus* and the Round herring *Etrumeus teres* make up the rest). Large pilchard fisheries also exist along the Pacific coast of North America, and off the coasts of South Africa, Australia and New Zealand. FAMILY: Clupeidae, ORDER: Clupeiformes, CLASS: Pisces.

PILL BUG, name for those species of *woodlice that can roll up when disturbed. Formerly they were swallowed as pills, for their supposed medicinal properties.

PILL MILLIPEDES, short-bodied millipedes with 17 to 23 pairs of legs. The dorsal shield of the second body ring is larger than the others and is called the shield. Pill millipedes push their way through soil and litter and use the shield like the blade of a bulldozer. When the animal rolls-up into a 'pill', the dorsal shield on the tail or telson which is shaped like a quarter-sphere, overlaps the head and fits snugly into a special groove on the second shield. Apart from the Pill millipedes, some of the Flat-backed millipedes can also roll up.

In the male the ring before the telson carries two pairs of modified legs which are used as claspers in copulation. In the female this ring does not have legs. The species of *Spaerotherium,* found in Africa and the Indo-Australian region, are the largest 'pills' and can reach 3½ in (9 cm) long and 2 in (5 cm) wide. The Pill millipedes are mainly Palearctic and include the common European *Glomeris* with 17 or 19 pairs of legs according to the sex. Many species of this genus have characteristically patterned plates on the back, the patterns being variable within a species. In some species over 20 colour and pattern varieties have been described. ORDER: Pentazonia, CLASS: Diplopoda, PHYLUM: Arthropoda. J.G.B.

PILOTFISH *Naucrates ductor,* a small fish habitually associated with sharks and larger fishes and related to the mackerels and tunas. This pelagic fish is found all over the world in tropical and temperate oceans. The name comes from its alleged habit of not only accompanying sharks and sometimes other large fishes but of actually leading them to their prey. The pilotfish feeds on the scraps of food left by its host and thus deserves the name commensal (literally 'feeding from the same table'). Pilotfishes swim round sharks, making brief sorties and returning, but it is doubtful if they act as pilots. V. V. Shuleikin calculated that sharks swim three times as fast as a pilotfish. He suggested the pilotfishes are carried along by the shark's boundary layer, that is, the layer of water over its surface which travels at the same speed as the shark.

Pill millipedes, like some other armoured animals, such as sowbugs, armadillos and pangolins, respond to danger by rolling into a ball.

Young pilotfishes are often found sheltering amongst the tentacles of jellyfishes, a habit shared with the young of the Horse mackerel and the Portuguese man-o'-war fish.

The pilotfish has a mackerel-like body with the first dorsal fin reduced to a few low spines. The second dorsal fin and the anal fin are moderately long and are opposite each other. The body is dark blue on the back and silver on the sides with about six vertical dark bars on the flanks which fade with age. The fish grows to about 2 ft (60 cm) in length.

Fishes of the genus *Seriola*, and especially *S. zonata*, also have an association with sharks. This fish can be distinguished from the rather similar pilotfish by the presence of seven small spines joined by a membrane in front of the soft-rayed dorsal fin (four to five separated spines in *Naucrates*). Two other fishes have been reported as associating with sharks, the Rainbow runner *Elagatis bipinulatus* and the Starry jack *Caranx stellatus*, both of which have been seen escorting Grey sharks (*Carcharinus*) off the Galapagos Islands. FAMILY: Carangidae, ORDER: Perciformes, CLASS: Pisces.

PILOT WHALES, several species of large dolphins with a worldwide distribution. The North Atlantic species, *Globicephala melaena*, is also called the Ca'aing whale or blackfish. Adults are about 25 ft (8 m) in length and they are found in schools of several hundreds. As the name implies Pilot whales have a rounded forehead which bulges forward of the lower jaw. They are black overall but for a white patch below the jaw. The flippers are distinctive being relatively long and narrow, about one-fifth of the body length.

Pilot whales are highly social, yet nervous, and as a result of this fall an easy prey particularly in the Faroes where the economy of the Faroese has been to a considerable extent dependent upon them. When a school approaches the islands the boats congregate and form a line to the seaward of the school which is then driven towards a bay. A few are lanced and driven onto the beach and the remainder follow where they can be dispatched at leisure. The remarkable feature is that although some may escape to sea the social sense is so strong they return to the remainder.

The North Atlantic Pilot whale is found as far south as Scotland and New Jersey. There is evidence of some migration but how far is not certain. A very similar animal is found round the Cape of Good Hope and New Zealand and is said to be the same species. The other species are very similar externally but have skull differences. *G. scammoni* is the Pilot whale of the North Pacific and *G. edwardi* lives off the Indian and South American coasts. *G. macrorhyncha* has a rather shorter flipper and is found on the north coast of America. All three are entirely black.

The Slender blackfish *Feresa attenuata* is interesting as it was once thought to be very rare, only four records being known from around the world. Then in 1963 a school of 50 or so was seen around Hawaii and one was captured and kept on the Island of Oahu. In the same year a school of 14 was also seen off Japan. They were captured and transferred to Ito aquarium where unfortunately all except one died within a week, having refused to feed. The survivor took sardines, squids, sauries and Horse mackerel but died of pneumonia after 21 days.

These blackfish are about 7 ft (204–244 cm was the size range of the 14 Japanese animals). They are dark grey with white lips and white over the lower abdomen and white or pale grey between the flippers. All the Japanese animals had pale wavy stripes along the sides when alive but these faded after death. Very little is known about them but presumably as in the case of other Cetacea, the rarity probably reflects the rarity of trained observers in the right parts of the world. FAMILY: Delphinidae, ORDER: Cetacea, CLASS: Mammalia. K.M.B.

PINEAL ORGAN, the posterior member of a pair of tiny processes which develop in the mid-line from the roof of the posterior part of the forebrain of vertebrates, and project upwards towards the roof of the skull. The anterior member of the pair is known as the *parietal organ.

In some animals, such as the lampreys and possibly larval amphibians, the pineal organ may become differentiated at the tip to form what appears to be a light-sensitive structure, capable of distinguishing light from dark. In most vertebrate animals, however, the pineal organ appears to be glandular, and may be part of the endocrine system. Much remains to be discovered about the exact nature of its function or functions. It has been totally lost in most nocturnal and burrowing lizards, and all snakes.

PIN FEATHER, the term for a feather in the early stages of its growth before it has emerged from the sheath. In this condition the numerous feather barbs are wrapped up together in an elongated bundle and have a very different appearance from that seen after the sheath has broken.

PINION, the term used in a number of senses connected with a bird's wing. In a poetic sense it may refer to the whole wing, or it may be applied to the end joint only, which bears the primary feathers. Or again, it may refer to a single primary feather. It is also used as a verb, in which case a 'pinioned' bird is one which has had the end joint of one wing removed complete with primaries. This makes the bird lop-sided and unable to fly. A more humane alternative is clipping the primaries of one wing, a process that has to be repeated at intervals as the feathers regrow.

PINNIPEDIA, a group of aquatic mammals comprising the true seals, sealions, Fur seals and walruses, the three former groups sometimes known collectively as seals. The order Pinnipedia, although related to the order Carnivora, is now regarded as distinct. It is divided into three families: Phocidae, the true seals; Otariidae, the sealions and Fur seals; and Odobenidae, the walruses. Studies of skulls and chromosomes suggest that pinnipeds arose from carnivore ancestry; otariids and odobenids being closer to the dog-bear stock, and phocids closer to the otters. The very early history of the order is not known and the earliest fossil seals show that they differed relatively little from present day forms. The earliest known fossils are from Middle Miocene deposits in the United States, but the greatest development of phocids was in the waters of central Europe and Asia; otariids developed along the Pacific coast of North America, and walruses in the North Pacific.

Pinnipeds have streamlined bodies with forefeet and hindfeet modified into flippers usually by elongation of digits which have a web of skin between them. The tail is short, and external ears are reduced or absent. Fur is present, but is sparse on walrus and Elephant seal. The fine underfur hairs of Fur seals are abundant and provide the soft fur coats of commerce, while the longer guard hairs form the main part of the coat in phocids and sealions. Body temperature ranges from 97·7–99·5F (36·5–37·5C) and there is a thick layer of blubber over the body. Fur seals are insulated from their cold environment by blubber and thick fur. Phocids contract peripheral blood vessels allowing their skin to cool to almost water temperature, while their inner body temperature remains constant. Milk dentition is feeble, lasting about six months in otariids and shed about the time of birth in phocids. Permanent cheekteeth vary from simple cones to complexly cusped structures. Annual rings are present in the dentine and cement of canines and it is possible to estimate age by them. The alimentary canal is uncomplicated, but the stomach frequently contains large numbers of pebbles, the exact function of which is unknown. The kidney is composed of a large number of small units or renules, each like a miniature kidney. The lungs have myo-elastic valves in the bronchi which may prevent collapse of the lung when the seal is diving and under pressure, and may also keep the residual air in the more rigid parts of the lung where nitrogen absorption is less easy, thus preventing the animal from suffering from the 'bends'. The eyes are adapted to see clearly in air and under water, but since a lacrimal duct is absent the tears run down the face. Hearing is probably the most important sense. A variety of underwater sounds has been recorded and some food is probably found by echolocating, as totally blind seals are still well nourished. Only one pup is produced each year, and breeding behaviour varies from the polygamous harems of the sealions, Fur seals and Elephant seals, where one male controls a harem of 20 or more females, to the monogamous family groups of male, female and pup in the Hooded and Harp seals.

Seals can remain under water for about half an hour and must therefore keep their brains supplied with oxygenated blood for as long as possible. The large quantity of blood can store much oxygen and has a reduced sensitivity to CO_2. The blood flow round the body is reduced by contracting the peripheral blood vessels, and also by a drastic reduction in the heart rate to about a tenth of its normal speed. Weddell seals dive regularly to depths of 980–1,310 ft (3–400 m) and can remain under water for up to 40 minutes.   J.E.K.

PIN WORM *Enterobius vermicularis,* a nematode parasite which lives in the large intestine of humans. It is particularly common in children in warm countries, and infection rates of 40% have been recorded. The adult parasite attaches itself to the wall of the gut of its host, and when the female is ready to lay her eggs she migrates to the anal region of the host, where the eggs are deposited. The irritation that results often causes the host to dislodge the eggs by scratching, and these may be ingested again from contaminated fingers. If no re-infection occurs, the initial infection dies out in about a month. SUBORDER: Ascardina, ORDER: Rhabditida, CLASS: Nematoda, PHYLUM: Aschelminthes.

PIPEFISHES, a family of highly elongated and rather specialized fishes related to the trumpetfishes, shrimpfishes and Sea horses. They have a world-wide distribution and although mainly marine include some freshwater species. The long, thin body is completely encased in bony rings but it is surprisingly flexible and prehensile. The fish is well camouflaged for a rather secretive life amongst weeds. The pelvic fins and the tail are often lacking. The prehensile body is developed to its greatest extent in the Sea horses, the head being bent at an angle to the body. There are pipefishes that approach this arrangement but still retain the head in the normal position.

The pipefishes show a most interesting method of caring for their young. In the most primitive forms (e.g. *Nerophis*) the

Most pipefishes, a family of highly elongated and specialized fishes, live in the sea. A few, like this *Syngnathus pulchellus*, of the Congo, have become adapted to a freshwater life.

fertilized eggs are stuck together on the underside of the male. In the next and more advanced group the eggs are embedded singly in a spongy layer that develops along the belly of the male. Finally, in forms like *Doryrhamphus* the bony plates encasing the body are enlarged to form a groove in which the eggs are placed. This is carried to the extreme in the Sea horses where the male has a distinct brood pouch.

There are six species of pipefishes found along British shores. One of the largest of these is the Great pipefish *Syngnathus acus,* a species which reaches 18 in (45 cm) in length. It has a small anal fin and a small tail. As in all pipefishes the rays of the dorsal fin are soft and flexible and each ray can be moved independently. This is important because like the Sea horses, the pipefishes swim by undulations of the dorsal fin. The small Worm pipefish *Nerophis lumbriciformis* rarely grows to more than 6 in (15 cm). The body is dark brown and the body plates are not easily seen. It is often found on the shore under stones and weeds. In July the males can be found with eggs stuck to the underside of their body.

Most pipefishes are rather drab in colour, but the male of the Straight-nosed pipefish *Nerophis ophidion* has a greenish body with blue lines along the abdomen. Some of the pipefishes are quite small. *Doryrhamphus melanopleura* from coral reefs of the Pacific region reaches only $2\frac{1}{2}$ in (6·5 cm) in length. It is bright orange-red with a longitudinal bright blue band from the snout to the tail, the latter being orange at its base, followed by blue with a white margin.

Most pipefishes live among corals or

weeds in shallow water, but a few live in burrows and *Corythoichthys fasciatus,* of the Indo-Pacific, inhabits the intestinal cavity of bêche-de-mer. *Syngnathus pelagicus,* on the other hand, is pelagic and lives amongst the sargassum weed floating at the surface in the Atlantic.

Some pipefishes can live contentedly in tropical aquaria provided that an adequate supply of live food is available. *Syngnathus spicifer* and *S. pulchellus* from the Congo are frequently imported but have rarely been bred in captivity. Even *Nerophis ophidion* from British coasts has populations in the fresh parts of the Baltic and has been kept in aquaria with only very slightly salted water.

The hobbyhorses or pipehorses are rather rare little pipefishes found largely in the Pacific. In many ways they bridge the gap between the pipefishes and the Sea horses. The genus *Acentroneura* contains small species which rarely exceed 3 in (7·5 cm) in length. The head is very slightly tilted from the main axis of the body and the tail is prehensile. To break the outline of the fish there are little sprig-like fringes irregularly scattered about the body, a type of camouflage also found in the young of some pipefishes (e.g. *Larvicampus runa*) but one that attains its greatest development in the Sea dragons. See Sea horses. FAMILY: Syngnathidae, ORDER: Gasterosteiformes, CLASS: Pisces.

PIPE SNAKES, once widespread, now comprise only three genera of non-poisonous snakes. They show many primitive features several of which are shared with the late Cretaceous and oldest known fossil snakes

Dinilysia and in some respects Pipe snakes are intermediate between the boas and shield-tails. Hindlimb vestiges are present as two spurs, close to the cloaca. There are two lungs but the left lung is less than a tenth the length of the right. On the underside there are enlarged belly scales, one to each vertebra, but these are not as wide as in most snakes. The skull bones are solidly joined and the jaws are not very flexible. Most Pipe snakes have a spectacle covering the eye but in the genus *Anilius* the eye is beneath the head scales. .

Most Pipe snakes belong to the genus *Cylindrophis* found in Ceylon and from Burma to the Malay Archipelago. Another genus, *Anomochilus,* is found in Malaya and Sumatra. The third genus, *Anilius,* occurs in South America. All the family are ovovivi-parous, giving birth to small litters of young, each of which may be half the length of the parent. All burrow underground or in surface litter. The skull is unsuitable for very large prey but they are recorded as eating eels and snakes as long as themselves. Some of the

Pipe snakes have interesting protective devices. The Guyanan pipe snake or False coral snake *Anilius scytale* is banded black and red, mimicking a poisonous snake of the same country. The Malayan pipe snake *Cylindrophis rufus* lifts its tail when molested, showing the crimson below as it waves it above its body, giving the appearance of a threatening head. FAMILY: Aniliidae, ORDER: Squamata, CLASS: Reptilia.   J.S.

PIPIDAE, a family of frogs, the only one in the so-called Aglossa, which means 'without a tongue', one of the adaptations to an aquatic life. Others are the absence of eyelids, a flattened body, powerful hindlegs and large webbed feet. There are four genera, and these fall into two distinct groups. There are the American forms of the genus *Pipa* and the African forms of the genera **Xenopus, Hymenochirus* and *Pseudohymenochirus.*

The strange-looking frogs of the genus *Xenopus* are known as 'platannas', a South African word meaning 'flat-handed'. All the members of the Pipidae, in fact, have this

character. When swimming in the water the front legs, which are small and feeble, are held out in front of the head with the fingers spread out in a fan. They act as feelers and as soon as they touch anything in the murky water which might be food they push it to the mouth. In *Pipa* this sensory function is aided by a star-like cluster of papillae at the end of each finger.

Pipa pipa, the Surinam toad, is found in the Amazon and the Orinoco. Its blackish-brown body is flattened making it difficult to see in muddy waters. The Surinam toad has an unusual method of breeding; the eggs develop in small pits in the female's back. During amplexus the male grasps the female just in front of her hindlegs and the two swim upwards in a loop in the water. At the top of the loop they are upside-down and at this point the eggs are released by the female and fall onto the belly of the male. They are then fertilized and move onto the female's back. They are pressed further up her back by movements of the male and then stick to her skin. The female then remains still while the

The African clawed frog *Xenopus laevis* is one of the tongueless frogs which are sometimes placed in a suborder Aglossa on their own.

skin of her back swells up around the eggs until each one is enclosed in a pit closed with a lid which is probably a hardened secretion of the female's skin. In them the eggs develop. In some species it is tadpoles which emerge while in others further development occurs and small frogs push off the lids of their pockets and swim out.

Hymenochirus is similar in some respects to *Xenopus*. Three of the toes have claws although the fingers are also partly webbed. ORDER: Anura, CLASS: Amphibia.   M.E.D.

PIPING CROWS, alternative name for *Australian magpies of the genus *Gymnorhina* in recognition of their loud melodious, warbling notes. These species are well-known for the chorus given by parties of birds, particularly at dawn. The small social groups gather in trees to give these calls which probably indicate communal territory ownership. FAMILY: Cracticidae, ORDER: Passeriformes, CLASS: Aves

PIPITS, small, sombrely-coloured terrestrial birds belonging to three genera, which together with the wagtails *Motacilla* and the Forest wagtail *Dendronanthus,* make up the family Motacillidae. They are generally brown, streaked with black above, and buffish white or yellow, with or without streaks, below. The sexes are usually alike. The tail is relatively long and is often bobbed up and down in a wagtail fashion. The bill is fine and pointed, the legs long and slender and the hind claw often very long. Although frequently quoted as being exceptional amongst passerines in possessing only nine pairs of primary wing feathers, pipits do in fact possess the normal quota of ten, the tenth pair being very much reduced.

Pipits are very much birds of open ground, inhabiting grassland, steppe and savannah country, usually in well-watered areas, alpine meadows in mountainous regions and arctic tundra, although a few species prefer areas with scattered bushes or trees. They walk or run but never hop. Most pipits occasionally perch on trees, particularly when disturbed, but few species do so habitually. The name 'pipit' is derived from the thin, twittering call uttered by many species in flight. The general similarity of pipits to larks has in some regions earned them the name 'titlarks'. However, they differ in the sides of the tarsus being covered with an unbroken sheath. Other features suggest a closer relationship to the Old World thrushes and warblers, Muscicapidae.

The genus *Anthus* contains some 34 species of confusingly similar colouration and cosmopolitan distribution. They are best represented in the Old World, occurring in suitable habitats throughout Africa (14 breeding species) and Eurasia (13 breeding species). One species occurs in Australia and

New Zealand, two in North America and seven in South America. The Antarctic pipit *A. antarcticus* is restricted to the subantarctic island of South Georgia and the New Guinea pipit *A. gutturalis* to the mountains of New Guinea. The other two genera, *Macronyx* (eight species) and *Tmetothylacus* (one species) are restricted to Africa.

Almost all pipits of the genus *Anthus* are brown above, buffish-white below and more or less heavily streaked, with prominent white outer tail feathers. One of the most widespread, Richard's pipit *A. novaezeelandiae,* occurs from New Zealand and the neighbouring subantarctic islands through Australia and Southeast Asia to India and also over much of Africa. Although absent from the Middle East and Europe as a breeding species, it has occurred irregularly on migration as far west as Britain. The Tawny pipit *A. campestris* prefers drier habitats than most pipits, occurring on sandy wastes, arid pastures, and barren rocky ground in southwest Asia, southern Europe and north Africa. Two of the commonest pipits in Europe, the Tree pipit *A. trivialis* and the Meadow pipit *A. pratensis,* although very similar in appearance, show quite different habitat preferences. The Tree pipit is a bird of wood edges, forest clearings and heaths with scattered trees. It seems that elevated perches are essential to Tree pipits during the breeding season as the erection of a line of telegraph poles across an otherwise

Male Golden pipit, of East Africa.

bare heath may lead to their colonizing the area. The Meadow pipit prefers rough grassland, moors and grassy tundra. It is replaced ecologically farther east by the Red-throated pipit *A. cervinus*. This is very similar in appearance to the Meadow pipit in winter, but in summer it has a brick red throat and breast, which makes it quite distinctive.

The pipit *A. spinoletta* of Eurasia and North America occurs in a number of populations which are readily separable into two groups: the Water pipits which are almost entirely inland forms of alpine meadows and arctic tundra, and the Rock pipits which are restricted to the rocky coasts and islands of western Europe from France to northern Scandinavia. The winter plumages are similar, but in spring the Water pipits undergo an almost complete body moult which gives a bluish grey tinge to the upper-parts, and an almost unstreaked breast with a pinkish wash. The Rock pipits, undergoing only a very incomplete spring moult, retain their sombre brown plumage throughout the year.

The common pipit of North America, Sprague's pipit *A. spragueii,* occurs in the prairie grassland of the central states and southern Canada. The closely related Correndera pipit *A. correndera* of South America occurs on open grassland and damp meadows from central Peru and southern Brazil to Tierra del Fuego and the Falkland Islands. Several pipits inhabit the grasslands and savannah of Africa, but two

Tree pipit, of Europe, bringing food to nestlings.

species, the Long-legged pipit *A. palli-diventris* and the local Sokoke pipit *A. sokokensis,* prefer forest clearings and fairly dense bush country. The Yellow-breasted pipit *A. chloris* of South Africa is exceptional amongst the *Anthus* pipits in that in spring the underparts are bright yellow.

The genus *Tmetothylacus* contains a single species, the Golden pipit *T. tenellus* which is restricted to East Africa. The male is almost entirely bright yellow, except for dark streaking on the back and a black pectoral band, whereas the female is dusky brown. It is somewhat intermediate between the true pipits and the wagtails, living in dry open scrub, perching freely on trees and wagging its tail conspicuously.

The genus *Macronyx* contains eight species of aberrant pipit known as the longclaws. The group is confined to Africa south of the Sahara. Longclaws are common and conspicuous birds of well-watered grassland, and cultivated open country, particularly where there is a scattering of bushes. They are larger and stouter birds than true pipits, with heavier bills and very long hind claws. It has been suggested that the extreme

elongation of the claws, which may be as long as 2 in (5 cm) in some species, facilitates running through long grass. Although the colour of the upperparts resembles that of other pipits, the underparts of most longclaws are bright yellow, with a more or less well defined black pectoral band. This is most extensive in the Yellow-breasted longclaw *M. croceus* and forms a black gorget, giving the species a remarkable resemblance to the unrelated meadowlarks of North America, which occur in similar habitats. In the Rosy-breasted longclaw *M. ameliae* the yellow is replaced by rosy-red.

Pipits are almost invariably ground nesters. The nest is a well-made cup of dried grasses, lined with finer materials and well concealed in a depression in the ground in low vegetation, in the side of a tussock or occasionally amongst stunted bushes. The Rock and Water pipits, however, commonly nest amongst boulders or in crevices on cliff faces. There is a tendency for the clutch size to vary with latitude, species in equatorial regions laying as few as two or three eggs, those at high latitudes up to six or seven. The eggs are typically whitish or dirty pink,

heavily streaked or spotted with brown.

The song is poorly developed, occasionally no more than a monotonous repetition of one note, although more usually it consists of a tinkling sequence of similar, rather thin and feeble notes which may or may not end in a trill. It is usually delivered from a short song-flight which commonly takes the form of a rapid ascent to some height and then a slow fluttering descent back to earth with the wings and tail pointing upwards. The Tree pipit is one of the most accomplished performers, giving a pleasant melodious song in a short song-flight which usually ends on a tree top. Some of the longclaws, notably the Rosy-breasted longclaw, deliver a plaintive whistling song whilst soaring or hovering, sometimes at great height.

The food of all pipits is mostly insects, although a few seeds may be taken in winter. Several African species are particularly fond of termites. The Rock pipit has a more varied diet of small worms, sandhoppers and periwinkles, in addition to a wide variety of insects.

Most pipits live singly or in pairs through-

Piranhas, South American river fishes, are credited with unusual ferocity, yet some species, including the Red piranha, are kept as aquarium fishes.

out the year but a few species regularly congregate in small groups or loose flocks outside the breeding season. Some species are long-distance migrants, particularly those breeding at high latitudes. The majority, however, are either sedentary or make only limited movements. High montane species usually descend to lower levels in winter and several African species undertake local movements associated with the rains. The way in which the shape of the wing has become adapted to the needs of the bird is well illustrated in the pipits. Pointed wings are the most efficient for long-distance flights and, even within species, slight variations in the wing shape can usually be correlated with the distances the various forms migrate. The longest-distance migrants, the Tree pipit and the Pechora pipit *A. gustavi,* have only three primaries in the wing point but the remaining palearctic migrants, travelling lesser distances, have four, while most of the sedentary pipits of Africa have five, giving the wing a very blunt, rounded shape. FAMILY: Motacillidae, ORDER: Passeriformes, CLASS: Aves. D.A.S.

PIRANHAS or caribes, small but very ferocious freshwater fishes from South America belonging to the family Characidae. They are renowned for their carnivorous habits and are amongst the most infamous of all fishes. Travellers' tales relate cases where large animals and even men have been attacked and the flesh picked off their bones in a very short space of time. At river crossings in South America a look-out is kept for the shoals of piranhas so that people

fording the river can be warned. There are several species involved, the largest growing to about 15 in (38 cm). The jaws are short and powerful and are armed with sharp cutting teeth. Their main diet is fish or mammals but they are reputed to be strongly attracted to the smell of blood so that a single bite will draw hundreds of other members of the shoal to the same spot.

The White piranha *Serrasalmus rhombeus* of the Amazon is one of the largest species. The body is olive to silver with irregular dark blotches. The Red piranha *Rooseveltiella nattereri,* also from the Amazon, grows to 12 in (30 cm) and has an olive-brown back, light brown flanks and numerous bright silver spots on the body. The belly and the fin bases are, appropriately enough, blood red; the dorsal and anal fins are black.

Provided that one is not squeamish, the piranhas make interesting aquarium pets. They are not unattractive but must be provided with live food to keep them in the best condition. If 20 or more are kept together they will attack anything that moves in the water. If only one or two are kept, however, they will cower in the corners of the tank until they have 'egged' each other on to attack. As in the phenomenon known as 'feeding frenzy' in sharks, it appears that intensive feeding is stimulated by the sight of others also attacking. FAMILY: Characidae, ORDER: Cypriniformes, CLASS: Pisces.

PIROPLASMS, minute single-celled parasites which occupy the red blood cells of vertebrates and are best known as the

causative organisms of a variety of serious diseases in cattle throughout the world. Under the general heading of piroplasms there are two distinct groups of organisms. *Babesia* inhabits the red cells of vertebrates and divides inside them to form two or occasionally four daughters which invade fresh blood cells. There are no other stages in the blood. In the second group, represented by *Theileria,* the stages of division occur in endothelial cells and the products of this division enter the red blood cells but do not divide any further in them. In both of these groups the parasites are transmitted from host to host by ticks and the actual cycles within the ticks are obscure. It is not known for certain, for example, whether there are any special sexual stages. The cycle within the tick is of interest because in some cases the parasites pass via the eggs to the next generation of ticks. This method of transmission is known as transovarian transmission and this is important because it ensures that a tick which spends its life on a single host produces offspring which will continue to spread the infection.

Among the diseases of cattle caused by piroplasms are red-water fever in Africa, America, Asia, Australasia and Europe and east coast fever in Africa. These diseases cause considerable losses among cattle. There is also a disease of dogs caused by these parasites. Man is occasionally infected with piroplasmosis but the only recorded cases are of people who have lost their spleens as the result of accidents. The piroplasms have long been classified with the *Malaria parasites which they resemble superficially, except that they do not produce any pigment. However, the apparent absence of any sexual forms and the life-cycle in the tick, in contrast to the mosquito, suggest that they should be separated from the Malaria parasites and this has been done in some recent classifications. More recent investigations have shown that at the electron microscope level the similarities between the piroplasms and the Malaria parasites are very marked, and the present tendency is to classify them as a distinct group somewhere close to the Malaria parasites. ORDER: Piroplasmida, CLASS: Piroplasmea, PHYLUM: Protozoa. F.E.G.C.

PISTOL SHRIMPS, relatively small shrimps with one pincer very much larger than the other. A shrimp with a body 1 in (2·5 cm) long may have one front pincer $\frac{4}{5}$ in (2 cm) long. The moveable finger of the enlarged pincer can be locked in the open position, and then suddenly snapped to the closed position, producing a sharp sound. This sudden discharge is used to stun prey, mainly by the shock wave rather than by direct contact. Some of the larger species, with bodies up to 2 in (5 cm) in length, can stun small fish with their pistol-like discharges. Some Pistol

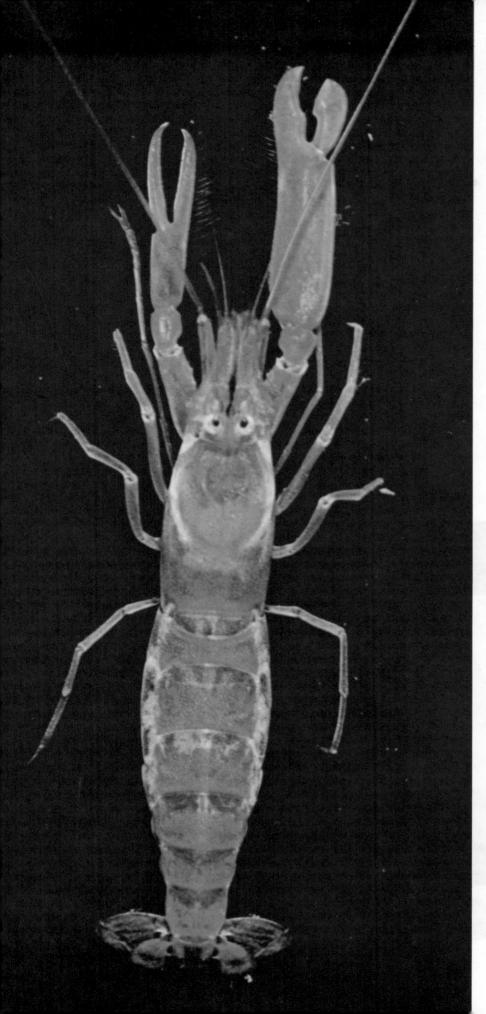

shrimps have been observed to catch worms with their small pincers and then to stun them by 'shooting' them with their large pincers.

The Pistol shrimps are often found in pairs in cavities in rocky shores, and some species are regularly found inside sponges. They may live for about eight years. FAMILY: Alpheidae, SUBORDER: Natantia, ORDER: Decapoda, CLASS: Crustacea, PHYLUM: Arthropoda.

PITHECANTHROPINES, erect-standing ape-men living 400,000–500,000 years ago whose relics were first found in Java in 1894. See man, the evolution of.

PITTAS, beautifully coloured ground-living birds which are very plump, with short wings and tail, and powerful legs and feet. They belong to the small family Pittidae and are generally regarded as being primitive members of the order Passeriformes. They form a very homogeneous group, very similar in size and shape, and can all be referred to the single genus *Pitta*. Because of their gorgeous colouration, they have been called 'jewel-thrushes'. The allusion to thrushes is ill-chosen, however, for they are not conspicuously thrush-like in appearance, nor related to them. The pittas are, without a doubt, among the most beautiful birds in the world. Few others have so many varied colours combined in their plumage. The male Green-breasted pitta *Pitta sordida* of Southeast Asia, for example, has a brown and black head, green back and breast, red under-tail coverts, blue rump and wings patterned boldly with blue, black and white. Other species display even more gaudy arrays of colour, but one or two, like the Banded pitta *Pitta guajana* of Malaysia, have a relatively sombre pattern of browns, relieved only by small splashes of bright colour. The females of most species are much duller than the males, and a few are quite drab-looking.

The group is centred around tropical Southeast Asia where most of the 23 species live. Two species occur in Africa and a few in New Guinea, tropical Australia and adjacent Pacific Islands. The Blue-winged pitta *Pitta brachyura* breeds outside the tropics in India, China and Japan, but migrates south in the northern winter, and is then often common in the forests of Ceylon, Malaya and Indonesia.

Pittas are characteristically birds of the forest, but they are not confined to any one vegetation type, being found in lowland and mountain rain-forest, bamboo thicket and coastal mangroves. When feeding, they move about quickly on the forest floor by hopping, but can fly rapidly if they have to.

Pistol shrimp *Alpheus glaber*, of European seas, stuns its prey with a snapping noise made with the large claw.

Their food is apparently very varied: spiders, ants and other insects, snails and seeds have all been found in the stomachs of shot specimens. Though they probably obtain all their food on the ground, they do fly into trees on occasion, and roost on branches at night. Generally speaking, pittas are shy birds, more often heard than seen, despite their showy appearance.

Their nests are large, untidy constructions of sticks, dead leaves and roots, built on, or near, the ground. The young remain in the nest for several weeks and are fed by both parents.

The pittas provide an interesting example of 'convergent evolution'. The 'niche' they occupy in the Asian and African forests—as small terrestrial birds scratching among the leaf litter for their food—is occupied in the American jungles by members of two families of pitta-like birds, not thought to be closely related to pittas. These are the antpittas *Gralleria* spp, belonging to the large family of antbirds (Formicariidae), and the gnat-eaters, or antpipits, which constitute the family Conophagidae. All these birds have evolved along similar lines (though probably starting from dissimilar ancestors) as they became adapted to the same way of life on the jungle floor. Thus they now resemble each other very much in size and shape—though the New World birds are not brightly coloured. FAMILY: Pittidae. ORDER: Passeriformes, CLASS: Aves.   P.W.

PITUITARY, an endocrine gland attached by a short stalk to the underside of the brain in vertebrates. It produces a number of *hormones, probably at least ten in mammals, which are liberated directly into the blood stream. Through these secretions the pituitary controls a wide range of metabolic activities, either by acting directly on the structures concerned, for example, the stimulation of milk secretion by prolactin, or more commonly by influencing the activity of other endocrine glands such as the thyroid and adrenal glands and the endocrine cells of the gonads, which in turn act directly on the appropriate structures.

PIT VIPERS, a very important group of highly venomous snakes, of which the best known are the *rattlesnakes of North America. The Pit vipers are either placed in a separate family of snakes, the Crotalidae, or in a subfamily, the Crotalinae of the family of true vipers, Viperidae. In the latter classification the true vipers constitute the subfamily Viperinae. In this account the Pit vipers are regarded as a family in their own right because the differences between them and the true vipers, although few, are mostly clear-cut and probably indicate that the two groups are not very closely related.

Pit vipers are so called because they possess a double pit in front of, and slightly below, the eye. The two halves of this cavity are separated by a translucent membrane which is richly innervated and bears a large number of sensory nerve endings. The forward chamber of the cavity has a fairly obvious external opening, which may be more noticeable than the nostrils; hence the crotalids are sometimes known locally as 'four nostrils'. The posterior section of the pit also has an external opening, but this is usually hidden and is placed just in front of the eye. The double pit on each side of the head is accompanied in a deep hollow in the bone known as the maxilla. Experiments with rattlesnakes *Crotalus* and also with copperheads *Agkistrodon contortrix* appear to have demonstrated that the membrane in the pit is exceedingly sensitive to changes in temperature and that it is used by the snake to detect the presence of animals which are warmer than their surroundings. Pit vipers which have been blindfolded are able to follow the movements of warm-blooded prey very accurately up to distances of about 6 ft (1·8 m), but they only strike when near enough to reach the prey. The only teeth present in the upper jaw are the long, curved fangs which are in paired sockets in the maxilla to allow for periodic replacement on each side. However, smaller teeth are present on the lower jaw and the pterygoid and palatine bones of the palate, so that the prey can be held very firmly once gripped. The maxilla of Pit vipers is noticeably very short and rectangular, especially compared to that of non-poisonous snakes. This shape is closely correlated with the swinging, forward movement it makes when the snake strikes with the jaws open, allowing the long fangs to assume a vertical position and thus penetrate the prey. The cavity in the maxilla and the associated sensory pit are the most important characters that distinguish the Pit vipers or crotalids from the true vipers. True vipers also tend to have longer poison fangs and shorter, thicker bodies than the Pit vipers.

Pit vipers are distributed through eastern Europe, much of Asia and Japan, and the Indo-Australian Archipelago, but their principal stronghold is in the New World, where live the rattlesnakes. Unlike the true vipers, the crotalids are absent from Africa.

The South and Central American genus of crotalids known as *Bothrops* includes several very poisonous, long fanged species. One of the most important of these is the fer-de-lance *B. atrox* which occurs throughout Brazil, Peru, Central America and much of Mexico, as well as many West Indian Islands, and attains a length of 10 ft (3 m). The fer-de-lance (literally, the iron of the lance) is named from the characteristic shape of its head. It frequently hampers the development of new areas for agriculture in many parts of

Blue-winged pitta, of southern and eastern Asia. Pittas are considered by some people the most beautiful of all birds.

Crossed Pit viper *Bothrops alternatus*. Pit vipers have a pit on each side, used as heat-detectors to strike at warmblooded prey.

tropical America since it occurs most commonly in forests and near running water. After the ground has been cleared, the fer-de-lance may return, especially to sugar and banana plantations. Although the immature snakes are tree climbers, adults of this species tend to remain on the ground. When excited, the fer-de-lance vibrates its tail vigorously against the ground and creates a rapid tapping sound which serves to alarm predators and enemies. The young probably feed mainly on amphibians such as frogs but adults prey primarily on mammals such as opossums and rats. Another well known species is the jararaca *Bothrops jararaca* which is the cause of many serious cases of snakebite in Brazil. The jararaca grows to a length of 5 ft (1·5 m) and is pale velvety brown or olive, with yellow marks having black margins on the sides of the body. The largest Pit viper is the tropical American bushmaster *Lachesis muta* which may reach 12 ft (3·6 m) and is one of the most feared venomous snakes. The bushmaster is a forest dweller and, although widely known and respected, is nowhere common. Other Pit vipers, of the genus *Agkistrodon,* are well known in North America. The copperhead *A. contortrix* and the cottonmouth or moccasin *A. piscivorus* are both fairly common and highly venomous. Halys pit viper *A. halys* occurs over much of Central Asia and extends into eastern Europe, where it is found in the area of the Volga delta.

Most Pit vipers, except the bushmaster and some Old World Pit vipers, are ovoviviparous, that is, the eggs hatch inside the body of the mother and the young are born alive. The bushmaster buries its eggs in the litter of the forest floor.

The non-poisonous kingsnake *Lampropeltis* is one of the few enemies of rattlesnakes. When a rattlesnake is threatened by a kingsnake it lowers its head and arches the middle section of the body off the ground and attempts to fend off its attacker with the arched body loop. This posture makes it difficult for the kingsnake to grasp its prey's head in order to swallow it.

In areas having cold winters rattlesnakes often aggregate in large numbers, together with tortoises and frogs, to hibernate. For example, hundreds of Great Basin rattlesnakes *Crotalus viridis* annually congregate in underground channels near Lake Bonneville, Utah. It is clear that many must travel long distances in order to assemble there and it is possible that this annual migration represents a learned behaviour pattern on the part of the adult snakes. FAMILY: Crotalidae, ORDER: Squamata, CLASS: Reptilia.   M.J.P.

PLACENTA, a name from Latin meaning literally a 'flat cake' and first used to describe the structure of that shape which attaches the developing human embryo and foetus to the wall of the uterus. It is the organ responsible for the transmission of material between mother and embryo before birth. But all placentae are not cake-like. Virtually all possible forms of transfer mechanism have been used in the various viviparous animals and methods of placentation. Although transfer is obviously the primary function of the placentae are not cake-like. Virtually all living organisms, has led to this structure being used for other purposes associated with the pregnant state. In many species of animals, for instance, it has important endocrine roles, producing hormones, required in

pregnancy. The placenta therefore can be considered as the structure which acts as the essential contact bridge between the mother and her totally dependent foetus (or foetuses) and, as well, acts to some extent as an endocrine supporter of the whole maternal-foetal state. The placenta is essentially a product of the developing ovum or egg and therefore must be considered as a part of a foeto-placental complex.

When the ovum is released by the ovary and fertilized it eventually comes to be in the cavity of the uterine horn or, as in the case of the human species, in a central common uterus or womb. As it moves freely towards the area where it will eventually settle and develop, division of the single-celled ovum occurs to form, firstly, a ball of cells, a morula, which then develops a central cavity to form a hollow ball of cells, the blastocyst. Within the blastocyst a few cells form a small knob which usually projects into its cavity. Of the whole mass, these are the only ones which develop into the embryo and foetus. The circumferential cells of the ball are responsible for forming the supporting structures of the developing embryo, the surface chorion, the placenta and placental membranes and the umbilical cord by which the embryo is attached to this placental system.

In some animals such as the viviparous fishes and some reptiles the egg has a considerable amount of yolk which serves, as in the oviparous animals, as a food store. But extra nutrition as well as respiratory exchange is achieved by attachment of the yolk sac and the surrounding chorion to the uterus so forming what is called a yolk sac placentation. Some reptile species do produce actual fusion of the chorion and the underlying allantois, a sac developed particularly for respiratory exchange and of great importance in mammals, with the maternal uterine wall in a fairly complex manner.

Among the marsupials the degree and character of attachment of the embryo to the uterus varies with the length of embryonic development in the uterus, though some show much the same complexity as the specialized lizards.

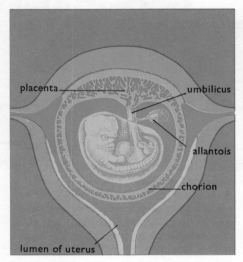

Section through mammalian womb showing the developing embryo attached by the placenta to the uterine wall.

It is among the eutherian mammals that placentation generally takes in its full range of patterns. In many species the whole chorionic sac becomes connected to the uterine wall and transfer of materials occurs over the whole surface, but in others much more developed systems occur whereby areas of the chorion become more highly specialized achieving a more intimate relationship with maternal tissues. These are the more circumscribed and specialized placentae such as the human placenta from which the name 'cake-like' arose.

The important feature of a placenta is the close contact between the foetal blood vessels in the placenta and those of the mother in the uterine wall. The foetal circulation is connected to the placenta by the umbilical arteries and vein and the blood flow maintained by the foetal heart. Obviously the closer the relationship between the bloods without actual mixing the better.

In an epithelio-chorial placenta as found in the hoofed animals (Artiodactyla, Perissodactyla), whales, pangolins and lemurs, the wall of the uterus retains its surface epithelium as does the chorion and the blood vessels of each lie deep to each surface epithelium. The minimum separation of bloods is therefore four cells thick, two epithelial surfaces and the blood vessels' lining endothelia. Hence it is essential to have a very large surface area. The separation is reduced in the carnivores, the sloths and Tree shrews by chorionic digestion of the surface epithelium of the uterus. The chorion now comes into contact with the endothelium of the maternal blood vessels, and this is known as an endothelial-chorial placenta. If further digestion of the maternal tissues occurs the maternal blood vessel walls are broken down and the chorion is now directly in contact with the maternal blood stream. This is a haemo-chorial placenta as found in many primates including man, rodents, bats and most insectivores. Being more efficient it can be more circumscribed.

The epithelio-chorial placenta, being only in contact with the uterine wall, is readily shed by the uterus when the foetus is born without damage to the maternal tissues; it is said to be non-deciduous. The more invasive varieties can only be lost by separation through the uterine tissues and birth is of necessity associated with some degree of maternal bleeding and need of repair. These are known as deciduous placentae. In fact, in many of the haemochorial placentae, such as that of man, the blastocyst actually digests the lining wall or endometrium of the uterus and comes to lie within it. The endometrium then heals over the blastocyst and as it grows it does so fully surrounded by endometrium. The true placenta forms on the deep aspect of the endometrium in which the blastocyst is contained; i.e. nearest the uterine wall. When the baby is born, bursting of the membranes include bursting out of the now very thin layer of stretched endometrium which covers the chorion. The placenta separates from the uterus as a result of rupture of the uterine blood vessels and tissues when the uterus contracts down after expulsion of the baby. Bleeding between uterus and placenta produces a clot which seals off the broken blood vessels and forms the basis for endometrial repair.   K.M.B.

PLAGUE GRASSHOPPERS, two species of *locust in Australia, known respectively as the Large plague locust *Chortoicetes terminifera* and the Small plague locust *Austroicetes cruciata.*

PLAICE *Pleuronectes platessa,* perhaps the most popular of all the edible European flatfishes. The common name derives from an Old French word for flat. The plaice is one of the most easily identified species because of the irregular orange spots on the upper surface which persist after the fish is dead (similar spots in the flounder soon disappear when the fish is out of water). The blind side is a translucent white. Unlike the flounder, there are no rough scales on the head or at the start of the lateral line, but there are small tubercles between the eyes. In contrast to most of the flatfishes, the plaice is a sedentary species, found mainly over sand or gravel. It is, therefore, very susceptible to overfishing and the maintenance of a fishery depends on strict control of catches to balance the natural replacement each year. Experiments have been conducted in the rearing of young plaice for restocking depleted areas and also in the transferring of plaice from British North Sea coasts, where they are numerous, to the eastern shores of the North Sea where growth conditions are better. Plaice grow to 33 in (83 cm) and may reach 15 lb (6·7 kg) in weight. FAMILY: Pleuronectidae, ORDER: Pleuronectiformes, CLASS: Pisces.

PLAINS WANDERER *Pedionomus torquatus,* a small quail-like bird closely related to buttonquails, but placed in its own separate family. It is confined to open grasslands of southeastern Australia. The role of the sexes is reversed, the female being bigger, more brightly-coloured, the male incubating the eggs and caring for the young. This species differs from buttonquails in possessing a hind toe, in the hairy texture of its feathers and in having a clutch of four large, pear-shaped eggs. It also tends to move in a very upright posture, raised on the toes, unlike the crouching postures of buttonquails. FAMILY: Pedionomidae, ORDER: Gruiformes, CLASS: Aves.

A plaice can be recognized by its red spots which persist when the fish is dead. Plaice can change colour to match the colours of the sea-bed on which they are lying, as is shown in these pictures of the same specimen.

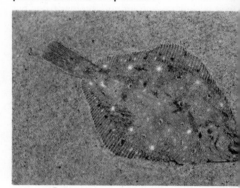

PLANARIANS, generally regarded as the most primitive of the many-celled bilaterally symmetrical animals or Metazoa. Nevertheless, they have shown remarkable powers of adaptability and include such types as the parasitic flukes and tapeworms.

It is necessary to look at the distinguishing features of the Platyhelminthes, best seen in the Turbellaria, and then of the Tricladida, to understand the distinctive organization of the planarians. The group as a whole are often said to be triploblastic, i.e. three layers of cells can be recognized by their origin in the early embryo, their position relative to each other and their functions. An outer single layer of cells, the ectoderm, which covers the flatworm has many functions among which are protection and sensation. The latter involves light-sensitive areas (eyes) and chemosensory cells, both concentrated at the front end. The ectoderm is ciliated in patches on the ventral surface and also on either side of the head where the cilia and chemo-sensory cells are concentrated in small slits called auricular sense organs, concerned with locating food. A major function of the ectodermal cells is the production of mucus of two main types so important in the economy of flatworms. In Turbellaria the mucus is used to assist locomotion by providing a carpet on which the animal crawls. It also facilitates the capture of prey, gives protection against desiccation and perhaps deters would-be predators. The latter function is, however, usually attributed to small rods of protein (rhabdites) which are uniquely turbellarian. They are produced in thousands by sunken ectodermal cells and are stored in the outer cells. When the flatworm is roughly handled they are released into the surrounding water and quickly dissolve. Their deterrent effect on predators can be demonstrated by smearing a piece of earthworm with mucus, including rhabdites, and feeding it to a fish. It will be rejected, although the fish will readily swallow untreated earthworm.

The innermost layer of cells, called the endoderm, forms the gut which is, of course, concerned with digestion and absorption of food. Indicative of the primitive nature of flatworms is the fact that there is only one opening to the gut which serves both for the intake of food and the rejection of unwanted materials, a function of the anus in more advanced animals. The third layer, the mesoderm, lies between the ectoderm and the endoderm. This comprises the muscles and the reproductive organs; the excretory and nervous systems are derived from ectoderm which has sunk into the mesoderm. The mesoderm also includes several kinds of cells in a semi-fluid medium. Their functions are not well known, but some are concerned with the transport of food and excretory products, others, called neoblasts, with regeneration. Flatworms have no special circulatory systems.

One of the major contrasts with more advanced animals such as annelids (segmented worms) is the absence of a body cavity (coelom) in flatworms. This is a space lying within the mesoderm and separating the outer body wall from the inner gut wall.

The triploblastic, acoelomate condition is characteristic of flatworms in general, including the parasitic types. The Turbellaria to which the planarians belong are the free-living members of the phylum. They comprise several orders, including the Acoela, minute mainly marine species lacking a true gut, the Rhabdocoela, rather larger worms with a wide range of habitats and having a sac-like gut, the Tricladida, still larger, mainly freshwater in habit and the Polycladida, the largest, all marine, with a many branched gut. The triclads are distinguished from the rest by possessing a three-branched gut, one branch in front, the other two to the rear. They also have a protrusible tubular pharynx and a characteristic arrangement of reproductive organs.

The term planaria not only refers to the freshwater triclads, technically known as the Paludicola but also to the marine species (Maricola) and the terrestrial species (Terricola). There are other, more complicated differences which distinguish these suborders, especially the details of the reproductive systems.

Adult planarians are relatively large, measuring $\frac{2}{5}$–$1\frac{1}{2}$ in (10–35 mm) in length. They are elongate and typically flattened dorso-ventrally. Much larger species measuring up to 10 in (250 mm) in length have been reported from the ancient and large Lake Baikal in Russia. The head is variable, it may be square, rounded or triangular and many species have anterior lateral projections called tentacles. Eyes are usually present either paired or more numerous and arranged around the anterior border of the animal. Many species are pigmented, usually in dull shades with black, brown and yellow predominating but some lack pigment and appear white although the coloured gut contents often show through. A flatworm possesses both male and female reproductive systems. It has a centralized nervous system in the mesoderm within the ventral muscle layers. In contrast to more advanced invertebrates there is no concentration of nerve cells to form ganglia.

Planarians are found in a wide range of freshwater habitats at high and low altitude from small ponds to large inland seas, from ditches and springs to large rivers. They are also an important element of cave faunas and speciation in such isolated habitats has been considerable. Typical freshwater species are found in the brackish waters of the Baltic and it is an unusual experience for a freshwater biologist to collect such planarians from seaweed in the company of typical marine

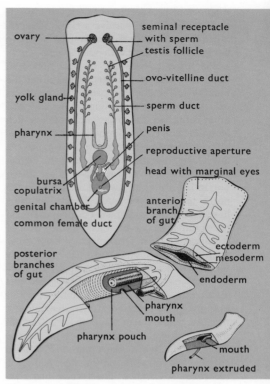

Top: a generalized plan of the reproductive organs of a planarian. Centre: *Polycelis tenuis*, a common planarian 8–12 mm in length, dissected to display the arrangement of the digestive system with the pharynx in the resting position; shape and eye pattern is also shown. Bottom right: the same planarian with the pharynx everted ready to feed.

animals. In lakes, where the species have a characteristic pattern of distribution according to lake type, planarians often form a large part of the *littoral fauna and reach their greatest abundance in water a few inches deep although some species are found in much deeper water. There is also a typical zonation of species in streams from headwater to coastal plain. Planarians avoid strong light and rest on the undersurfaces of stones and leaves of aquatic plants and also in the leaf axils of semi-emergent vegetation. They are probably more active at night but can easily be stimulated to move in daylight by placing a piece of fresh liver or slit earthworm in their vicinity when they will seek out the food. Planarians glide smoothly over the substratum by means of waves of contraction in the ventral longitudinal muscles, assisted by the cilia; they are not able to swim.

There are considerable differences in the ability of planarian species to tolerate organic pollution but all are sensitive to toxic substances such as the heavy metals, copper and lead. Individual species, for example *Polycelis nigra*, may tolerate a wide range of natural conditions being found in high, minerally poor lakes and in low, minerally rich lakes. Other species are much more restricted, especially spring species, such as *Crenobia alpina,* and cave species. In some cases this is due to inability to survive a rise in temperature but in others restriction may be due to competition for food with other species.

Planarian species are to be counted in hundreds rather than thousands although the number will undoubtedly rise as more places are searched. An interesting feature of speciation is the fact that large, ancient lakes such as Baikal and Ohrid (Jugoslavia) have a large number of endemic species. For example, the latter lake holds more species than the British Isles. Planarians are world-wide in distribution but a majority of species occur in the north temperate latitudes. Recent analysis has suggested that dispersal of planarians on the grand scale can be traced to the effect of *Continental Drift. Dispersal by other means, such as the traditional bird's feet is relatively unimportant and a narrow strip of sea, such as the Menai Straits in North Wales, presents an effective barrier. Man's trading activities are now being reflected in their distribution; thus a common American species *Dugesia tigrina* is found in several places in Europe and Britain while a common European species, *Dugesia polychroa,* has just been recorded in Canada. The former has been spread by man's trading in fish for aquarists.

Multiplication of planarians can be achieved by asexual methods via a process of transverse fission, with each part regenerating a new individual, and by sexual methods. Some populations of a species are able to multiply in both ways, for example, *Crenobia alpina,* but usually at different seasons. Other populations may be restricted to one or other method. Cytological studies have indicated, in part, the reason for this. Those populations reproducing only asexually usually have an odd number (3, 5 or 7 etc.) of chromosome sets in their cells instead of the more usual double set (diploid) and are therefore not able to produce viable gametes. In cases where both methods are used, mechanisms which determine type and season are not fully understood, but temperature and food supply seem important. One of the unusual features of sexual reproduction is that in some European species it is a form of pseudogamy; that is, sperm only serve to activate egg development and contribute no chromosomal material to the fertilized egg. Normal fertilization is the rule in diploid populations.

The life-cycle of planarians does not involve larvae, nor, except in one species, resistant stages. During copulation both individuals behave as males and an exchange of sperm occurs. It is received into the bursa copulatrix and is soon transferred to the seminal receptacles at the top of the ovovitelline ducts, adjacent to the ovaries. Several days or weeks after copulation, cocoons are laid containing a number of fertilized eggs together with a lot of yolk cells, which initially serve as food for the young.

Cocoons are relatively large, 1–3 mm in diameter and are glued to the undersurfaces of stones or leaves in shallow water. At first, they are orange-yellow but darken within a few hours by a quinone tanning process comparable with the hardening of insect cuticle. After several weeks or months, according to temperature, 1–20 young, depending on species, hatch by a rupture of the cocoon. The young are small replicas of the adult except for their immaturity. They become adult in several months if food is plentiful. *Polycelis tenuis,* a common British species may be taken as an example. It commences laying oval stalkless cocoons in late March. Hatching reaches a peak in May with 2–7 young per cocoon. These do not become adult until the following spring. Planarians show remarkable ability to withstand starvation and an adult measuring $\frac{3}{5}$ in (15 mm) length may shrink to $\frac{1}{8}$ in (3mm) and then grow again when fed. While some species such as *Dendrocoelum lacteum* are annuals, others which have this ability to shrink, are potentially long lived; *Dugesia benazzi* has been kept in the laboratory for 21 years. In nature the average life-span is probably 2–3 years.

Planarians are often erroneously referred to as scavengers. They are in fact predators feeding on small freshwater oligochaetes, crustaceans, insect larvae and gastropod molluscs. They are quickly attracted to prey behaving abnormally, such as those trapped in mucus or the surface film. The muscular pharynx is pushed through the body wall in a weak place. The softer body tissues of the prey are then sucked out. Planarians do not feed on microscopic animals, plants or detritus. It has been shown recently that although there is overlap in their diet, each of the British lake species has a different main prey which reduces interspecific competition.

Because of their primitive nature and pronounced ability to regenerate, planarians have been used extensively in laboratory experiments. The classical work on regeneration was carried out on planarians and they have also figured in research on physiological ageing using radiation techniques. Control of cell differentiation together with the development and maintenance of metabolic gradients in the whole organism have also been studied extensively in these organisms. Our understanding of old age, malignant tumours etc., in man may stem ultimately from such work. Latterly, we have seen the development of an interest in planarian behaviour especially in relation to the mechanisms and biochemical aspects of learning and memory. The study of planarian cyto-genetics has shed much light on the role of polyploidy (multiple chromosome sets) in animal speciation. Finally, because of their unique position between the primitive, radially symmetrical Cnidaria and the more advanced bilaterally symmetrical

animals, Turbellaria, if not planarians, have been conspicuous in the various theories of metazoan evolution. ORDER: Tricladida, CLASS: Turbellaria, PHYLUM: Platyhelminthes.   T.B.R.

PLANKTON, collective name for plants and animals, usually small, often microscopic, that drift in the, mainly, surface waters of lakes, rivers and seas. Their presence in vast numbers is not normally appreciated as few of them are visible to the naked eye. If, however, a net of fine silk gauze is towed through the water, a layer of plankton is retained on the inside of the net. When this is rinsed into a jar a fine suspension of microscopic plants and animals is obtained in which a number of larger transparent animals are floating.

Particularly in the oceans, all these are at the mercy of the movements of the water in which they live. They are carried long distances over the surface of the globe by the well defined current systems set up by the prevailing winds. The word 'plankton' is from the Greek, meaning 'that which is drifting and wandering'.

Plants. Despite the enormous volumes of water in the seas and lakes, there is only a relatively shallow layer of water near the surface which is penetrated by sunlight, an essential energy source for any plant for the manufacture of food from dissolved carbon dioxide and inorganic ions. Ponds and lakes frequently support fairly large plants floating at or near the surface. In the oceans by far the greater proportion of the plant life is microscopic in size and confined to the first 200–400 ft (60–120 m).

The phytoplankton, the plant life of the plankton, is made up of four main constituents: the diatoms, peridinians, coccolithophores and the nanoplankton. The diatoms are of many shapes ranging from $\frac{1}{1000} - \frac{1}{30}$ in (0·075–1·0 mm). The protoplasm of their bodies is enclosed in a shell of highly ornamented silica which helps the organism remain afloat. The peridinians, about the same size as the diatoms, have distinctive shapes. Their shells are made of cellulose and they have two flagella which help to drive them through the water. Coccolithophores are much smaller, seldom more than $\frac{1}{500}$ in (0·05 mm) in diameter. They have a single flagellum and their surfaces are protected by small disks of lime. Like the diatoms and peridinians the coccolithophores contain green chlorophyll and usually a small droplet of oil which serves as a food reserve and also helps to buoy the organism up. When the plants die they sink to the floor of the ocean and these oil droplets by slow accumulation century after century are believed to be the source of the world's reserves of petroleum. The nanoplankton is so small that fine-mesh tow nets are required to collect it.

Marine zooplankton, the two largest are the copepod (crustacean) *Calanus finmarchicus* and the zoea larva of the Masked crab *Corystes cassivelaunus*.

Animals. Amongst this suspension of plant food are animals which strain off the single-celled plants in a manner referred to as *suspension feeding. Most of these animals are fairly small although a few of them are considerably larger and reach 2 in (5 cm) in length. They include the single-celled *foraminiferans and *radiolarians and many small crustaceans such as *copepods. The animals of the plankton, or zooplankton, are much less numerous, though more varied, than the plants. In a cubic foot of sea water there are roughly 20,000 plants against only 120 animals. Something like that proportion is needed in order to maintain the balance of life in the oceans. When one of the zooplankton eats a quantity of phytoplankton only 10% of the material consumed is converted into flesh. Similarly, the larger animals that feed on the zooplankton also conserve only 10% of their food as flesh.

Food webs. The herbivorous animals are in turn consumed by other larger, carnivorous animals, such as *jellyfish, *Sea gooseberries

and *arrow-worms. All of the creatures of the planktonic *food web so far described are characterized by their transparent bodies which are modified for flotation, having either extensions such as spines as hydrofoils, or a jelly-like consistency. These animals represent an important part of the food web of lakes and oceans. In the seas they are preyed on by certain fish, such as herring, pilchard and Basking shark, and also by the largest mammals that have ever existed, the Whalebone or Baleen whales.

Dead or dying remains of the plankton rain down on brittlestars, sponges, worms and bivalves inhabiting the sea-bed. These sieve off the nutritious particles as food. Other animals feed on them including the bottom dwelling fish. Midwater fish feed on plankton-eating fish such as the herring, so that although relatively few fish feed directly on living plankton, all of them are ultimately dependent upon it.

Most of the animals of the plankton are highly adapted to spend their entire life in

surface waters. However, this rich food supply is often exploited by the young stages of animals which, when mature, swim in deeper waters or lie on the bottom. Many insects have freshwater planktonic larvae. Those of shore dwelling animals such as barnacles, winkles and crabs are taken in plankton samples considerable distances offshore. All these larvae are visitors to surface waters and where breeding is restricted to certain months of the year they make a seasonal appearance in plankton samples. They may be taken in great numbers. At times the plankton of the North Sea is dominated by fish larvae or eggs. Temporarily, they become part of the overall food web and many are taken as food by other animals so that only a fractional percentage survive.

Productivity. The creatures that live the year round in the surface waters are themselves capable of reproduction. The plants only replicate themselves if they are able to synthesize plenty of food, and the production

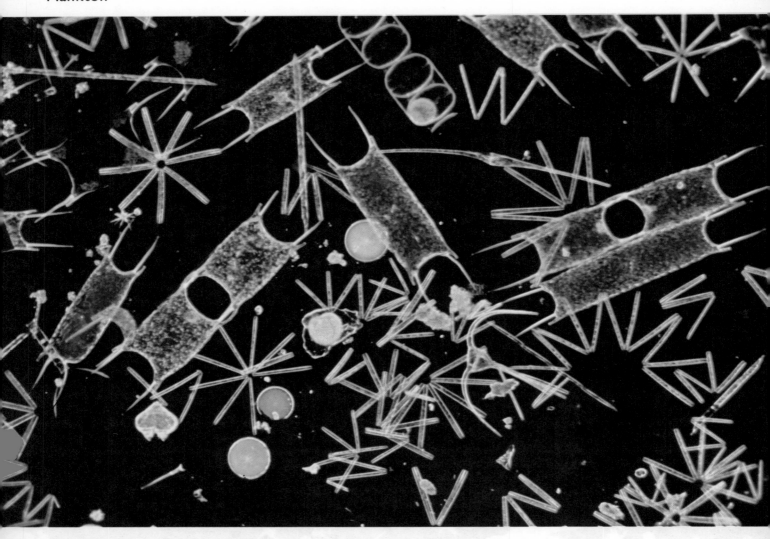

Phytoplankton from the English Channel containing various species of diatoms and dinoflagellates.

of new plant cells is closely linked to the availability of the raw materials for this purpose. The essential minerals and salts come from land drainage and are replenished by the bacterial breakdown of dead plants and animals and the excreta of live animals.

The study of the *biomass of the creatures of the plankton, the rate of reproduction of the plants, the so-called productivity of the plankton, is receiving world wide attention by scientists today. A clear understanding of the factors influencing the productivity of the plankton, the nature of the food web, including information regarding each link of the feeding chains, is being sought. This is essential if the lakes and oceans with their potential wealth of food are to be harvested in a controlled fashion to provide high yields.

The warmer surface waters of the tropics have a relatively sparse plankton of uniform density throughout the year. Their yield of fish is correspondingly small. Temperate waters, particularly coastal and above the continental shelf, have a denser plankton, with increased productivity in spring and

autumn. This has been correlated with a higher concentration of nutrients, and results in good catches containing large reserves of nutrients. Nutrient-laden cold water which has run off the Antarctic continent drifts slowly northwards along the floor of the oceans. Precipitation is less in the Arctic and this ocean is enclosed by submarine ridges but there is a well defined current moving southwards at intermediate depth in the Atlantic Ocean. Local upwelling of this water supports a rich plankton off Bermuda, the west coast of Africa and areas of the tropical Pacific, for example.

Vertical mixing and enrichment of the surface layers of lakes and seas occurs in temperate regions when the surface water cools in the autumn, becomes less dense, and sinks. Horizontal mixing of water masses from different sources is also accompanied by a rich plankton and good yields of fish. Hence the excellent catches of cod and herring in the Barents, Norwegian and North Seas which, receiving water from various sources, benefit from the strong stream of water from the

Atlantic Ocean (Gulf stream), which passes north of the British Isles.

Planktonic indicators. When particular animals, for example arrow-worms, are associated with water of a particular area, they are referred to as planktonic indicators. The movements of water may be traced by reference to those animals which behave in the manner of labels or current-bottles which are thrown into the sea. The origins of the water from which they are collected subsequently, though far afield, are then known. There are animals living deeper in the ocean which, being carried by the deep currents, are by definition also planktonic. They are much less frequent, are not of course accompanied by plant food, and are usually red orange or white in colour. Some are *bioluminescent, a phenomenon also seen amongst surface dwelling forms.

Some of the deeper dwelling planktonic animals, such as Opossum shrimps, migrate long distances to the surface at night to feed. More local migrations of the surface plankton have been extensively studied. In general a day/night vertical migration occurs. This is beneficial to plants, which may lie deeper at midday to avoid damage from too intense illumination by the sun, and by rising to the surface towards evening maintain themselves in optimum light conditions for longer periods of time. The depth at which individual animals are taken depends upon the nature of their food and their enemies, and is influenced by geographical distribution and the season of the year. Many of them follow the diurnal rhythm of the plants, but go deeper in daylight to reduce predation.

Fertilization. Fertilizing freshwater ponds to increase fish yields originated in antiquity. In warm waters in the Middle and Far East it is a commercial proposition and used to increase yields of carp. To the same end domestic fowl hutches are built over ponds in parts of central Europe and China, and decaying vegetation is added to *Tilapia* ponds in Africa. The addition of fertilizers to ponds and lochs in North America and Scotland has improved sport fishing. The consequence of this practice may be variable and unpredictable and the final result may not be according to plan. For example, in shallow inland waters growth of bottom dwelling plants may be favoured which will change the whole character of a stretch of water.

The phenomenal expense of a programme of fertilization of the sea makes it a less probable area of exploitation by this means. Further, though many freshwater fish feed directly on the plankton, few marine fish do so, and many commercial fish are two or three stages removed from the food production of the planktonic plants. This makes it more difficult to ensure that they benefit from the added minerals and salts, and not some other, less useful member of the community. Pilot experiments in more restricted shore areas have not been satisfactory since they are not the normal grounds of the fish of economic importance. Tapping the richer reserves of nutrients in deeper water may be attempted in the future. Taking plankton itself from the sea as food is ten times as expensive, weight for weight, as commercial fishing. A more rational use of the world's fisheries can improve our supply of food from the oceans today.

However, we are harvesting the plankton of a bygone epoch. Many of the plants of the plankton are encased in a glassy siliceous material, which persists on the bed of the ocean as an ooze. Deposits formed long ago have been upheaved and now form rocks, which are mined and used for insulation and polishing. Crude oil of the Rumanian and Californian fields contains traces of planktonic creatures which sedimented in particular conditions at the bottom of the sea. The refined derivatives power the motor cars of today.

W.A.M.C.

PLANTCUTTER *Phytotoma rutila,* a single bird species constituting the family Phytotomidae, very like a finch or cardinal in appearance, with a heavy bill and short crest. The sexes differ, males being brownish-grey streaked with black dorsally, with black wings and tail marked with white. The crown and underside are red, the latter becoming paler on the belly. The female is brown. The plantcutter occurs in the Andean region from Peru south to mid-Argentina and Chile. It lives in open scrub, feeding on fruit and parts of plants and is often a pest. It builds a typical open nest, with two to four greenish, dark-spotted eggs. The voice is harsh. FAMILY: Phytotomidae, ORDER: Passeriformes, CLASS: Aves.

PLANULA. In the *Cnidaria the fertilized egg gives rise to a ciliated larva known as a planula. After fertilization the zygote divides to form a ball of cells each of equal size. Cleavage is said to be radial and indeterminate, any cell can be removed without the embryo lacking certain parts, it is just smaller. This ball of cells then arranges into two cell layers, an outer ectoderm and an inner endoderm, in a variety of ways, the most common being by inward migration of cells either from one or both ends. These cell movements lead to the formation of a solid, mouthless and generally ciliated larva, the planula. In shape the planula is usually rather elongated with a broader anterior end. After a short free-swimming existence, during which time the inner cells or endoderm have become organized into a definite layer around an internal cavity, or enteron, the planula settles and develops into a polyp. The planula may be retained by the female parent; for example, in Oaten-pipes hydroid, until it has developed into a small polyp or actinula larva which is then released, or as in Sea anemones when small anemones are released.

PLASTRON, the lower half of the shell of tortoises and turtles. It is connected to the upper half of the shell, the carapace, by a bony 'bridge'. The structure is comprised of nearly fused bony plates covered with shields or scutes of a hornlike substance. The shields provide colour and pattern to the shell and are useful in identification. Although not all are present in all species, these shields are named, from front to back, the gulars, intergular, humeral, pectoral, abdominal, femoral and anal. A small shield at the forward edge of the 'bridge' is called the axillary; that at the rear edge the inguinal.

The name 'plastron' is also used for the thin film of air carried on the undersurface of aquatic insects, trapped usually in a pile of short bristles, and for the layer of air trapped in the surface of some insect eggs.

PLATYPUS *Ornithorhynchus anatinus,* four-legged amphibious animal which, with the echidnas, comprises a distinct subclass of the Mammalia, the Prototheria or egg-laying mammals. It was first observed by white men in November 1797 and a description of it was sent by John Hunter, governor of the penal colony at Port Jackson in New South Wales, to the former judge-advocate of the settlement David Collins, who had returned to England. Collins, in his *An Account of the English Colony in New South Wales* 2nd Ed 1804, says 'Although the settlement of Port Jackson had now been established within one month of ten years, yet little had been added to the stock of natural history which had been acquired in the first year or two of its infancy. The kangaroo, the dog, the opossum, the Flying squirrel, the kangaroo rat, a spotted rat, the common rat, and the large fox-bat (if entitled to a place in this society) made up the whole catalogue of animals that were known at this time; with the exception which must now be made of an amphibious animal of the mole species, one of which had lately been found on the banks of a lake near the Hawkesbury. In size it was considerably larger than the land mole. The eyes were very small. The forelegs, which were shorter than the hind, were observed, at the feet, to be provided with four claws, and a membrane, or web, that spread considerably beyond them; while the feet of the hindlegs were furnished, not only with this membrane, or web, but with four long sharp claws, that projected as much beyond the web, as the web projected beyond the claws of the forefeet. The tail of this animal was thick, short, and very fat; but the most extraordinary circumstances observed in its structure was its having, instead of the mouth of an animal, the upper and lower mandibles of a duck. By these it was enabled to supply itself with food, like that bird, in muddy places, or on the banks of the lakes, in which its webbed feet enabled it to swim; while on shore its long and sharp claws were employed in burrowing; nature thus providing for it in its double or amphibious character. These little animals had been frequently noticed rising to the surface of the water and blowing like the turtle.'

This description is accurate except perhaps for the numbers of claws on the hands and feet; all the platypuses I have seen had five digits on each, those of the hands being armed with long blunt claws and those on the hindfeet with long sharp claws. As Hunter describes, the webbing on the hand projects beyond the ends of the claws, being carried by five long leathery extensions of the digits. When walking on land this extraneous web is folded back under the digits. The claws on these are used for the construction of the burrows to which they retire after swimming and feeding. All feeding is done in the water and the prey consists of various crustaceans, molluscs, aquatic insect larvae, and even large flying insects like the cicada *Melampsalta denisoni*, which may fall into the water. The platypus lives only in freshwater lagoons, lakes and the pools in small and large rivers. It is a beautiful little animal with a streamlined body and a tail like that of a beaver. The body is covered with a dense very fine fur about 0·75 in (1·5 cm) long somewhat concealed with coarser long hairs, but the tail is covered with coarse bristle-like hairs, densely on the dorsal surface and very sparsely on the ventral surface.

An adult male platypus is about 20 in (51 cm) long (a length of 26 in or 65 cm has been recorded) and weighs 4·2 lb (1·9 kg); adult females are much smaller weighing 2½–3 lb (1·1–1·3 kg). The legs are short and stout, the ankles of the males bearing a curved spur about 0·75 in (1·9 cm) long. This spur is hollow and communicates with a duct which emerges from a gland situated on the dorsal side of the upper hindleg. The gland secretes a poisonous substance during the breeding season; the function of the apparatus is unknown. There is no scrotum, the testes being internal as they are in reptiles. The number of chromosomes in the cells of the body is 53 in the males and 54 in the females. The chromosomes resemble those of reptiles in that there are large chromosomes and very small microchromosomes. There is evidence that suggests the sex determining mechanism depends on the presence of two X chromosomes in the females and only one in the males, a Y chromosome not being detectable. Thus the spermatozoa of the platypus would be of two types: one carrying 26 chromosomes and the other 27. An egg fertilized with a spermatozoon carrying 26 chromosomes would give rise to a male platypus with 53 chromosomes in the cells of its body. There is only one opening for the passage of faeces, urine and reproductive products; this is situated on the ventral surface of the base of the tail. There is, however, no difficulty in determining the sex of a platypus since the females never have the spur on the ankle.

The eyes are situated dorsally on the broad flattened head and immediately posterior to the eye is the external opening of the ear. There is no external pinna, and both the eye and ear are situated in a groove or fold of fur. Both the eye and ear openings are closed by the apposition of the lips of this groove when the animal is under water. The duck-billed muzzle is formed from anterior prolongations of the widely separated premaxillary bones and the mandibles or lower jaws, covered by darkly pigmented soft naked skin. This is extended back over the front part of the face on the dorsal surface and on the ventral surface back under the throat. The nostrils are located on the dorsal surface of the bill near the anterior end. The

delicate skin covering the muzzle apparatus contains innumerable sense organs innervated by branches of the trigeminal nerve which is absolutely and relatively enormous. The sense organs are tactile in function and since the eyes and ears are closed under water, the sense of touch of the muzzle is presumably the only means of locating food. Much mud and grit is ingested along with food and this doubtless helps in grinding up the crustaceans taken in.

Very young platypuses have molariform teeth, the exact dental formula is hard to determine but at least two teeth occur in the upper jaw and three in the lower. In the adult the teeth are replaced by horny plates situated on a flattened area of the lower jaw just anterior to the coronoid process and on a lateral projection of the posterior portion of the maxillary bone. The horny plates serve to crush the food some of which is then stored temporarily in cheek-pouches; doubtless larger items pass direct to the stomach since the cheek-pouches are small. The stomach, as in the echidna, has no gastric glands so presumably all digestion takes place in the intestines.

The platypus is found in fresh waters throughout Tasmania and the eastern coast of Australia as far north as Iron Range in Cape York Peninsula. It also occurs west of the Great Dividing Range in the Murray and Murrumbidgee river systems and it is still thought to be present in the Onkaparinga and Glenelg rivers just within the borders of South Australia. In northern Queensland it has been recorded as far west as the Leichhardt River which flows into the Gulf of Carpentaria. Within these river systems and the creeks, lakes, ponds and pools associated with them platypuses are found in a variety of habitats ranging from the freezing waters of the Australian Alps to the warm rivers and lagoons of tropical Queensland. Platypuses spend little of their time in the water, maybe a total of three or four hours a day in the winter, less in summer; nobody knows for sure since inidentified animals have not been studied; maybe observation of tagged animals will provide an answer to this question. The platypus spends most of its time in burrows which it digs in the soft earth of the banks of the waterways, or in sunning itself in the open. The entrances to the burrows are said to be above water level. There are two types of burrow: one used for shelter and another for breeding; the latter is constructed and inhabited by a pregnant female only and is not shared with any other platypus, male or female.

In 1884 W. H. Caldwell demonstrated that platypuses do not produce their young as other mammals do, but lay eggs. Copulation takes place in the water and fertilization is followed by an unknown period of gestation in the left uterus only, the right ovary

and oviduct being non-functional. The female then retires to the complicated nesting burrow where she has excavated a brood chamber containing a nest of grass, leaves, reeds and so on. Generally two eggs are laid, sometimes three; the eggs adhere to one another their shells being sticky when laid. Nobody knows how the eggs are incubated (there is no pouch as in the echidna), nor for how long; equivocal evidence suggests the period may be between seven and ten days. After hatching the tiny young about 0·65 in (17 mm) long, are suckled by paired mammary glands which open at a pair of milk patches or areolae on the ventral surface. These milk patches are not well defined like those of echidnas but are hidden by thick fur, consequently scientists find them very hard to detect but the newly hatched platypus presumably has no such difficulty, possibly sense of smell helps it. The young are surprisingly like new-born marsupials with their enormous, strong forelimbs and rudimentary hindlimbs, save that an egg tooth and caruncle are present on the head, which are used for breaking out of the keratinized egg shell. Doubtless the relatively great forelimbs of the newly hatched are used for clinging to the fur over the milk patches. As the young grow the mammary glands become very large reaching almost from the armpits to the pelvis longitudinally and up around the flanks laterally. The glands are made up of alveoli and ductules as they are in other mammals. Analysis of a sample of milk shows that, in its fatty acid content, it is like that of marsupials, insectivores, and echidnas, with the difference that there is about 8% lauric acid in the platypus milk whereas it is scarcely detectable in the other types of milk mentioned.

As far as is known copulation takes place in the months of August and September and the young emerge from the breeding burrow for the first time in December and January and are about 12–14 in (30–35 cm) long, i.e. not much smaller than their mothers. They growl, squeak, and play like puppies.

The body temperature of the platypus is about 86–89°F (30–32°C). It is not known whether or not platypuses can hibernate. Platypus blood contains a lot of haemoglobin (up to 21g/100ml) and the oxygen capacity of the blood is high compared with that of other mammals. The high oxygen capacity of its blood enables the animal to maintain a large store of oxygen which helps in diving and staying under water for long periods. The platypus can in fact stay under water for about nine minutes without harm. As in other diving animals the heart rate slows down when the platypus dives, a phenomenon known as bradycardia. FAMILY: Ornithorhynchidae, ORDER: Monotremata, SUB-CLASS: Prototheria, CLASS: Mammalia.

M.E.G.